MW01242463

Marriage, Divorce, & Remarriage

The Uniform Teaching of Moses, Jesus, & Paul

Samuel G. Dawson

Gospel Themes Press
2028 S. Austin, Suite 906
Amarillo, TX 79109-1960
www.gospelthemes.com

Except where otherwise indicated, all Old Testament Scripture quotations are taken from the New American Standard Bible, © 1960, 1962, 1963, 1968, 1971, 1972, 1973, 1975, 1977 by The Lockman Foundation. Used by permission. Except where otherwise indicated, all New Testament Scripture quotations are taken from the American Standard Version New Testament, © 1901, 1929 Thomas Nelson & Sons.

Published by:
    Gospel Themes Press
    2028 S. Austin, Suite 906
    Amarillo, TX 79109-1959 USA

ISBN 978-0-938855-56-9

Library of Congress Cataloging in Publications Data.

Dawson, Samuel G., 1943-
    Marriage, divorce, & remarriage: the uniform teaching of Moses, Jesus, & Paul
    346 p.
    Includes bibliography and indexes.
    1. Marriage—United States—Religious aspects—Controversial literature—Christianity. 2. Divorce—Religious aspects—Controversial literature—Christianity. 3. Remarriage—Religious aspects—Controversial literature—Christianity. I. Title.
ISBN 0-938855-56-5

Printed and bound in the United States of America.

3 4 5 6 7 8 9 10

Table of Contents

Chapter 8: Unscriptural Divorce & Remarriage: A Variety of Answers   177

Chapter 9: Rights of Those Unjustly Put Away   205

Chapter 10: Remarriage of the Put-Away Fornicator   223

Introduction

This book presents the fruits of nearly twenty-five years of the author's study of the Bible's teaching on marriage, divorce, and remarriage. Of course, the Bible has much to say about marriage: both what makes it and how those involved in it should conduct themselves toward each other. Likewise, it has much to say about violations of marriage, which may lead to divorce. Finally, it teaches concerning remarriage, a natural consequence of divorce.

Aside from the controversial nature of the subject, there are many reasons to justify such a study. First, it is a Bible subject. God has revealed his will on the subject and desires that we understand his teaching on it. Second, the high rate of divorce in society demands, if we're going to teach members of society, that we teach God's view of divorce and remarriage to those striving to live according to the Gospel so that they may bring their lives into harmony with it.

It is nearly unnecessary to cite statistics to substantiate this point. In recent years, divorces nationally number nearly two-thirds the number of marriages entered into annually. In Houston, Texas, in a recent year, there were eighty-five percent as many divorces as marriages. When the author began to realize the seriousness of this study, *Time Magazine* of February 11, 1966 had this to say concerning the high rate of divorce: "400,000 U. S. couples are being divorced each year. 500,000 children are involved. Two-thirds of them are under the age of ten. More than 6,000,000 Americans are now divorced or separated, and divorce seems to breed divorce: probably half of all divorced Americans are the children of divorced parents." With the advent of the twenty-first century, divorces in America approach 1,200,000 per year, and the total number of divorced Americans approaches sixty million. Nationally the chance of divorce is one for every two marriages. In the West, it is nearly 4 times that of the Northeast, and in one California county, San Mateo, the ratio is 70 divorces for 100 marriages.

The tens of millions of divorced and remarried Americans have tremendous effects on the efforts of many to teach the Gospel of Christ. Many believe there is no use in carrying the Gospel affirmatively to the divorced, and consequently they don't. Such a situation reminds us of the predicament Mormons found themselves in when they believed Negroes could not be in their priesthood, and they didn't carry their message affirmatively to them.

Another reason to invest time and energy in such a study is to deal with the moral quagmire people involve themselves in when divorce occurs. While we do not say that all involved in divorce are sinners (even God divorced Israel), no divorce takes place without sin. Likewise, divorce always takes place with much grief. It never takes place without broken hearts, broken homes, broken lives, and broken friendships. In many divorces, the parties involved can have every mental attitude which is in opposition to God, i.e., envy, strife, jealousy, hatred, emulation, wrath—they may all be there. Much more is involved than just the separation of a husband and wife.

The greatest reason for the study is preventive. A thorough understanding of the Bible's teaching on marriage, divorce, and remarriage will help prevent many from getting involved in the clutches of treacherous divorce. This study will help us deal with people we're teaching the gospel, to help people who have been through all kinds of marital problems, breakups, and remarriages conclude what God would have them to do to bring their lives into harmony with his will.

In the nineteenth-century restoration movement in America, great preachers of those days such as McGarvey, Lard, and Campbell didn't encounter such problems with the frequency we do today, nor did Christian teachers of the first half of the twentieth century. Thus, their writings don't deal much with the subject, and the religious papers of their day didn't carry a great deal of questions, arguments, or news of debates concerning the subject as we see it in our time.

A Plea for Open Minds as We Begin Our Study

Any time a controversial question is approached for study, it is good to remind ourselves of the great personal need to attempt to have an open mind as we approach such a study. Some wise person said that in such cases there are four possible attitudes people might have toward such a study. The first attitude is, "I know what I believe and you're not teaching it." This is merely an attitude of *prejudice*, which renders useless any study of God's word on this or any other subject. The second attitude is, "I know what I believe and God's word must fit." This is merely *preconceived morals*, and again, if that is the reader's attitude, he might as well stop reading with this sentence. Another attitude one might have is, "How can I get around this teaching and still be pleasing to God?" This attitude of *rebellion* also renders all study useless. Of course, our hope is that we might all have the attitude of Samuel in I Sam. 3.10, when he said, "Speak Lord, thy servant heareth." Samuel's open heart and attitude of humble submission to God's will was the secret of his being a great servant of God, and it is the secret to our being successful students of God's will on any controversial topic.

Many Bible passages bear this out. In Prov. 18.15, we find, "The mind of the prudent acquires knowledge, and the ear of the wise seeks knowledge." If we're going to be wise, we must seek the truth regardless of whether or not we presently agree with it, or our behavior is in harmony with it. Many Bible students admire the Berean Jews of whom Luke said in Ac. 17.11, "Now these were more noble than those in Thessalonica, in that they received the word with all readiness of mind, examining the scriptures daily, whether these things were so. Many of them therefore believed." In John 8.32, Jesus said, "Ye shall know the truth, and the truth shall make you free." Many preachers, elders, and other Christians are a*nything but free* on the subject of divorce and remarriage. They're afraid to be questioned on the subject, afraid to give answers to others or to preach on the subject, and afraid for the subject to come up in private or public discussions. The only thing that will free us from such bondage on any subject is God's truth on the subject.

Eugene Britnell, an influential preacher, writer, and debater of the mid-twentieth century, once said: "The man who refuses to give honest consideration to teaching on any subject, must (1) believe that he is incapable of learning, or (2) think that he knows all there is to know on the subject, or (3) knows that he is wrong and does not intend to change. In our search for truth, may we be free from: (1) the cowardice that shrinks from new truth, that is, new to us; (2) the laziness that is content with half-truths; and (3) the arrogance that thinks it knows all truth already." (*The Sower,* Jan. 1978, p. 2.) Scripture has much to say about each of these characteristics.

Of the one who thinks he is *incapable of learning,* Prov. 1.5 says, "A wise man will hear and increase in learning, and a man of understanding will acquire wise counsel." So such a man is not wise, to say the least. Prov. 15.14 goes further and calls him a fool, for "The mind of the intelligent seeks knowledge, but the mouth of fools feeds on folly."

Of the one who *thinks he knows all there is to know on the subject,* Prov. 12.15 says, "The way of a fool is right in his own eyes, but a wise man is he who listens to counsel." Prov. 28.26 says, "He who trusts in his own heart is a fool, but he who walks wisely will be delivered."

Of the one who *knows that he is wrong and does not intend to change,* Prov. 17.10 says, "A rebuke goes deeper into one who has understanding than a hundred blows into a fool." Prov. 27.22 says, "Though you pound a fool in a mortar with a pestle along with crushed grain, yet his folly will not depart from him."

Of the *cowardice that shrinks from truth new to him,* Prov. 28.1 says, "The wicked flee when no one is pursuing, but the righteous are bold as a lion."

Of the *laziness that is content with half-truths,* Prov. 13.4 says, "The soul of the sluggard craves and gets nothing, but the soul of the diligent is made fat." Prov. 26.16 says, "The sluggard is wiser in his own eyes than seven men who can give a discreet answer."

Of the *arrogance that thinks it knows all the truth already,* Prov. 14.16 says, "A wise man is cautious and turns away from evil, but a fool is arrogant and careless," and Prov. 16.5, 18 says, "Everyone who is proud in heart is an abomination to the Lord, assuredly, he will not be unpunished. Pride goes before destruction, and a haughty spirit before stumbling." Surely none of these characteristics ought to infest the heart of one involved in a serious study of the subject before us.

One last quotation to prompt us to see the need for an open mind before we begin our study in earnest is the following:

> We do not start our Christian lives by working out our faith for ourselves; it is mediated to us by Christian tradition, in the form of sermons, books and established patterns of church life and fellowship. We read our Bibles in the light of what we have learned from these sources; we approach Scripture with minds already formed by the mass of accepted opinions and viewpoints with which we have come into contact, in both the Church and the world. It is easy to be unaware that it has happened; it is hard even to begin to realize how profoundly tradition in this sense has moulded us. But we are forbidden to become enslaved to human tradition, either secular or Christian, whether it be "catholic" tradition, or "critical" tradition, or "ecumenical" tradition. We may never assume the complete rightness of our own established ways of thought and practice and excuse ourselves the duty of testing and reforming them by Scriptures. (J. I. Packer, *"Fundamentalism" and the Word of God* [Grand Rapids, MI: William B. Eerdmans Publishing Co., 1958], pp. 69-70.)

A Plea for Confidence in God's Word

We also plea for confidence in God's word. God's word has the answers to our questions on this and every controversial topic God wants us to understand. In II Tim. 3.16, Paul said, "Every scripture inspired of God is also profitable for teaching, for reproof, for correction, for instruction which is in righteousness: that the man of God may be complete, furnished completely unto every good work." As Paul affirmed, God's word furnishes us completely unto the work, which lies ahead, and we need to have confidence in that fact.

In II Pet. 1.3, Peter affirmed that God "hath granted unto us all things pertaining unto life and godliness." If life-wracking problems concerning divorce and remarriage pertain unto real life, eternal life, life with God, and how to be pleasing to God, we need to have confidence that God has granted us the answers in his word.

In Hosea 4.6, God said of Israel of old, "My people are destroyed for a lack of knowledge." Ignorance of that word is our problem, and nothing else. In Ac. 17.30, Paul told the Athenians, "The times of ignorance therefore God overlooked; but now he commandeth men that they should all everywhere repent." Those times of ignorance are gone. In Eph. 4.17-18, Paul affirmed that we're not like them: "This I say therefore, and testify in the Lord, that ye no longer walk as the Gentiles also walk, in the vanity of their mind, being darkened in their understanding, alienated from the life of God, because of the ignorance that is in them, because of the hardening of their heart."

Thus, our solution is to find out what the Bible teaches on our subject, as we keep our "heart with all diligence, for from it flow the issues of life." Keeping an open mind may well be the hardest work, requiring the most energy and attention, any of us has to do. It's more important than faith in God, faith in Christ, being baptized into Christ, or being a Christian, for all those are negated without an open mind. The lack of open-mindedness is tragic: Jesus was killed for the lack of it; the apostles were persecuted for the lack of it. All kinds of personal and church problems are caused by the lack of open-mindedness. We simply must desire the truth above our family, the pressures of friends, and our own personal convenience

The wise man said in Eccl. 12.12, "And furthermore, my son, be admonished: of making many books there is no end; and much study is a weariness of the flesh." Serious Bible study is hard work. It's much easier to let our parents or the preacher and the elders do our studying for us. But serious Bible study is a work that absolutely must be done in order for us to understand our God's will on the subject.

A Plea to Refrain from Maligning Motives

Many times in religious controversy, those who differ cannot seem to refrain from maligning the motives of those with whom they disagree. We close this chapter with a plea to refrain from such as we involve ourselves in our study. We shouldn't malign the unknown motives of others because it is a prerogative solely of deity. Paul said in I Cor. 2.11, "For who among men knoweth the things of a man, save the spirit of the man which is in him? Even so, the things of God none knoweth, save the Spirit of God." We simply do not know the motives of a person unless he reveals them. In Ac. 1.24, when the apostles wanted to know whom God had selected as a replacement apostle, they addressed God thusly: "Thou, Lord, who knowest the hearts of all men." God alone knows the hearts of other men. We do not, and never have. When we assign improper motives to those with whom we disagree, we blaspheme God by assuming powers that belong only to him. In Ro. 1.29, in the list of sins God holds all men responsible for, whether they have heard of God or not, whether they believe in his existence, whether they've ever heard a gospel sermon is "malignity," the very sin of which we speak. Yet often, on the present subject, maligning the character of another is often done.

Thus, as we begin this important study of this controversial subject, may we all strive to be honest with ourselves, to treat God's word, and treat each other in such a way that we can all grow in knowledge and understanding.

Chapter 1

What Makes a Marriage?

Highlights

- *Cohabitation doesn't make a marriage, but is a right of one, with application to Roman Catholic concept of annulment.*
- *Betrothal in Old Testament was marriage, not engagement, required divorce to put asunder, as illustrated by case of Joseph and Mary.*
- *Husband and wife bound to each other in marriage, not to God, not to law of God.*
- *Civil government's interest in marriage.*
- *Marriage in OT was common law marriage with no waiting period, and was private, as was divorce.*

As we turn our attention to marriage, it is customary on studies of this subject to define what makes a marriage by listing standard components required to make a marriage. Such lists usually contain things like a covenant being required, a relationship recognized by God, marriage that is in harmony with the laws of the land, mutual love, submission of the woman to the man, etc. Usually, cohabitation or sexual intercourse is on the list as well. Some get so exuberant in making their lists that they add the requirement that both parties be Christians, that they live together in harmony with all the laws of God, etc. Thus, they add that the husband always treats his wife as Christ loved the church and that the woman always submits to her husband as the church submits to Christ.

If such lists were valid, probably very few of us would be recognized as married, because all of us lack some component in

these lists. Many have confused what *ought to be* in a marriage
with what actually *makes* a marriage. Surely both parties in a
marriage should be Christians, but it might just be that atheists
and Muslims can marry as well. Granted, God would desire that
both parties live together in harmony with all his will, but most
people who are married, even highly successfully, do not know
all of his will, much less live in harmony with all of it. Thus, we
wish to develop a less humanly idealized, but scriptural definition
of marriage, for such understanding will help us significantly
when we consider divorce (the departure of parties from each
other) and remarriage.

The Beginning of Marriage

New Testament writers didn't define marriage, but rather
assumed their readers would know what marriage was from the
Old Testament. Since that's no longer such a safe assumption,
we begin with the beginning of marriage itself in Gen. 2.18-25:

> Then the Lord God said, "It is not good for the man to
> be alone; I will make him a helper suitable for him. And
> out of the ground the Lord God formed every beast of
> the field and every bird of the sky, and brought them to
> the man to see what he would call them; and whatever
> the man called a living creature, that was its name. And
> the man gave names to all the cattle, and to the birds of
> the sky, and to every beast of the field, but for Adam there
> was not found a helper suitable for him. So the Lord God
> caused a deep sleep to fall upon the man, and he slept;
> then He took one of his ribs, and closed up the flesh at
> that place. And the Lord God fashioned into a woman
> the rib which He had taken from the man, and brought
> her to the man. And the man said, "This is now bone of
> my bones, And flesh of my flesh; She shall be called
> Woman, Because she was taken out of Man."
>
> For this cause a man shall leave his father and his mother,
> and shall cleave to his wife; and they shall become one

flesh. And the man and his wife were both naked and were not ashamed.

"Cleaving" vs. "One Flesh"

From this passage we first notice the words "cleave" and "one flesh." These words refer to two aspects of marriage, which we need to understand clearly at the beginning of our study. Many times people confuse these two terms, and many preachers treat them without distinction, saying, "When one cleaves, he is one flesh." This is not so, as we'll soon see. Before we do, let's notice Jesus speaking of the origin of marriage in Mt. 19.4-6. When the Pharisees interrogated him on our subject, he said:

> And he answered and said, have ye not read, that he who made them from the beginning made them male and female, and said, For this cause shall a man leave his father and mother, and shall cleave to his wife; and the two shall become one flesh.

In Eph. 5.31, as Paul paralleled the relationship between Christ and his church with a husband and his wife, he said:

> For this cause shall a man leave his father and mother, and shall cleave to his wife; and the two shall become one flesh.

To understand how "cleaving" and "one flesh" are different, we want to first consider the Old Testament's use of the terms "taking a wife" and "cleaving."

"Taking a Wife"

As noted above, New Testament writers didn't have to define marriage because in teaching the Jews first, they could rely on Jews knowing what the Old Testament taught on the subject. Since generally we're not so familiar with the Old Testament's teaching on marriage anymore, we'll take some time to get acquainted with it. In Gen. 4.19, we read of Lamech, the first bigamist of the Bible: "Lamech *took* unto himself two wives." In Gen. 6.1-2, Moses speaks of the sons of God marrying women of the world solely because of their physical attractiveness, saying, "they *took* unto themselves wives of the daughters of men and came into them." In Gen. 11.29, Moses said that "Abraham and Nahor *took* them wives." In Gen. 24.3-4, Abraham instructed his servant not to "*take* a wife for my son Isaac" from among the Canaanites.

The concept of *taking a wife* corresponds to the agreement of a man and a woman to live together as husband and wife. In Gen. 24.67, after the servant brought Rebekah to Isaac, Moses said that "Isaac *took* Rebekah, and she became his wife." Notice that they were married without a preacher reading a ceremony out of the Bible in a church building; there was no justice of the peace or other agent of the state, and there was no license, but they were married. They were as bound together as husband and wife as anyone ever was.

Similarly, in Gen. 25.1, at the death of Sarah, Abraham *took* another wife. In Gen. 26.34, Esau "*took* to wife Judith." In Gen. 27.46, Jacob *took* a wife, speaking of Leah. In Gen. 28.1, he *took* Rachel for a wife.

Notice in particular Gen. 34.8, the process of the father *giving* his daughter and the prospective husband *taking* her for a wife: and Jacob "*took* her and *went in unto* her." The "going in unto her" comprises sexual intercourse, for we see in Gen. 6.4 that it produced children. In Gen. 29.21 and 23 "going in unto" is used of Jacob and Rachel producing their children, and in Gen. 38.2-3 Judah *went into* his wife, and she produced a son.

Thus, there was a *taking* of a wife to make the marriage, and a *going into* the wife, *not to make her his wife*, but because she was his wife. This is made even clearer in Gen. 29.18 where Laban said to Jacob, "I give her." Jacob couldn't steal her, that would have been kidnapping. In Gen. 29.21, Jacob said, "*Give* me my wife that I may *go in unto* her." Notice that Jacob wasn't going into her to make her his wife, but because she was his wife. *Going in to her was a right of marriage, not a condition of marriage.*

Many times we hear the term "consummate a marriage," as in two young people getting married in a church ceremony and then getting killed in a car wreck on their honeymoon before they could "consummate the marriage." Such language is not the healthy words of the teaching of Christ, but rather Roman Catholic language.

Cohabitation Doesn't Make a Marriage

To further see that sexual intercourse doesn't make a marriage, we give three arguments: (1) Old Testament teaching, (2) the case of Joseph and Mary, and (3) further notice of the concept of cleaving.

The Old Testament Treated Betrothed Virgins as Married

In modern times we use the term "betrothed" to mean engaged. We see it so used on the Society page of the Sunday paper every week. It means that a couple has made a covenant or agreement to get married at some later time. However, in the Old Testament betrothed people weren't fiancés, they were husband and wife, the giving and taking of the woman had been done. They had made a covenant or agreement to live together as husband and wife. In Dt. 22.22-24, we read:

> If a man is found lying with a married woman, then both of them shall die, the man who lay with the woman, and the woman: thus you shall purge the evil from Israel. If there is a girl who is a virgin engaged [ASV—*betrothed*] to a man, and another man finds her in the city and lies with her, then you shall bring them both out to the gate of that city, and you shall stone them to death: the girl, because she did not cry out in the city, and the man, because he has violated his neighbor's *wife*. Thus you shall purge the evil from among you.

Notice that a man who violates a betrothed virgin has violated his neighbor's wife, not his neighbor's fiancée. Since she was a virgin and a wife, cohabitation wasn't necessary to make her a wife. Cohabitation didn't "consummate" their marriage, for she was already a wife. To see this even further, consider the difference in penalties between violating a betrothed virgin and an unbetrothed one. In Dt. 22.28-29, we read:

> If a man finds a girl who is a virgin who is not engaged [ASV—betrothed], and seizes her and lies with her and they are discovered, then the man who lay with her shall give to the girl's father fifty shekels of silver, and she shall become his wife because he has violated her; he cannot divorce her all his days.

Sometimes we hear preachers say that there was no distinction between fornication and adultery in the Old Testament. Here we see some differences, at least. Fornication with an unbetrothed virgin was punishable by (1) paying a fine, (2) marrying the woman, and (3) never divorcing her. Adultery with a betrothed virgin was punishable by death since a man's wife had been violated. If we can understand the difference between the death penalty and a fine, we can understand the difference between unbetrothed and betrothed virgins. Again, cohabitation wasn't necessary to make her a wife; she was one already by the fact that she was betrothed.

The Case of Joseph and Mary

In Mt. 1.18, we read the account of Joseph and Mary, who were faithful Jews living under Dt. 22.22-29:

> Now the birth of Jesus Christ was on this wise: When his mother Mary had been betrothed to Joseph, before they came together she was found with child of the Holy Spirit.

So Joseph and Mary were betrothed, they were husband and wife, not fiancés, and she was a virgin, because they had not come together. Indeed, cohabitation wasn't necessary for them to be husband and wife. In verse 19, we have:

> And Joseph her husband, being a righteous man, and not willing to make her a public example, was minded to put her away privily.

Notice that Joseph is identified as her husband. The word "put away" is the standard word for divorce, and is the same word Jesus used in Mt. 19.9, when he said, "Whosoever shall put away his wife." Although they had not cohabited, they were so married that he was going to divorce her, something not done with fiancés. In a later discussion of divorce under the Mosaic Law, we'll talk more about Joseph's options with Mary, but suffice it to say that he would certainly have been a troubled young man. He loved this woman, they were married, and according to Jewish tradition, they wouldn't live together until after the marriage feast. All of a sudden, he found out that she was pregnant, and he knew he hadn't had relations with her. In his mind, he knew she had been unfaithful to him, so he wanted to get away from her. Interestingly, Matthew said he was a "righteous man" in so doing, but rather than making her a public spectacle, he wanted to do it privily, literally "on the side."

We continue reading in verse 20:

> But when he thought on these things, behold, an angel of the Lord appeared unto him in a dream, saying, Joseph, thou son of David, fear not to take unto thee Mary thy wife, for that which is conceived in her is of the Holy Spirit.

Thus, the angel recognized that Mary was his wife, not his fiancée, and that cohabitation wasn't necessary to "consummate" the marriage.

Concluding this account, we read in verse 24:

And Joseph arose from his sleep, and did as the angel of the Lord commanded him, and took unto him his wife.

For the third time, Matthew said that Mary was his wife, not his fiancée; thus, this virgin woman, who knew not a man, was married.

Cleaving Isn't Cohabitation

The third argument we give to show that marriage doesn't require cohabitation is just that the word "cleaving" simply doesn't mean cohabitation. This is easily shown by noticing passages where the word cleaving (Greek *kollao*) cannot include cohabitation. For example, in Ac. 9.26, when Paul as a new Christian assayed to *join* himself to the saints in Jerusalem, the word "join" is from this same word *kollao*. Paul wanted to cleave to these brethren, but it was cleaving in fellowship, in mind, in purpose, not in cohabitation. In Ac. 10.28, when Peter saw his vision commanding him to preach the gospel to Gentiles for the first time, he said:

Ye yourselves know how it is an unlawful thing for man that is a Jew to join himself to or come into one of another nation.

The word "join" is the same word translated "cleave," *kollao*. Peter affirmed that he couldn't keep company with Gentiles, with no reference to sexual cohabitation at all. The reader is urged to note other examples where this same word is used without reference to cohabitation in Lk. 15.15, Lk. 10.11, Ac. 8.29, Ac. 5.13, and Ac. 17.34. In the context of marriage, cleaving means marriage, having the right to become one flesh. Thus, cohabitation was never a condition of marriage, but rather a right of it.

Young people need to be aware that cohabitation doesn't establish a marriage. If they make a covenant to live together as husband and wife, and they stand before their friends and take vows regarding that covenant, they're married, just like Jacob and Rachel, Joseph and Mary, whether they ever cohabit or not.

As mentioned earlier, Roman Catholicism gave us the concept of consummating a marriage, a concept bereft of scriptural basis. Following from that concept, though, is their concept of annulment, essentially their substitute for divorce. While maintaining an apparently strict stance against divorce, even for fornication, Catholics annul marriages by the tens of thousands each year in this nation. The practice began by voiding marriages that had not been consummated by cohabitation, a concept we've seen to have no scriptural basis at all. Now, they've extended the practice to annulling the marriages of prominent politicians who've been married for decades and have large numbers of children and grandchildren, by going back and finding a lack of sincerity, mental reservation, etc. to declare that the marriage "never existed."

Noting that cohabitation was never a condition of marriage may also help us deal later on with a sometimes-offered solution to marriage and divorce situations in local churches. Sometimes when a church discovers a questionable divorce and remarriage situation within their midst, they propose that the couple continue to live in the same house, but the man lives on one floor, and the woman on another to insure that they do not cohabit. One well-known preacher recounted to the author once how he advised such a couple to hang a sheet from the ceiling in their bedroom extending down to the middle of their bed, so they could continue to sleep in the same bed, but assure that they weren't cohabiting. Notice, by giving up the cohabitation, they weren't giving up the marriage at all—the preacher was letting them stay in the marriage, but denying them the right of it. Surely these brethren were sincerely trying to solve the problem, but a misunderstanding of what constitutes marriage seriously undermined their efforts.

In addition, recognizing that cohabitation is not a condition of marriage will help us with several proposed answers to unscriptural divorce and remarriage situations we'll confront later in this book. The Moyer position, briefly, was based on the assumption that when a married man committed adultery with a woman not his wife, the first act of adultery broke his old marriage ties and the second act married him to the second woman. We'll have more to say about this position in Chapter 8, "A Variety of Answers," but for now we simply remark that cohabitation alone outside of marriage never broke a marriage (we'll establish this later), and it never made one.

Conclusion

We now have a Bible definition of marriage. Marriage, first of all, is an agreement to live together as husband and wife. As will become important later in our study, we note that it's not a covenant to commit fornication, but to share life in a marriage with its responsibilities, joys, pleasures, sorrows, miseries, and all the other experiences of life. Sexual cohabitation is a right of marriage and not the consummation of such.

In addition, we read in Mal. 2.14 that God is a witness to this covenant. After their return from Babylonian captivity, the Jews wondered why God was punishing them again. God explained:

> Because the Lord has been a witness between you and the wife of your youth, against whom you have dealt treacherously, though she is your companion and your wife by covenant.

Thus, God witnesses our marriage covenants, even the covenants of atheists, who don't even believe in God.

God also joins the husband and wife together, for Jesus said in Mt. 19.6:

> What therefore God hath joined together, let not man put asunder.

The result of God's joining the man and woman is that they are bound to each other. In Rom. 7.2, Paul said:

> For the woman that hath a husband is bound by law to the husband while he liveth.

The word "bound" is the Greek word for *tied* (see Mt. 21.2 where Jesus used this same word to tell his disciples to find a donkey *tied* to a tree). Notice in verse 1 that Paul said, "I speak to men who know the law." This is what men who knew the Old Covenant knew, that a husband and wife were bound to each other. Likewise, Paul said in I Cor. 7.27 that the husband is bound to the wife:

Art thou bound unto a wife? Seek not to be loosed.

It is emphasized that we should use scriptural language when discussing this or any Bible subject. Many times, preachers speak of people being bound to God in marriage, but scripture nowhere uses that language, any more than it speaks of consummating marriage by cohabitation. Men who knew the law in Paul's time didn't know of either one. People who know the law in our present day don't either. Notice the following quotation from Roy Deaver, legendary preacher in churches of Christ during most of the twentieth century:

In the marriage situation there are THREE sets of handcuffs—not one set. The husband is handcuffed to God (to the law of God); the wife is handcuffed to God (the law of God); and the husband and the wife are handcuffed to each other. The marriage law is God's law, and all men are amenable to that law. When the wife is guilty of fornication the husband has the right to put away the wife—to take off the handcuffs by which he is bound to the wife. But he is still handcuffed to the law of God, and the wife (the guilty party) is still handcuffed to the law of God. The law of God allows the husband (the innocent party) to form another marriage union. But, the law of God does not allow the wife—the guilty party—to form another marriage union. The guilty party is still handcuffed to the law of God—not to the husband she sinned against. (Roy Deaver, quoted by J. D. Thomas, *Divorce and Remarriage* [Abilene, TX: Biblical Research Press, 1977], p. 55.)

Men who knew the law didn't know anything about one set of handcuffs, much less three. Likewise, they didn't know anything about anyone being handcuffed to God or to the law of God. If we know the law, neither will we.

Incidentally, Rom. 13.1 and Tit. 3.1 teach that Christians should do all things in harmony with the law of the land. In most counties in the United States of America, this means that to be married, the man and woman must have a blood test, a marriage license, and a ceremony performed by an agent of the state, that is, a justice of the peace, magistrate, minister, etc. While we certainly believe that Christians should obey the law of the land, and urge people to do so, we'll realize the more we progress through this study that government's involvement in both marriage and divorce has in large part brought on this entire controversy.

Government's interest in marriage isn't whether we have the right to marry or not, whether we treat each other right or not, or whether we divorce on scriptural grounds or not. Government's interest in our marriages is based on one thing: property for taxation purposes. Government wants to make sure it has our property in the right account in their computers while we're married. If we divorce, they want to know about it to separate our property in their computer databases, and that's it. We've read nothing about licenses, blood tests, and agents of the state in the Bible's teaching on making marriages. It is the author's present opinion that these are not conditions of marriage, but conditions of being in harmony with the law of the land, and to this, civil government agrees by recognizing common-law marriages. Depending on the county or state, civil government recognizes as marriage the relationships of people who have been living together as husband and wife for a period of months or years, and who wish to be considered as married. The point is that not even civil government recognizes the license, blood test, and ceremony performed by an agent of the state as absolute conditions of marriage.

The reader may not be comfortable to admit it at first, but without the interference of civil government, marriage in the Bible was a common-law marriage with no waiting period. Isaac took Rebekah into his tent and knew her *with no waiting period.* Joseph and Mary were married and according to tradition, were waiting until the marriage feast to begin cohabiting. If they had cohabited before the marriage feast, they wouldn't have been viewed as sinners (Jesus' detractors, looking for anything at all to convict Jesus of, never dreamed of his being illegitimate), but just having broken a tradition, like viewing the bride in a wedding dress before the ceremony.

Marriage in the Bible was an individual, private affair. As we'll see later on, so was divorce. Joseph was going to divorce Mary privily, with no court, lawyers, etc. involved. Much of the controversy around marriage and divorce evolves around the involvement of civil government in such affairs, despite our protestations that the laws of man ought not to affect our behavior on the subject. It is the author's considered opinion that we might all be better off if marriage and divorce were still private affairs, rather than governmental, not even considering the tax benefits. We, of course, have inherited this situation. Rather than leave marriage private as God arranged it, Roman Catholicism made marriage "a sacrament of the church" (a term as foreign to the Bible as "consummation of marriage" and "handcuffs"). When denominations began to arise in the fifteenth and sixteenth centuries, they brought that concept along with them. In the American restoration movement, when people strove to rid themselves of denominational allegiance and practices, they brought the concept still further. Today we think it unnatural when someone questions whether local churches ought to be involved in weddings with their preacher officiating as the agent of the state. We cannot read any such thing in the Bible—we should be forthright enough to admit its origin within Roman Catholicism instead of the pages of scripture. At such times as this, we need to recall the words of Paul in I Tim. 6.3 as he pronounced God's displeasure at "any man [who] teacheth a different doctrine, and consenteth not to sound words, even the words of our Lord Jesus Christ."

Chapter 2

Violations of Marriage

Highlights

- *Fondling is sexual intercourse.*

We begin this chapter by noting briefly I Cor. 7.1-7, a paragraph which, unlike the rest of I Corinthians 7, describes a "normal" or "happy" marriage:

> Now concerning the things whereof ye wrote: It is good for a man not to touch a woman. But, because of fornications let each man have his own wife, and let each woman have her own husband.

Note Paul's plural use of fornication. There are many different kinds of fornication, several of which we'll discuss in this chapter. Paul affirmed that God's answer to man's need to avoid every kind of fornication is for him to have his own wife.

In verses 3-7, Paul discussed the responsibilities of the husband and wife to each other in the sexual realm:

> Let the husband render unto the wife her due: and likewise also the wife unto the husband. The wife hath not power over her own body, but the husband: and likewise also the husband hath not power over his own body, but the wife. Defraud ye not one the other, except it be by consent for a season, that ye may give yourselves unto prayer, and may be together again, that Satan tempt you

not because of your incontinency. But this I say by way
of concession, not of commandment. For I would that all
men were even as I myself. Howbeit each man hath his
own gift from God, one after this manner, and another
after that.

We notice these verses to remind us of the closeness of the
marriage relationship—surely the closest human relationship that
exists. Marriage is easily closer than the parent-child relationship, closer than any business or work relationship, closer than
the teacher-student relationship, or closer than any other human
relationship we might think of.

Because of the intimacy of the marriage relationship, violations of marriage incur a heavy penalty. As the author of Hebrews
said in Heb. 13.4:

Let marriage be had in honor among all, and let the bed
be undefiled: for fornicators and adulterers God will
judge.

As we'll eventually see, any separation but death is invariably
involved with sin. When divorce takes place, whether for a
scriptural reason or unscriptural, sin has taken place. Thus, all
should contemplate, whether we're married or not, that there is
no way short of death to be freed from the bond of marriage
without sin.

This chapter basically develops accurate definitions of two
words: fornication and adultery. Some readers will think the
definitions of these words are so simple that reading this chapter
is unnecessary and skip on to the next chapter, but the author
urges the reader not to do so. Misuse of these two words is at the
root of so many disagreements on this topic, and of misunderstanding of the seriousness of sexual sin. It can be safely said that
nearly all disagreements on marriage, divorce, and remarriage
have, at their basis, misunderstandings of what fornication and
adultery are.

Many who think the definitions of these two words are too
elementary to spend an entire chapter on are the very ones who
need to consider these two words the most. Many years ago, I

began work with a congregation containing an elderly, retired preacher whom I had known since my youth. He had at least forty years experience over me, and I was impressed when one day at lunch soon after I moved to his city, that he brought up questions concerning marriage, divorce, and remarriage. This made me feel not so naïve on the subject if he had been preaching a half century and still had such questions. In our conversation, he was using the words fornication and adultery in a way that showed he was confused about their meaning. I finally asked him if he thought he had a clear understanding of the difference between fornication and adultery. "I think I do," he replied. "Isn't adultery the King James Version translation and fornication the American Standard Version translation?" I replied no, that I thought it was more basic than that.

As simple as we think these two words are, the author practically guarantees that you will learn something significant from this chapter that makes it well worth reading carefully.

Fornication

The Greek word for fornication is *porneia*, containing the root of our English word pornography. Thayer, in his lexicon, defines the word *porneia* as "illicit sexual intercourse in general." Many times it's translated harlotry or whoredom, but it's always used of the same Greek word, *porneia*.

We should notice that the New American Standard Version translates the word *porneia* as "immorality," a terrible translation at this point, for there are many types of immorality which have nothing to do with sexual sin. Bank robbery is immoral, but it's not fornication. Putting poison in public drinking water supplies is immoral, but it has nothing to do with our subject. Torturing a child is immoral, but again, it's not fornication, which essentially is a sexual sin.

First of all, we notice that while there's no real dispute about the above definition of fornication, there are some real misunderstandings about what the definition means. For example, what is "intercourse"? Most men tend to think that intercourse implies coitus or sexual penetration of a woman by a man. Women tend to have a broader idea of what constitutes illicit sexual intercourse. In 1875, when Thayer's lexicon was published, the word intercourse meant "activity or involvement," and didn't necessarily have the sexual connotation it does in our minds today.

Many times we see, particularly in older literature, someone speaking of "maritime intercourse at the waterfront," not speaking of anything sexual, but referring to a type of particular activity. We might read of "financial intercourse on Wall Street," again not referring to anything sexual at all.

Several years ago a friend of the author returned from a trip to Pennsylvania and brought him a bumper sticker which said, "I spent 45 minutes in INTERCOURSE, PA," with the PA in tiny type. This of course, was supposed to produce a laugh. There is a town named Intercourse, Pennsylvania. When the town was named, people understood that the term intercourse wasn't particularly a sexual term. To them, the bumper sticker wouldn't have had the desired humorous effect at all. The early settlers of that town wanted the world to know that they were an active, thriving, bustling community. A similar example of such a word now would be City of Industry, California. When we mention that town's name, no one thinks anything sexual about it. Like Intercourse, Pennsylvania, the citizens of the City of Industry, California merely wanted the world to know how industrious and productive they are. Thus, intercourse has a sexual connotation in our time that isn't inherent in the word, and many assume an interpretation of coitus or penetration that is not in the definition.

Thus, fornication or sexual intercourse, that is, sexual activity or involvement, probably has a much broader interpretation than most of us have given it. For example, in Ezek. 23.1-3, Ezekiel was given an allegory of two sisters (Oholah and Oholibah) representing the divided kingdoms of Israel and Judah before they went into captivity for their idolatry, immorality, and trust of other nations rather than God. Of these two nations, God said:

> The word of the Lord came to me again, saying, Son of
> man, there were two women, the daughters of one
> mother; and they played the harlot in Egypt. They played
> the harlot in their youth; there their breasts were pressed,
> and there their virgin bosom was handled.

The word harlot in this passage in the Greek Old Testament is the same root word as our word *porneia* in the New Testament. These women were committing fornication, except in modern times we would call this petting, wouldn't we? We would tend to say that two teenagers doing this wouldn't be committing fornication. But what would we say if we were asked, "Is pressing a woman's virgin breasts sexual activity or involvement?" What did Ezekiel say? He said it was fornication, and if we use the word intercourse correctly, we will, too.

Many years ago the author and his wife were acquainted with a young lady who graduated from a prominent "Christian college." She was preparing for marriage, and was having serious problems coming to terms with an affair she had with a married professor while at the college. She related how she and this professor would often meet at a motel near the college, take off their clothes, lay on the bed, and fondle each other for hours, being careful "not to go all the way, lest we commit fornication." We should ask ourselves: was that sexual activity or involvement? Surely it was; it was fornication.

In recent years, a former President of the United States admitted having some kind of sexual relationship with a young intern working under him. Our news media, political leaders, social commentators, etc., were all in a tizzy wondering what "having sex" or "having a sexual relationship" actually means. A contemporary *TIME Magazine* article contained this statement:

> So the lawyers for Paula Jones tried to avoid any possible ambiguity by drafting a galactically broad definition of sex that would include touching of any erotic kind, fondling, oral sex or actual intercourse. ("Nation," *TIME Magazine,* August 17, 1998.)

This is typical. To the average person, touching of any erotic kind, fondling, and oral sex are not "actual intercourse" or actual sexual activity! If we know what sexual activity or involvement is, we know what fornication is, for they are one and the same— "illicit sexual intercourse in general" as Thayer said.

Old Testament Prohibitions

Fornication was a serious sin in the Old Testament and we've already noticed one passage dealing with it, Dt. 22.28-29:

> If a man finds a girl who is a virgin, who is not engaged [ASV "betrothed"—SGD], and seizes her and lies with her and they are discovered, then the man who lay with her shall give to the girl's father fifty shekels of silver, and she shall become his wife because he has violated her: he cannot divorce her all his days.

Again, the Mosaic penalty for committing fornication was mandatory marriage, the payment of a fine, and a prohibition against divorce for life.

In Ex. 22.16-17, while at Mt. Sinai, Moses told the Jews:

> And if a man seduces a virgin who is not engaged [ASV "betrothed"—SGD], and lies with her, he must pay a dowry for her to be his wife. If her father absolutely refuses to give her to him, he shall pay money equal to the dowry for virgins.

Notice the right of the father to refuse "to give" the man his daughter, in which case the man couldn't "take" her to be his wife, as we noticed in the previous chapter.

In Lev. 19.29, Moses warned of national consequences of fornication:

> Do not profane your daughter by making her a harlot, so that the land may not fall to harlotry, and the land become full of lewdness.

This passage may remind us of passages where Israel was told that capital punishment was required in the Old Testament because unjustly shed blood defiled the land, i.e., it required the blood of the murderer to cleanse the land of unjustly shed blood. Many times we become indignant when murderers are running free, or receiving trivial sentences for their heinous acts, saying indignantly, "Surely God notices all this unrequited blood and our nation is in danger!" True, but God also notices how rampant fornication defiles a nation. What must he think of our nation? How indignant do we get about it? We don't begin to take fornication as seriously as God does.

In Lev. 21.9, we learn more about how serious fornication was to the priesthood of Israel:

> Also the daughter of any priest, if she profanes herself by harlotry, she profanes her father, she shall be burned with fire.

This "harlot" is a fornicator. We've already seen that a typical harlot received mandatory marriage, the payment of a fine, and no divorce for life. This harlot received a much more severe sentence because she dishonored her priestly father.

In Dt. 22.20-21, we read of the seriousness of a woman representing herself as a virgin at marriage when she actually wasn't:

> But if this charge is true, that the girl was not found a virgin, then they shall bring out the girl to the doorway of her father's house, and the men of her city shall stone her to death because she has committed an act of folly in Israel, by playing the harlot in her father's house: thus you shall purge the evil from among you.

Passages like these might be multiplied, but this sample should demonstrate sufficiently that fornication was a serious sin in the Old Testament.

New Testament Prohibitions

Just as the Old Testament did, the New Testament also condemned fornication. In I Cor. 6.9-10, Paul said:

> Or know ye not that the unrighteous shall not inherit the
> kingdom of God? Be not deceived: neither fornicators,
> nor idolaters, nor adulterers, nor effeminate, nor abusers
> of themselves with men, nor thieves, nor covetous, nor
> drunkards, nor revilers, nor extortioners, shall inherit the
> kingdom of God.

In Gal. 5.19-21, Paul included sexual sin in the works of the
flesh:

> Now the works of the flesh are manifest, which are these:
> fornication, uncleanness, lasciviousness of which I fore-
> warn you, even as I did forewarn you, that they who
> practice such things shall not inherit the kingdom of God.

So fornication is a serious matter in the New Testament as
well. The kingdom of God will not be inherited by those guilty
of illicit sexual activity or involvement in general.

Adultery

The concept of adultery is probably the most important concept to understand correctly on this entire subject. Until recently,
there was nearly unanimous acceptance of its definition. Later on
in this volume, we will discuss several recent attempts to redefine
the word. For now, we use the standard definition used for
hundreds of years by renowned lexicographers of our time. Of
course, it's possible for lexicographers to be mistaken, but we
will amply demonstrate that their definitions are right because
their definition agrees with the definition given by God himself.

Thayer defines adultery as "unlawful intercourse with another's wife." Vine, in his *Expository Dictionary of New Testament Words*, defines it as "unlawful intercourse with the spouse
of another." From these definitions, we see that while fornication
is the general term involving all kinds of illicit sexual activity,
adultery requires the participation of at least one married person.
While many kinds of fornication may not involve the spouse of
another, adultery must. Every time the word adultery occurs in

the Bible, in both the Old or New Testament, there is always a spouse in the context.

Jesus agreed with this definition, for in Mk. 10.11, he said:

> And he saith unto them; Whosoever shall put away his wife, and marry another, committeth adultery against her.

Notice that adultery is against the spouse.

In Rom. 7.2-3, a critical passage because it contains God's definition of adultery, Paul agreed that adultery requires participation of at least one spouse:

> For the woman that hath a husband is bound by law to the husband while he liveth; but if the husband die, she is discharged from the law of the husband. So then if, while the husband liveth, she be joined to another man, she shall be called an adulteress.

The woman who commits adultery in this passage has a husband, and he's mentioned five times! If a woman who doesn't have a husband commits adultery when she joins another man, this passage would make no sense at all. A spouse is absolutely required for adultery to be committed.

When Paul said "she shall be called an adulteress," he used the word *chrematizo*, which is here translated "called." This very interesting word only occurs nine times in the New Testament and it always refers to a pronouncement by God. Thayer said the word means "a divine calling, a calling from heaven." It's the word used in Mt. 2.12 where the wise men were "*warned of God* in a dream that they should not return to Herod" to protect the baby Jesus. It's the word used in Heb. 8.5 of Moses being "*warned of God* when he is about to make the tabernacle." It's the word used in Ac. 11.26, where Luke recorded that "the disciples were *called* Christians first in Antioch." Sometimes people wonder who called them Christians. Was it their friends? Their enemies? Did they call themselves that? If we understand the meaning of *chrematizo* to be a divine calling, a calling from heaven, we understand that God called the disciples Christians.

Thus, understanding how this word is used through the New Testament, Paul actually said in Rom. 7.2-3 that when a woman who has a husband joins herself to another man, God calls her an adulteress. Here is an inspired definition of adultery, i.e., unlawful sexual intercourse with the spouse of another.

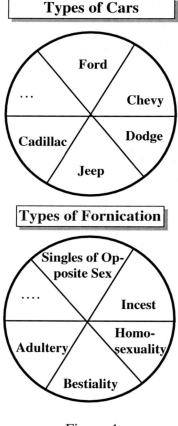

Figure 1

Distinction Between Fornication and Adultery

In Figure 1, we illustrate the difference between fornication and adultery. The top of the chart "Types of Cars," is a general term, then there are specific types of cars: Chevys, Fords, Jeeps, etc. Obviously, all Chevys are cars, but not all cars are Chevys. So it is with fornication. There are many types for fornication: bestiality (illicit sexual activity involving an *animal*), incest (illicit sexual activity involving a *relative*), homosexuality (illicit sexual activity involving *people of the same gender*), and adultery (illicit sexual activity involving a *spouse*). All incest is fornication, but not all fornication is incest, because not all fornication

Types of Fornication

INCEST

> cannot be committed together by persons
> unrelated, just as

BESTIALITY

> cannot be committed together by two persons,
> just as

HOMOSEXUALITY

> cannot be committed together by two persons of
> opposite sex, just as

ADULTERY

> cannot be committed together by two single
> persons

Figure 2

involves relatives. So fornication is illicit sexual intercourse in general, while adultery, incest, homosexuality, and bestiality are all specific types of fornication.

Figure 2 further illustrates the differences in sexual sins. As the chart illustrates, incest cannot be committed together by two people who are unrelated. Notice: two unrelated people can commit a lot of fornication together, but by definition, they cannot commit incest together, try as though they might! If a husband and wife propose over breakfast to commit incest together all day long, they cannot, try as though they might! Surely they can commit a lot of sin together, but we cannot call all sin incest. Incest is a very particular kind of fornication.

Similarly, two people cannot commit bestiality together. There must be an animal involved. Two people of the opposite sex cannot commit homosexuality together. By definition, someone of the same sex must be involved.

Likewise with adultery. Two people who are not spouses cannot commit adultery together, try as though they might. By definition, a spouse must be involved. Surely they may commit a lot of sin, but we don't brand everything we don't like adultery. Adultery is a very specific sin: illicit sexual intercourse involving a spouse.

Figure 3 illustrates how adultery in the Old Testament excluded fornication committed by two single people. In Lev.

Adultery in Old Testament Excluded Fornication by Two Singles

Lev. 20.10 - "committed adultery with another man's wife"..."committed adultery with his neighbor's wife"

Jer. 29.23 - "committed adultery with their neighbors' wives"

Ezk. 16.32 - "A wife that committed adultery that taketh strangers instead of her husband"

Hosea 4.13 - "your brides committed adultery"

Hosea 2.2 - "She is not my wife, and I am not her husband, . . . let her put away her adultery"

Penalties Differed!

Dt. 22.22 - Adulterers killed
Dt. 22.28 - Single fornicators fined

Figure 3

20.10, Moses wrote of those who "committed adultery with another man's wife," and those who "committed adultery with his neighbor's wife." In Jer. 29.23, Jeremiah spoke of those who "committed adultery with their neighbors' wives." Hos. 4.13 speaks of those whose "brides committed adultery." Again, every passage in the Bible speaking of adultery has a spouse in the context.

We also want to be sure to notice Hos. 2.2, which in latter days has been used to say that someone without a spouse can commit adultery. God said concerning Israel:

> Contend with your mother, contend, for she is not my wife, and I am not her husband. And let her put away her harlotry from her face, and her adultery from between her breasts.

Here God said that Israel was not his wife, and he was not her husband, yet she was guilty of adultery. Is this proof that a person with no spouse can commit adultery with another spouseless person? Not at all. God didn't divorce Israel until she committed adultery. Her adultery was the very reason God put her away. After God put Israel away, she no longer was married to God, and God was no longer her husband. But she was a spouse when she committed adultery, wasn't she? Rather than being a passage, which shows spouseless people can commit adultery, it's just another passage where adultery is mentioned where there is a spouse in the context.

Brethren Agree that Adultery Requires a Spouse

Before we leave our study of these two definitions, we increasingly notice that people who should know better say there's no distinction between fornication and adultery. Consider how that would have been accepted by Jews who knew anything at all about the Bible's teaching on fornication and divorce. They knew if a man committed fornication with an unbetrothed virgin that he had to marry her, pay a fine, and couldn't divorce her all his life (Dt. 22.28). However, a man who committed adultery with another man's wife, and it was provable (we'll talk about how in the next chapter), the penalty was death (Dt. 22.22). As surely as those people could know the difference between a fine and the death penalty, we should all be able to know the difference between fornication and adultery.

Given that the major lexicographers agree with God's definition of adultery, it matters little what legendary Bible students and teachers believe about it. In view of some brethren of late beginning to use new definitions of adultery that no one ever heard of until the last few years (some of which we'll talk about in Chapter 6), we present here a sampling of well-known preachers who in their writing and speaking demonstrate that we've always understood adultery to be fornication necessarily involving a spouse. These quotations could be multiplied by several factors, but these should make the point.

Bryan Vinson:

> It is understood that fornication, as distinguished from adultery, is simply an illicit sexual relationship, whereas adultery more specifically denotes such an act between two persons where either or both are *married* [emphasis mine—SGD] to other persons. (*Preceptor*, April 15, 1965.)

Jay Bowman:

> Adultery—illicit sexual intercourse by a *married* [emphasis mine—SGD] person. (*Tract on Marriage*, p. 2.)

Gene Frost:

> Adultery is voluntary sexual intercourse by a *married* [emphasis mine—SGD] man with another than his wife or by a *married* [emphasis mine—SGD] woman with another than her husband. (*Dabney-Frost Debate* [Fort Worth, TX: The Manney Co., 1959], p. 113.)

Roy Lanier, Sr.:

The word "fornication" is a broader term than "adultery" and includes all forms of sexual impurity. Paul uses fornication to express the sin of *married* [emphasis mine—SGD] people in I Cor. 5.1, 2. Jesus used the broad term when speaking of the exception, so as to allow divorce for all sexual impurity which occurs after marriage. Adultery means, illicit sexual intercourse on the part of *married* [emphasis mine—SGD] persons. (*Marriage, Divorce, Remarriage* [Shreveport, LA: Lambert Book House, n.d.], pp. 16, 34.)

Maurice Barnett:

Adultery: to have unlawful intercourse with another's wife, to commit adultery with. (*Alien Sinners and the Law of Christ* [Phoenix, AZ: Westside Church of Christ].)

J. T. Smith:

In answer to question in McCollum-Smith Debate:

Question 5: Do you agree that the definition of adultery is limited to sexual intercourse with the spouse of another? Yes.

J. D. Thomas:

From the above definitions we may say that *fornication* means any and all kinds of illicit sexual intercourse or union (including homosexuality) while *adultery* simply means intercourse where one (or both) is *married* [emphasis mine—SGD] to someone else...It is needful that these definitions be carefully in mind, because some strange meanings have been given to them apparently in the hope of justifying some unholy union. (*Divorce and Remarriage* [Abilene, TX: Biblical Research Press, 1977], p. 5.)

Notice particularly this last statement: "It is needful that these definitions be carefully in mind, because some strange meanings have been given to them apparently in hope of justifying some unholy union." Could be! As we'll see, some new definitions no one ever heard of until the last quarter of the twentieth century have arisen. A few preachers say two single people can commit adultery. If they can, there's no difference between fornication and adultery between two single people, yet there was a distinction in the sin and the punishment in the Bible.

Old Testament Teaching on Adultery

There are several instructive examples of Old Testament heroes being involved with adultery. In Gen. 12.11-20 we have the first example involving Abram:

> Now there was a famine in the land; so Abram went down to Egypt to sojourn there, for the famine was severe in the land. And it came about when he came near to Egypt, that he said to Sarai his wife, See now, I know that you are a beautiful woman; and it will come about when the Egyptians see you, that they will say, This is his wife, and they will kill me, but they will let you live. Please say that you are my sister so that it may go well with me because of you, and that I may live on account of you. And it came about when Abram came into Egypt, the Egyptians saw that the woman was very beautiful [Sarai was sixty-five years old at this time—SGD]. And so Pharaoh's officials saw her and praised her to Pharaoh; and the woman was taken to Pharaoh's house. Therefore he treated Abram well for her sake, and gave him sheep and oxen and donkeys and male and female servants and female donkeys and camels. But the Lord struck Pharaoh and his house with great plagues because of Sarai, Abram's wife. Then Pharaoh called Abram and said, What is this you have done to me? Why did you not tell me that she was your wife? Why did you say, She is my sister, so that I took her for my wife? Now then here is

your wife, take her and go. And Pharaoh commanded his men concerning him; and they escorted him away, with his wife, and all that belonged to him.

This is an embarrassment of Abram, who would become the father of all the faithful, being upbraided by a pagan king who realized he nearly committed adultery with another man's wife. Even pagans realized that adultery was a serious sin against God.

In Gen. 26.6-11, Abram's son Isaac had the same problem:

So Isaac lived in Gerar. When the men of the place asked about his wife, he said, She is my sister, for he was afraid to say, My wife, thinking, the men of the place might kill me on account of Rebekah, for she is beautiful [Rebekah was about sixty years old here—SGD]. And it came about, when he had been there a long time, that Abimelech king of the Philistines looked out through a window, and saw, and behold, Isaac was caressing his wife Rebekah. Then Abimelech called Isaac and said, Behold, certainly she is your wife! How then did you say, She is my sister? And Isaac said to him, Because I said, Lest I die on account of her. And Abimelech said, What is this you have done to us? One of the people might easily have lain with your wife, and you would have brought guilt upon us. So Abimelech charged all the people, saying, He who touches this man or his wife shall surely be put to death.

Again, this pagan king had a clear measure of the seriousness of adultery. He realized that for one of his citizens to commit adultery was to defile the whole land, to the extent that he was willing to impose the death penalty in order to deter such. Would that our government was so earnest in deterring sin.

In Gen. 39.6-9, Joseph, son of Isaac and grandson of Abram had a similar experience with the ruler's (Potiphar) wife in Egypt:

[Potiphar—SGD] left everything he owned in Joseph's charge; and with him around he did not concern himself with anything except the food which he ate. Now Joseph was handsome in form and appearance. And it came about after these events that his master's wife looked with desire at Joseph, and she said, Lie with me. But he refused and said to his master's wife, Behold with me around, my master does not concern himself with anything in the house, and he has put all that he owns in my charge. There is no one greater in this house than I, and he has withheld nothing from me except you, because you are his wife. How then could I do this great evil, and sin against God?

This passage teaches that adultery is not just against one's spouse, and the spouse of the partner, but also against God.

In addition to these examples of the seriousness of adultery in the Old Testament, there were also specific prohibitions of adultery in Ex. 20.14 in the Ten Commandments, Lev. 18.20, and Lev. 20.10, where the death penalty is pronounced upon the guilty:

If there is a man who commits adultery with another man's wife, one who commits adultery with his friend's wife, the adulterer and the adulteress shall surely be put to death.

There were restrictions on using the death penalty for adultery which we'll notice in the next chapter, "Divorce under Moses."

New Testament Prohibition of Adultery

The New Testament continues God's prohibition of adultery in Gal. 5.19-21, where Paul said:

Now the works of the flesh are manifest, which are these: fornication [which includes adultery—SGD], uncleanness, lasciviousness, of which I forewarn you, even as I did forewarn you, that they who practise such things shall not inherit the kingdom of God.

Chapter 3

Divorce Under Moses

Highlights

- *Most adulterers under Moses' Law couldn't be stoned to death.*
- *God not loose on divorce in Old Testament.*
- *Some rabbis of Jesus' time correctly understood Deuteronomy 24, and we can too.*
- *Dt. 24.1-4 authorized divorce only for fornication, and both parties could remarry.*

We come now to what must be the most critical part of our study, Moses' teaching on divorce. The author didn't always feel that Moses' teaching was so important, but in recent years he came to realize he was giving the Old Testament's teaching on the subject completely inadequate attention. Understanding Moses' teaching is critical because it helps us understand Jesus' teaching, which he gave in the context of discussions with his fellow Jews regarding Moses' teaching. Jesus' discussion with the Pharisees in Mt. 19.1-12 was about Dt. 24.1-4. Men to whom Paul spoke in Rom. 7.1-3, "who know the law," knew the passages we're about to study. If we don't know the Old Testament teaching, Rom. 7.1-3 wasn't addressed to people like us: it was addressed to a more knowledgeable people. The author can nearly guarantee that our study of divorce under Moses will stimulate your thinking concerning both the teachings of Moses and Jesus. You, like the author, will probably conclude this study thinking much more highly of God and God's will concerning divorce than we have in the past.

Plan of Study

Old Testament

Not for fornication	*For fornication*

New Testament

Not for fornication	*For fornication*

Figure 4

Strategy for Study

In the next few chapters of this book, we intend to follow the study strategy depicted in Figure 4. First, we will cover the Old Testament's teaching on divorce in cases of fornication. Second, we will cover the Old Testament's teaching in the not-for-fornication case. Third, we will proceed to the New Testament's teaching on divorce not for fornication, and last, the New Testament's teaching on divorce for fornication. When we finish these four sections of our study, we should be able to fill out the empty sections of Figure 4.

We begin our study of divorce under Moses by noting that Moses dealt with three situations involving adultery: (1) cases where adultery was verified, (2) cases where adultery was suspected after marriage, and (3) cases where fornication was suspected before marriage.

Adultery Verified—Death

In Lev. 20.10, Moses said:

If there is a man who commits adultery with another man's wife, one who commits adultery with his friend's wife, the adulterer and the adulteress shall surely be put to death.

In Dt. 22.22, Moses said:

If a man is found lying with a married woman, then both of them shall die, the man who lay with the woman, and the woman; thus you shall purge the evil from Israel.

In cases where the death penalty was carried out, of course, it was not really a case of divorce. With both of these passages, we need to keep in mind the condition God put on all exercise of the death penalty in Mosaic times, a condition which, if neglected, will cause us to make a serious mistake on divorce in the Old Testament. Moses was very explicit that capital crimes were only to be punished with death if there were a plurality of witnesses to the offense. In Dt. 17.6, he said, "On the evidence of two witnesses or three witnesses he who is to die shall be put to death; he shall not be put to death on the evidence of one witness." In Num. 35.30, we read, "If anyone kills a person, the murderer shall be put to death at the evidence of witnesses, but no person shall be put to death on the testimony of one witness." In Dt. 19.15, Moses again said, "A single witness shall not rise up against a man on account of any iniquity or any sin which he has committed; on the evidence of two or three witnesses a matter shall be confirmed."

Thus, a man couldn't just suspect his wife of adultery and have her put to death. It couldn't be done on the basis of rumor. No one could be put to death for any sin without the testimony of at least two witnesses. This was actually the situation Joseph, husband of Mary, was in. From his point of view, he knew she was an adulteress, but he couldn't have had her stoned because there were no witnesses.

Since most people then and now are so inconsiderate that they commit their adultery privately, not in front of two or three witnesses, the death penalty could not be exercised except on the most blatant cases. Realization of this fact exposes the serious mistake in the statement, "There was no divorce for adultery in the Old Testament because all adulterers were put to death," even when it was made by the author himself for many years.

Adultery Suspected—Law of Jealousy

Num. 5.12-28 described what a Jewish husband could do when he wasn't sure if his wife had been unfaithful to him and there were no witnesses:

> If any man's wife goes astray and is unfaithful to him, and a man has intercourse with her and it is hidden from the eyes of her husband and she is undetected, although she has defiled herself, and there is no witness against her and she has not been caught in the act, if a spirit of jealousy comes over him and he is jealous of his wife when she has defiled herself, or if a spirit of jealousy comes over him and he is jealous of his wife when she has not defiled herself, the man shall then bring his wife to the priest, and shall bring as an offering for her one-tenth of an ephah of barley meal; he shall not pour oil on it, nor put frankincense on it, for it is a grain

offering of jealousy, a grain offering of memorial, a
reminder of iniquity.

Then the priest shall bring her near and have her stand
before the Lord [probably in front of the tabernacle, as
the altar is mentioned further down—SGD], and the
priest shall take holy water in an earthenware vessel; and
he shall take some of the dust that is on the floor of the
tabernacle and put it into the water. The priest shall then
have the woman stand before the Lord and let the hair of
the woman's head go loose, and place the grain offering
of memorial in her hands, which is the grain offering of
jealousy, and in the hand of the priest is to be the water
of bitterness that brings a curse. And the priest shall have
her take an oath and shall say to the woman, If no man
has lain with you and if you have not gone astray into
uncleanness, being under the authority of your husband,
be immune to this water of bitterness that brings a curse;
if you, however, have gone astray, being under the
authority of your husband, and if you have defiled yourself and a man other than your husband has had intercourse with you, then the priest shall have the woman
swear with the oath of the curse, and the priest shall say
to the woman, The Lord make you a curse and an oath
among your people by the Lord's making your thigh
waste away and your abdomen swell; and this water that
brings a curse shall go into your stomach and make your
abdomen swell and your thigh waste away. And the
woman shall say, Amen, Amen.

The priest shall then write these curses on a scroll, and
he shall wash them off into the water of bitterness. Then
he shall make the woman drink the water of bitterness
that brings a curse, so that the water which brings a curse
will go into her and cause bitterness. And the priest shall
take the grain offering of jealousy from the woman's
hand, and he shall wave the grain offering before the
Lord and bring it to the altar; and the priest shall take a
handful of the grain offering as its memorial offering and

offer it up in smoke on the altar, and afterward he shall make the woman drink the water. *When he has made her drink the water, then it shall come about, if she has defiled herself and has been unfaithful to her husband, that the water which brings a curse shall go into her and cause bitterness, and her abdomen will swell and her thigh will waste away, and the woman will become a curse among her people.* [emphasis mine—SGD] But if the woman has not defiled herself and is clean, she will then be free and conceive children.

Of course, this would be an excruciatingly humiliating experience for a man to put his wife through. It is apparent that in a case where there were no human witnesses to her marital unfaithfulness, that God would be the witness. This test was done in the presence of God, with an oath before God, and God would indicate whether she was unfaithful or not. If the indication was that she was guilty, "the woman will become a curse," that is, she would be set apart for destruction. This would be death as an adulterer with God as the witness to her adultery and high-handed lying in his presence. If she were put to death, of course, there would be no divorce.

Joseph, who lived under this law, could have put Mary through this test, at least if the High Priest of his time were still engaging in this practice. The excruciating nature of this ordeal gives meaning to Matthew's statement that "Joseph, being a righteous man, was mindful to put her away privily." Even though Joseph was convinced that Mary was an unrepentant pregnant adulteress, he was not willing to humiliate her to this extent.

Fornication Suspected Before Marriage

In Dt. 22.13-19, we read of the seriousness of a man unjustly defaming his wife when he suspected marital unfaithfulness:

If a man takes a wife and goes in to her and then turns against her, and charges her with shameful deeds and publicly defames her, and says, I took this woman, but when I came near her, I did not find her a virgin. Then the girl's father and her mother shall take and bring out the evidence of the girl's virginity [a garment, v17—SGD] to the elders of the city at the gate. And the girl's father shall say to the elders, I gave my daughter to this man for a wife, but he turned against her, and behold, he has charged her with shameful deeds, saying, I did not find your daughter a virgin. But this is the evidence of my daughter's virginity. And they shall spread the garment before the elders of the city. So the elders of that city shall take the man and chastise him, and they shall fine him a hundred shekels of silver and give it to the girl's father, because he publicly defamed a virgin of Israel. And she shall remain his wife; he cannot divorce her all his days.

The 100-shekel fine for a man to falsely defame his wife was enormous. Scholars agree that 100 shekels was about 100 months' wages. If a man of our time made $4,000 per month, this fine would amount to $400,000. A Jewish man would have to sell himself into slavery to pay such an amount. Thus, Jewish men would be extremely careful about defaming their wives, and we see God's love in protecting wives from this abuse.

Of course, if the wife were guilty, verses 20-21 teach that she was stoned to death, so divorce was not an option in this case, either.

Divorce for Indecency or Unseemliness— Dt. 24.1-4

We now come to the major text on divorce in Moses' teaching. These are the verses Jesus discussed with the Pharisees in Mt. 19.1-9. Again, these are verses that "men who know the law" to whom Paul wrote in Rom. 7.2-3 knew. Moses said:

When a man takes a wife and marries her, and it happens that she finds no favor in his eyes because he has found

some indecency [ASV "unseemliness"—SGD] in her,
and he writes her a certificate of divorce and puts it in
her hand and sends her out from his house, and she leaves
his house and goes and becomes another man's wife, and
if the latter husband turns against her, and writes her a
certificate of divorce, and puts it in her hand and sends
her out of his house, or if the latter husband dies who
took her to be his wife, then her former husband who sent
her away is not allowed to take her again to be his wife;
since she has been defiled: for that is an abomination
before the Lord, and you shall not bring sin on the land
which the Lord your God gives you as an inheritance.

The key question of this passage is, and apparently has been
for at least two thousand years, the meaning of the word "indecency" or "unseemliness." This was essentially what the controversy was about in Mt. 19.3, where the Pharisees questioned Jesus
about the grounds for divorce: "Is it *lawful* for a man to put his
wife away for every cause?" The only law they could have
referred to was Moses' law. In Mt. 19.7, they referred to this very
passage in Deuteronomy when they asked, "Why then did Moses
command to give a bill of divorcement, and to put her away?"

History tells us that some rabbis of Jesus' time said that
"indecency" referred to fornication. Others said it could include
trivial reasons. If a man found a prettier woman, he could put
away his present wife because she was indecent. If his wife
burned the bread, or spun [yarn—SGD] in the streets, that would
be indecent enough. Some in our day might say their wives are
indecent if they sleep past 5 a.m. and only fix one kind of gravy
for breakfast.

One tragic thing that has happened as a result of the rabbinical
controversy in Jesus' time is that many throw up their hands and
say, "If they couldn't understand what indecency was in Jesus'
time, how can we hope to now?" We need to have more confidence in God's word than that. Additionally, it wasn't that the
Jews couldn't understand, it's just that some of them didn't
understand. Some of them did understand! Whether indecency
implied fornication or something less than that, some rabbis were
entirely correct, and Jesus endorsed the teaching of those rabbis!

We'll present the evidence for our position momentarily, but let's realize that when rabbis of our day disagree on something like whether baptism is sprinkling or immersion, we don't throw up our hands and say, "Well, if they can't understand it, how can we?" Remember Ps. 119.104, where the Psalmist said, "Through thy precepts I get understanding," and Ps. 119.105, "thy word is a lamp unto my feet and a light unto my pathway." We need to have confidence in God's word that it contains the answers.

Rather than go through a word study of what "indecency" means, it's customary for most teachers on this subject to assume that since adulterers were stoned to death, divorce wasn't an option for them, so indecency must be something other than adultery. This is the road the author went down for about fifteen years until he realized that the vast majority of adulterers were not stoned; and rightly so, because of a lack of witnesses.

Once someone makes that assumption, though, it's easy to assume that God allowed divorce for reasons less than fornication in the Old Testament, then Jesus finally straightened the mess out when he came into the world. Notice the following typical statement of this position:

> Jesus referred here to the Old Testament law of Deuteronomy 24:1-4 which allowed a man to put away his wife for indecent conduct short of adultery, but Jesus said such a practice will no longer be tolerated." (Ron Halbrook, *Searching the Scriptures, XXXII,* #9, September 1991, p. 11.)

One can be an extremely good fellow and take this position. I know, because I did myself for many years. One can make this statement quickly, without defining the word translated "indecency," without displaying any word study of what it means, and go directly to the New Testament's teaching on divorce. I know, because I did the same thing myself for many years. But I'm not going to do it any more.

There's something basically wrong with taking the position that God would allow Jewish men to put away their spouses for something less than fornication. Recall that we studied in Deuteronomy 22 how God prevented men from defaming their wives by ordering a huge fine, about eight years' wages, for defaming their wives. Why would God allow those same men to defame and stigmatize their wives by divorcing them here, when he wouldn't allow them to defame and stigmatize them only two pages back in their Bibles? If a man could divorce without the basis of adultery here without payment of a fine, why would a man risk violating Deuteronomy 22 with false accusations of fornication that could backfire on him and result in his being sold into economic bankruptcy or slavery? Did God allow Jewish men to so treat their wives just as long as they handled the paperwork, the bill of divorcement, correctly? If so, that seems to be the ultimate emphasis on bureaucratic formality over treating their wives humanely, doesn't it? That would make God think more of the paperwork than he did the wives! To take the position that Deuteronomy 24 allowed divorce for reasons short of adultery seems incompatible with Mal. 2.14, where God told a later generation of Jewish men, "I hate divorce," unless, of course, one thinks that God was rather loose on divorce, looser than most of us would permit preachers to be, then God finally got his act together just before he sent Jesus into the world.

We don't tolerate such a view of God on other subjects such as when we're discussing premillennialism. We note that doctrinaire premillennialists teach that God intended to establish his kingdom when Christ came into the world the first time, but because the Jews rejected Christ, God was forced to suspend the kingdom and will establish it when Christ comes back the next time. We point out to them that God's plans aren't thwarted by men and that God doesn't cave in because of what men do. Yet many of us have exactly that view of God, if we believe that God caved in and permitted loose divorce because the Jews were so rebellious. To so argue is to make the same argument premillennialists make. May it never be!

I believe, and am about to prove, that the word "indecency" here refers to fornication in this passage, and that the passage authorized, but didn't demand, the husband to divorce his wife for her fornication. I further believe that God didn't want him to divorce her, even for fornication, unless he couldn't work the problem out, or if his wife wouldn't repent, then he was authorized to put her away, just like God did with Israel, and Joseph was going to do with Mary until he found out she wasn't an impenitent fornicator. Further, when she was put away for her fornication, she was authorized to remarry.

Word Study of *Gervah*—Nakedness

The Hebrew word translated "indecency" is *gervah*, which means nakedness, without argument. The word holds this meaning all the fifty or so times it occurs in the Old Testament. While everyone who writes on this subject realizes this, it's customary for most of us to make statements like, "The word *gervah* basically means nakedness, and it's usually used in a bad sexual connotation. But since adulterers were stoned to death, it wasn't adultery. So the best guess is that the word refers to some sexual sin short of adultery." While we won't discuss every time this word is used in the Old Testament, we will give the reader a list of every time the word occurs (which will enable the reader to study every occurrence of *gervah*). Instead, we will discuss all the different ways the word is used.

Nakedness of Land

First of all, as Figures 5-6 show, there are two times where the word is used, not of sexual or even personal nakedness at all, but of the nakedness of a land. In Gen. 42.9 and 12, the Jews were told "to see the nakedness of the land" in order to see how defenseless it was. In these two passages, the word *gervah* has no sexual connotation at all.

Personal Sexual Nakedness, Not Sexual Activity, Just Shameful or Inappropriate

Next, *gervah* is used of personal sexual nakedness not involving sexual activity, but in cases where such nakedness was shameful or inappropriate to the circumstances. For example, in Gen. 9.22 Noah's sons saw the nakedness of their father, and took it lightly. In Gen. 9.23, they covered their father's nakedness.

Deut. 24.1-4 - "Indecent"

from NAKEDNESS - Heb: GERVAH

Nakedness of lands or cities

Gen. 42.9 - to see the NAKEDNESS of the land ye are in
Gen. 42.12 - to see the NAKEDNESS of the land

Summary: Not personal nakedness or sexual activity, but uncovered, defenseless land

Shameful personal nakedness with no sexual activity

Gen. 9.22 - Noah's sons saw NAKEDNESS of their father
Gen. 9.23 - covered the NAKEDNESS of their father
Gen. 9.23 - they saw not their father's NAKEDNESS
Ex. 20.26 - priest's NAKEDNESS not to be discovered when ascending altar
Ex. 28.42 - linen breeches to cover their NAKEDNESS
Dt. 23.12-14 - two things uncovered here
        excrement - covered with spade
        personal nakedness - covered by going outside the camp
Isa. 20.4 - Assyrians will carry off Egyptians NAKED into captivity
Isa. 47.3 - Babylon's personal NAKEDNESS will be shown in punishment
Ezek. 16.8 - God covered Israel's NAKEDNESS at the beginning
Ezek. 16.37 - Egyptians, Chaldeans will see Judah's NAKEDNESS

Summary: Improper sexual nakedness without sexual activity

Illicit or Legitimate Sexual Activity

Lev. 18.6 - NAKEDNESS of a blood relative
        v19 - marry to uncover nakedness, to lie with, etc.
Lev. 18.7 - NAKEDNESS of father, NAKEDNESS of mother
        one honorable, one dishonorable - incest
Lev. 18.8 - the NAKEDNESS of thy father's wife
        one honorable, one dishonorable - incest
Lev. 18.10 - the NAKEDNESS of thy son's daughter
        incest with granddaughter
Lev. 18.10 - daughter's daughter's NAKEDNESS thou shalt not uncover
        incest with granddaughter
Lev. 18.11 - the NAKEDNESS of thy father's wife's daughter
        incest with stepsister
Lev. 18.12 - the NAKEDNESS of your father's sister
        incest with aunt
Lev. 18.13 - the NAKEDNESS of your mother's sister
        incest with aunt

Figure 5

Indecency (Cont'd)

Illicit or Legitimate Sexual Activity (Cont'd)

Lev. 18.15 - the NAKEDNESS of your daughter in law incest with daughter
in law

Lev. 18.16 - the NAKEDNESS of thy brother's wife
one honorable, one dishonorable, incest with sister in law

Lev. 18.17 - the NAKEDNESS of a mother and her daughter

Lev. 18.18, 19 - marry a woman in addition to her sister to uncover her
NAKEDNESS
"uncovering nakedness" synonym of "lie"

Lev. 18.19 - NAKEDNESS during menstrual impurity

Lev. 20.11 - uncovered his father's NAKEDNESS incest

Lev. 20.17 - he sees relative's NAKEDNESS and she sees his NAKEDNESS
general incest

Lev. 20.18 - uncovers NAKEDNESS of menstruous woman
two things uncovered: personal nakedness, her discharge

Lev. 20.19 - NAKEDNESS of aunts

Lev. 20.20 - uncovered his uncle's NAKEDNESS

Lev. 20.21 - uncovered his brother's NAKEDNESS
Mk. 6.17-18, Mt. 14.1-4

Dt. 24.1 - he hath found some UNCLEANNESS in her

I Sam. 20.30 - the confusion of thy mother's NAKEDNESS

Lam. 1.8 - Babylon has seen Judah's NAKEDNESS

Ezek. 16.36 - thy NAKEDNESS discovered through your harlotries
harlotries in LXX is *porneia* (fornication in Mt. 19.9, 5.32)

Ezek. 22.10 - they discovered their father's NAKEDNESS
sexual sins of rulers of Israel

Ezek. 23.10, 18, 29 - Egyptians discovered Israel's NAKEDNESS
Egyptians unlawful relations with Israel
v29 - uses NAKEDNESS and *porneia* synonymously again

Conclusion: This isn't
spinning in the streets or burning the bread
But it is
illicit sexual activity, or fornication!

Some Rabbis were right!

Figure 6

There was no fornication here, no sexual activity, just personal sexual nakedness.

In Ex. 20.26 we get an idea of what personal sexual nakedness actually meant when Moses said, "And you shall not go up by steps to My altar, that your nakedness may not be exposed on it." This, again, involved no sexual activity, but it was just shameful and inappropriate for the priest's nakedness to be revealed while he was ascending the altar. In Ex. 28.42, Moses ordained linen breeches to cover their nakedness from their waist to their thighs. Hence, nakedness, at least for men, referred to their genital area, not their ankles or shoulders.

One extremely interesting passage is Dt. 23.12-14, where the reader should notice two things that were uncovered that need to be covered:

> You shall also have a place outside the camp and go out there, and you shall have a spade among your tools, and it shall be when you sit down outside, you shall dig with it and shall turn to cover up your excrement, since the Lord your God walks in the midst of your camp to deliver you and to defeat your enemies before you, therefore your camp must be holy; and He must not see anything indecent [Heb. *gervah*—SGD] among you lest He turn away from you.

The first uncovered thing that needed to be covered up was the person's personal nakedness while he tended his bodily needs. This was covered by going outside the camp for privacy. His excrement also needed to be covered, and that was accomplished with the shovel. This could have been accomplished inside the camp, but of course, the person's personal nakedness wouldn't have been covered there.

In Isa. 20.4, we read of the personal sexual nakedness of the Egyptians. This was not sexual activity, but the exposure of the Egyptians by the Assyrians as they carried them off into captivity. In Isa. 47.3, we read of the Babylonians' personal sexual nakedness being exposed as they were carried off into captivity themselves. Other examples of this use of *gervah* are given in Figures 5-6.

Seeing Someone's Sexual Nakedness Dishonorably—Either Illicit or Legitimate Sexual Activity

In Lev. 18.6, we read:

> None of you shall approach any blood relative of his to uncover nakedness, I am the Lord.

This is not speaking of changing a baby's diapers, or adults having an accidental glance at someone's personal nakedness. As we see in verse 19, marriage was for the right of uncovering nakedness. This use is synonymous with "lying with" a person. This passage is prohibiting incest.

In Lev.18.7, we see *gervah* used twice, once honorably, and once shamefully:

> You shall not uncover the nakedness of your father, that is, the nakedness of your mother. She is your mother; you are not to uncover her nakedness.

Uncovering the nakedness of the woman was honorable as the right of marriage for the father to do it, but dishonorable for her son to do it. There are a number of cases of *gervah* used this way, but let's notice in particular Lev. 20.21:

> If there is a man who takes his brother's wife, it is abhorrent; he has uncovered his brother's nakedness. They shall be childless.

This is the situation described in Mt. 14.1-4 and Mk. 6.17-18 where John the Baptist told Herod that it wasn't lawful for him to have his brother Philip's wife.

Dt. 24.1 is next in Figure 6, our present passage of interest, where the man wants to put his wife away because he has found some *indecency* in her. It should be obvious thus far that indecency isn't burning the bread or spinning in the streets in which no sexual nakedness is involved at all. So far we would just know indecency is a matter of sexual nakedness, at least from her waist to her thighs. In Ezek. 16.36, we have an extremely important passage where God described Jerusalem's unfaithfulness to him:

> Thus says the Lord God, Because your lewdness was poured out and your nakedness [Heb. *gervah*—SGD] uncovered through your harlotries [Gr. *porneia* in Septuagint—SGD] with your lovers and with all your detestable idols, and because of the blood of your sons which you gave to idols:

This passage is important because here *gervah* is used synonymously with *porneia*, the Greek word for fornication in the Septuagint (Greek Old Testament).

In Ezek. 23.29, God spoke again of Jerusalem's unfaithfulness being punished by the Babylonians:

> And they will deal with you in hatred, take all your property, and leave you naked and bare. And the nakedness [Heb. *gervah*—SGD] of your harlotries [Gr. *porneia* in Septuagint—SGD] shall be uncovered, both your lewdness and your harlotries.

This is speaking of the unlawful relations of the Egyptians with Israel, and is another example of *gervah* and *porneia* being used synonymously again. This isn't spinning in the streets or burning the bread, but it is illicit sexual activity or fornication. When some of the rabbis thought indecency referred to fornication, they were exactly right, weren't they?

Gervah Is Translated by *Askemon* in Septuagint

Another major clue to the meaning of *gervah* in the Old Testament is to see how it was translated in the Greek version, or Septuagint. The Greek word for *gervah* is *askemon*, and as Figure 7 shows, *askemon* is used just five times in the New Testament. Seeing how *askemon* is used in the New Testament will be extremely instructive, as to the meaning of "indecency" in the

"Indecency" is ASKEMON in LXX

Only 5 times in New Testament:

I Cor. 7.36 - "if any man thinketh that he behaveth himself
UNSEEMLY toward his virgin *daughter*. . . let him do what he will,
he sinneth not; let them marry"

> *daughter* added by translators
> *daughter* implies incest!
> same as I Cor. 7.2 - to avoid fornications

I Cor. 13.5 - love doth not behave itself UNSEEMLY

Rom. 1.27 - the men burned in their lust one toward another, men
with men working UNSEEMLINESS

Rev. 16.15 - Blessed is he that watcheth, and keepeth his garments,
lest he walk naked, and they see his SHAME

I Cor. 12.23 - the parts of the body, which we think to be less
honorable, upon these we bestow more abundant honor; and our
UNCOMELY parts have more abundant comeliness, whereas our
comely parts have no need

Conclusion: Greek word implies sexual nakedness
consistently in New Testament
Means fornication 4 of 5 times!
Some Rabbis were right!

Figure 7

Old Testament, and it will probably enlighten us on the meaning
of several New Testament passages as well.

First, in I Cor. 7.36, Paul said:

But if any man thinketh that he behaveth himself unseemly [from Gr. *askemon*—SGD] toward his virgin
daughter, if she be past the flower of her age, and if need
so requireth, let him do what he will, he sinneth not, let
them marry.

First of all, the word daughter in this passage is in italics,
indicating it was supplied by the translator. It is better omitted
for two reasons: (1) it authorizes incest, condemned elsewhere in
the Bible, and (2) it is not in keeping with the theme of I
Corinthians 7, avoiding fornication. The verse teaches the general
condition where it is good not to marry (verse 1): that if a man is
not able to contain his sexual desires toward his virgin, he should
marry her. This is just a special case of it being better to marry
than burning with unsatisfied sexual desire (verse 9). Here the
word *askemon* is used of a man either committing or about to
commit fornication with his virgin.

In I Cor. 13.5, Paul used this word when he said, "Love doth
not behave itself *unseemly* [Gr. *askemon*—SGD]." Again,
askemon, used for indecency in the Old Testament, is undoubtedly referring to indecency in the sexual realm, here to a spouse
who loves his partner not being sexually unfaithful to him or her.
It's not talking about temper tantrums, or merely being inconsiderate, but illicit sexual activity.

In Rom 1.27, Paul said:

...and likewise also the men, leaving the natural use of
the woman, burned in their lust one toward another, men
with men working *unseemliness* [Gr. *askemon*—SGD].

Here the word *askemon* is used with reference to homosexual
fornication.

In Rev. 16.15, Jesus said:

Behold, I come as a thief, Blessed is he that watcheth,
and keepeth his garments, lest he walk naked, and they
see his *shame* [Gr. *askemon*—SGD].

Here the word *askemon* is used of one seduced by the harlot to commit fornication.

The last New Testament passage where *askemon* occurs is I Cor. 12.23-24, where Paul said:

> ...and those parts of the body, which we think to be less honorable, upon these we bestow more abundant honor; and our uncomely [Gr. *askemon*—SGD] parts have more abundant comeliness.

Our uncomely parts here are probably not our toes, but this is undoubtedly a reference to covering our personal nakedness with clothing, whereas our more honorable parts have no need of such cover, our faces, our hair, our hands, etc.

In these five examples sexual nakedness was referred to each time, and fornication was referred to four out of the five times. When some of the rabbis said *gervah referred to fornication, they were right!*

Thus, to conclude the first part of our study of Dt. 24.1-4, we notice what Moses said:

> When a man takes a wife and marries her, and it happens that she finds no favor in his eyes because he has found some indecency [ASV "unseemliness"—SGD] in her, and he writes her a certificate of divorce and puts it in her hand and sends her out from his house...

Moses was very probably speaking of a man whose wife had committed sexual sin not punishable by death, and that's the reason "she finds no favor in his eyes." In Chapter 5 where we discuss Jesus' teaching on divorce under Moses, we'll be able to refine our interpretation of Dt. 24.1-4 even further.

Moses then said, "And he writes her a certificate of divorce and sends her out of his house." A sample copy of a certificate of divorce is given in Figure 8. As marriage was private in Moses' time, so was divorce; although, customarily the certificate was signed by witnesses, as many legal documents are today. Some writers suggest that the written document would serve several purposes. First, it might prevent hasty action on the part of the

Sample Writing of Divorcement

"On the _____ day of the week_____ in the month
_____ in the year _____ from the beginning of the
world, according to the common computation in the
province of _____, I, _____ the son of _____
by whatsoever name I may be known, of the town of
_____, with entire consent of mind, and without any
constraint, have divorced, dismissed and expelled thee
_____ daughter of _____ by whatsoever name thou
art called, of the town _____, who hast been my wife
hitherto, but now I have dismissed thee _____ the
daughter of _____ by whatsoever name thou art called,
of the town of _____ so as to be free at thy own disposal,
to marry one, from this day for ever. Thou art therefore
free for anyone who would marry thee. Let this be thy bill
of divorce from me, a writing of separation and expulsion,
according to the Law of Moses and Israel.

_____, the son of _____, witness
_____, the son of _____, witness

(from Hebrew *MISHNAH, ISBE, II*, p. 864)

Figure 8

husband. If he had to take long enough to compose the document
and secure witnesses to his action, he might not rashly send his
wife away because if he did and she remarried, she could never
be his wife again. Second, the certificate would be a measure of
protection for the put-away woman. It would show that she was
no longer married to the man, and, as we'll see momentarily,
show her right to marry another.

Could the Put-Away Person Remarry?

Moses then said, "And goes and becomes another man's wife." The question generally arises whether (1) Moses authorized the put-away woman to remarry, (2) whether he just recognized that most would without approval or authorization from God, or (3) whether Moses just stated that if she did remarry, she would not be able to remarry the first husband as a further regulation.

It's interesting to notice how casually Moses mentioned the remarriage of this put-away partner who had committed sexual activity not punishable by death. Recall that many times in the Old Testament when a certain sin or matter of uncleanness was committed, some fine or sacrifice was required. We've already seen that when a man committed fornication with a virgin, he had to pay a fine and marry her. There were trespass offerings for touching a dead body, a sore, or human waste, even by accident. For dozens of other infractions and trespasses, grain offerings or animal offerings were required.

However, when Moses dealt with the remarriage of a put-away sexual sinner, Moses said, "And she goes and becomes another man's wife," just like that. No fine, no grain offering, no pinch of salt, no turtledoves, no pigeons, lambs, goats, nor bulls. The remarriage of this put-away sexual sinner didn't seem to be controversial at all.

Further evidence that she could remarry is found in Lev. 21.7 where Moses said, "A priest shall not marry a woman divorced from her husband." This verse contains a necessary implication that she could marry any man except a priest, else the verse would have no meaning at all. Likewise, with Dt. 24.2-4, Moses said:

> ...and she leaves his house and goes and becomes another man's wife, and if the latter husband turns against her, and writes her a certificate of divorce, and puts it in her hand and sends her out of his house, or if the latter husband dies who took her to be his wife, then her former husband who sent her away is not allowed to take her again to be his wife; since she has been defiled: for that

is an abomination before the Lord, and you shall not
bring sin on the land which the Lord your God gives you
as an inheritance.

The fact that Moses prohibited the first husband from remarrying her after the second husband put her away or died necessarily implies that she could marry any other man (unmarried, of course). If she were prohibited from remarrying at all, the prohibition regarding her first husband would have no meaning.

Summary of Moses' Teaching on Divorce Thus Far

Our study of Moses' teaching thus far has elicited the following facts:

1. Moses authorized divorce for illicit sexual activity not punishable by death.

2. The put-away wife was authorized to remarry without sin.

We will further refine our interpretation of Dt. 24.1-4 in the following chapter, but for now, this is what "put away" meant to the Jews the four times that it is used in Mt. 19.3, 7, 8, and 9 when they questioned Jesus about this very passage. This is what those to whom Paul spoke in Rom. 7.2-3, "who know the law," knew. We cannot use Romans 7 to disagree with Moses' teaching without contradicting Deuteronomy 24. Under Moses, scriptural divorce freed both parties to remarry.

Chapter 4

Jesus Correctly Interpreted Moses to Jews

Highlights

- *Sermon on the Mount is Old Covenant teaching, not New Covenant.*

Before we conclude our study of Moses' teaching on divorce, we want to consider Jesus' teaching on divorce under Moses. Jesus' statements on divorce are found mainly in Mt. 5.32 and Mt. 19.3-12, in which both Jesus and the Pharisees, who were testing him on divorce and remarriage, referred to parts of Moses' teaching in Deuteronomy 24. Since Mt. 5.32 is in what is commonly called the Sermon on the Mount, we first want to examine the entire context of Jesus' teaching there by briefly analyzing the Sermon on the Mount, primarily from Matthew 5-7, generally considered the heart of Jesus' moral teaching. Beginning with Matthew 5 we read:

> vv1-2: And seeing the multitudes, he went up into the mountain: and when he had sat down, his disciples came unto him: and he opened his mouth and taught them, saying…

Thus, Jesus taught Israelites, Israelites who desperately needed to return to God and serve him in spirit and truth. Understanding what he taught in this sermon will help us place Mt. 5.32 in its proper context.

Views of the Sermon on the Mount

The Common View: Contrasting Covenants

In Matthew 5-7, we find the most complete account of the Sermon on the Mount. The common view of this passage is that Jesus contrasted his New Covenant with the Mosaic Covenant. The author for many years held this view himself. It's easy to see how one could so take the contrasts Jesus built, like "Ye have heard that it was said, but I say unto you." Since Malachi prophesied that the Messiah would bring a new covenant anyway, surely the Sermon on the Mount contrasted those two covenants.

A number of Bible scholars take this approach. Foy E. Wallace, in his *Sermon on the Mount and the Civil State* stated it this way:

> The whole of the Sermon on the Mount was therefore prospective and contemplative of the new covenant, the new dispensation and the new kingdom, from Pentecost to the end of time, and we now proceed to the examination of its principles. (Foy E. Wallace, Jr., *Sermon on the Mount and the Civil State* [Nashville, TN: Foy E. Wallace, Jr. Publications, 1967], p. 11.)

> Each beatitude states a gospel principle, a preview of the kingdom, and it is impossible to ignore Pentecost as the time foretold in these precepts, the immediate prospect of which accentuated the teaching. (*Ibid.*, p. 12.)

James Tolle, author of a helpful volume on the Beatitudes, sets forth the same approach:

> Thus the Beatitudes have been variously designated as the charter of the Christian life, the magna carta of

Christianity, the central document of the Christian faith, the living law of the new kingdom, and the code for Christian discipleship. (James Tolle, *The Beatitudes* [Fullerton, CA: Tolle Publications, 1966].)

The author now thinks that this position is not correct, but that Jesus was correctly interpreting the Mosaic Covenant to the Jews. The contrast was not between the Mosaic Law and Christ's New Covenant, but between the Law of Moses and what the Jews had made out of the Law of Moses. He did this to show them what every Israelite ought to be. Thus, we will soon see that all of the Sermon on the Mount was from the Law of Moses. This includes his teaching in the Beatitudes, his teaching on salt and light, and his teaching concerning attitude and action. It also encompassed his teaching concerning lust, love of enemies, the "golden rule," marriage, divorce and remarriage, and oaths—all of it!

Why This Study Is Important: Explaining the Mosaic Law

This study is important, first, because we should not misunderstand the most basic teaching of Jesus. Also, we should not apply its teaching to those to whom Jesus didn't intend it. Albert Sweitzer, the illustrious French missionary physician, thought that the Sermon on the Mount was a noble effort, but "not an ethic for every day." However, if Jesus was merely teaching correctly the Law of Moses, it is important to understand that man fully has the capacity to obey God sinlessly. When God was about to give the Mosaical Covenant to the Jews at Mt. Sinai in Ex. 19.5, he told them:

Now then, if you will indeed obey My voice and keep My covenant, then you shall be My own possession among all the peoples, for all the earth is Mine.

In verse 8, the people gave their reaction, as though they believed God did not ask too much for his fellowship with them to be based upon strict obedience to his covenant:

And all the people answered together and said, All that
the Lord has spoken we will do!

Of course, someone might think the Jews were naive in
supposing they could keep the covenant, but consider further. In
Dt. 5.27, when Moses gave them the covenant the second time,
the Jews again told him:

Go near and hear all that the Lord our God says; then
speak to us all that the Lord our God will speak to you,
and we will hear and do it.

Apparently, the Jews didn't think it was impossible to obey
God, even though they had been acquainted with the covenant
for forty years. In verse 28, God commended them for so thinking:

And the Lord heard the voice of your word when you
spoke to me, and the Lord said to me, I have heard the
voice of the words of this people which they have spoken
to you. They have done well in all that they have spoken.

Thus, neither did God think keeping the covenant was beyond
their ability. Lastly, in Dt. 30.11-14, that took place at the end of
Moses' life, God assured the Jews it was within their grasp to
obey the covenant:

For this commandment which I command you today is
not too difficult for you, nor is it out of reach. It is not in
heaven, that you should say, Who will go up to heaven
for us to get it for us and make us hear it, that we may
observe it? Nor is it beyond the sea, that you should say,
Who will cross the sea for us to get it for us and make us
hear it, that we may observe it? But the word is very near
you, in your mouth and in your heart, that you may
observe it.

Thus, God persuaded the Jews, and they understood that
keeping the Law of Moses was within their grasp. God never gave

them a law that was beyond their capacity to obey. The problem wasn't that the law was too difficult for them—the problem was they just didn't keep it flawlessly.

We'll also see that God included the vast majority of Jesus' teaching in the New Covenant later on, so it's attainable by Christians. The fact that Israel so misused the teaching Jesus rehearsed in this passage provides stern warnings for those of us striving to live by Christ's New Covenant. Our approach with each segment of the Sermon on the Mount will be (1) to understand the teaching, (2) to notice where we can find it in the Mosaic Covenant, (3) to notice that Jesus taught the same thing Moses did to the same people, (4) to notice where we may find the same teaching in Jesus' New Covenant (if that teaching is ever addressed to Christians), and therefore that it is binding upon Christians now.

The Beatitudes—Mt. 5.3-11

v3: Blessed are the poor in spirit: for theirs is the kingdom of heaven.

To be poor in spirit is to be humble. It's the opposite of arrogance, self-righteousness, and pride. Jesus taught that those Jews who were poor in spirit would be blessed or happy.

Old Covenant Teaching

The Old Covenant clearly taught God's people to be humble. In Isa. 66.2, God said:

> For My hand made all these things, thus all these things came into being, declares the Lord. But to this one I will look, to him who is humble and contrite of spirit, and who trembles at My word.

Likewise, in Isa. 57.15, we read:

The Sermon on the Mount, the Law of Moses, & the New Covenant

MATTHEW 5

vv1-9: Beatitudes

v3: Poor in Spirit

OT: Isa. 66.2, 57.15, Prov. 29.23
JESUS TO JEWS: Jn. 7.48, Lk. 18.9-14, Lk. 22.24-30,
       Jn. 13.6-12, Lk. 6.24
NEW COVENANT: Rom. 12.3, Jas. 4.6, 10, I Pet. 5.5

v4: Mourn

OT: Ps. 38.18, 51.4, Joel 2.12, 13, II Chron. 7.14
JESUS TO JEWS: Mt. 26.75, Lk. 18.13, Lk. 6.25
NEW COVENANT: II Cor. 7.10, I Cor. 5.2, Ac. 2.36-38,
       9.18-19, 8.39, 16.34

v5: Meek

OT: Ps. 37.11, 22, 29, 34, 149.4, Ezk. 2.3
JESUS TO JEWS: Mt. 5.5, Mt. 15.29
NEW COVENANT: Jas. 1.21, II Tim. 2.25, I Pet. 5.5,
       Eph. 5.21, 4.1-2, Col. 3.12-13
(Although no land promise)

v6: Hunger and Thirst

OT: Ps. 42.1, 63.1, Amos 8.11, II Chron. 15.15
JESUS TO JEWS: Lk. 18.9
NEW COVENANT: I Cor. 9.24, Phil. 3.13-14, Ac. 17.11

v7: Merciful

OT: Ps. 18.25, Hos. 6.6, II Sam. 22.26, Mic. 6.8
JESUS TO JEWS: Lk. 10, Mt. 9.13, Mt. 23.23, 24, Mt. 25.41-46
NEW COVENANT: Rom. 15.1, I Thes. 5.14, Eph. 4.32

v8: Pure in Heart

OT: Isa. 29.13, Prov. 4.23, Ps. 24.3-4, Ps. 73.1
JESUS TO JEWS: Mt. 23.25, 27, 28
NEW COVENANT: II Cor. 7.1, I Pet. 1.22, I Tim. 1.5

Figure 9

For thus says the high and exalted One who lives forever, whose name is Holy. I dwell on a high and holy place, and also with the contrite and lowly of spirit in order to revive the spirit of the lowly and to revive the heart of the contrite.

In Prov. 29.23, Solomon wrote:

A man's pride will bring him low, but a humble spirit will obtain honor.

Jesus Taught Jews the Same as Old Covenant

Thus, in this beatitude Jesus taught Jews who were not poor in spirit exactly what Moses taught. You can see their arrogance in Jn. 7.48, where in essence the rulers asked, "Have any of us great ones believed on him?" In Lk. 18.9-14 the Pharisees "trusted in themselves that they were righteous, and set all others at naught." In Mt. 18.1-4, even Jesus' Jewish disciples needed to humble themselves, hence the lesson with the child: "Except ye turn, and become as little children, ye shall in no wise enter into the kingdom of heaven." In Jn. 13.6-12 Jesus washed his disciples' feet to teach them humility while they argued about who was the greatest. Jesus told Peter if he didn't learn the lesson he was striving to teach, he would have no part with Jesus. Peter would have had no part with Moses, either. When he finished, he asked them, "Know ye what I have done?" They knew he had washed their feet! What they still needed to learn was that the greatest is one who serves, not one who stands around arguing "who is the greatest." If they didn't learn that, they would have no part with Christ. In Lk. 6.24 (Luke's account of the Sermon on the Mount) Jesus put the same lesson negatively when he said:

But woe unto you that are rich! for ye have received your consolation.

An examination of the context shows that Jesus didn't speak of physical riches, but of richness of spirit, arrogance, a lack of humility. The arrogant among the Jews were not destined to be happy, but woeful when the nation was soon destroyed, as both John the Baptist and Jesus announced. The arrogant among the

Jews already had their consolation. They had no future reward in the kingdom because of their lack of humility.

New Covenant Teaching

The New Covenant of Christ taught Christians the same thing about humility. In Rom. 12.3, Paul said:

> For I say, through the grace that was given me, to every man that is among you, not to think of himself more highly than he ought to think; but so to think as to think soberly, according as God hath dealt to each man a measure of faith.

In Phil. 2.5-8, Paul said Christians should have the attitude of Christ:

> Have this mind in you, which was also in Christ Jesus, who, existing in the form of God, counted not the being on an equality with God a thing to be grasped, but emptied himself, taking the form of a servant, being made in the likeness of men; and being found in fashion as a man, he humbled himself, becoming obedient even unto death, yea, the death of the cross.

In Jas. 4.6, 10, we find:

> But he giveth more grace. Wherefore the scripture saith, God resisteth the proud, but giveth grace to the humble....Humble yourselves in the sight of the Lord, and he shall exalt you.

In I Pet. 5.5, Peter said:

> Likewise, ye younger, be subject unto the elder. Yea, all of you gird yourselves with humility, to serve one another: for God resisteth the proud, but giveth grace to the humble.

Thus, we learn that if we have a know-it-all attitude, we're no different from the Jews of Jesus' day. Surely, God's word has all the answers, but not one among us does. A good example of humility is seen in Isaac Newton, the great genius who discovered calculus, who wrote toward the end of his distinguished career:

> I do not know what I may appear to the world; but to myself I seem to have been only like a boy, playing on the seashore, and diverting myself now and then by finding a smoother pebble or prettier shell than ordinary, while the great ocean of truth lay undiscovered before me. (James Tolle, *The Beatitudes* [Fullerton, CA: Tolle Publications, 1966], p. 18.)

We encourage those interested in further study on this point to note the following examples of humility: Gideon (Jud. 6.14-15—"Oh my Lord, wherewith shall I save Israel? Behold, my family is poor in Manasseh, and I am the least in my father's house"), Solomon (I K. 3.5-9—"And I am but a little child: I know not how to go out or come in"), Peter (Lk. 5.8—"Depart from me; for I am a sinful man, O Lord"), Paul (Eph. 3.6-8—"Unto me, who am less than the least of all saints"), and Jesus (Phil. 2.5-8). Examples of pride are also suggested for further study: Uzziah (II Chron. 26.15, 16—"But when he was strong, his heart was lifted up to his destruction"), the disciples of Christ (Mt. 18.1-4—"Who is the greatest in the kingdom of heaven," Mk. 9.33-35, Lk. 9.46-48, Lk. 22.24-27), Peter (Mt. 26.33-35—"Though all men shall be offended because of thee, yet will I never be offended"), Herod (Ac. 12.21-23), and the elder brother (Lk. 15.26-30), who was self-righteous (like the Pharisees in the context), didn't realize his own moral deficiencies, and his need for his father's forgiveness.

Conclusion

Obviously, Jesus' teaching concerning humility in the Sermon on the Mount is not new. It's the same thing Moses taught. It's not more noble than what Moses taught, nor is it too high for man to attain. It was attainable for the Jews, and it's attainable by us. Yet we can be God's people, like some Israelites, and miss humility by a mile!

v4: Blessed are they that mourn: for they shall be comforted.

"Mourn" here doesn't speak of crying at a funeral, but mourning over one's sinful condition. In I Cor. 5.2 Paul said that the Corinthians "did not mourn" over the condition of an impenitent fornicator among them. Rather than being puffed up about him, they should have mourned his wretched condition. There are at least three attitudes man can have toward sin: (1) indifference (see Jer. 6.15 where Israel lost the ability to be ashamed), (2) stubbornness (like King Saul, I Sam. 15.13-24), or (3) mourning over sin.

Old Covenant Teaching

The examples of David mourning over his own sins in Ps. 38.18 and Ps. 51.4 are good ones. For further study see also Isa. 6.5, Joel 2.12, 13, Mt. 26.75, Lk. 19.41, Dt. 4.29, 5.29, II Chron. 7.14, Hab. 1.4, Ezk. 9.4, Ps. 139.21, Ps. 119.136, Ezra 10.6, and Ps. 32.1, 2.

Jesus Taught Jews the Same as Old Covenant

Thus, we see that Jesus was teaching Jews (who weren't mourning over their sad condition) exactly what Moses taught. Recall the publican in Lk.18.13, who wouldn't even lift his eyes to heaven, in contrast to the self-righteous Pharisee ("God I thank thee, that I am not as the rest of men"). Likewise, Peter, in Mt. 26.75, went out and wept bitterly over his pitiful condition. Finally, remember the negative version of this beatitude in Lk. 6.25, where Jesus said:

Woe unto you, ye that laugh now, for ye shall mourn and weep.

Jesus warned the Jews who would not mourn at his and John's teaching that they would mourn and weep later—when the nation fell down around their ears!

New Covenant Teaching

We find the same teaching in the New Covenant. In Ac. 2.37, the first Jews to obey the gospel on the first Pentecost after Christ's resurrection were "pricked in their heart." Paul told us in II Cor. 7.10 that godly sorrow produces repentance unto salvation. This is why Jesus said the mourners would be comforted. We can see it in the conversion of Paul in Ac. 9.18-19, where he took food and was strengthened after his conversion to Christ. We can see the comfort of the Philippian jailer in Ac. 16.34 who "rejoiced greatly, having believed in God."

Conclusion

Certainly, Jesus' teaching in this second beatitude is not new, nor is it more noble than the Law of Moses. It wasn't too high for the Jews, nor is its counterpart in the New Covenant too high for Christians today. Yet we can be God's people (like the Jews of Jesus' day) and miss the proper attitude toward sin a great deal!

v5: Blessed are the meek: for they shall inherit the earth.

The word "meek" is a much-abused word today. While we think of a meek man as a Casper Milquetoast, a Mr. Peepers, or a "wimp," the Greeks used it to describe strength under control. They used it of horses that were tamed. They were not weak, but tremendously strong. Yet that strength had been brought under control. We might use the word meek to describe a rushing, turbulent river that a dam has tamed. The river still has great power, but the power has been brought under control. In Num. 12.3, "Moses was meek above all men," yet we remember his indignation at sin, shattering the tablets, burning the idols, etc., which demonstrated he was anything but a wimp. Someone suggested that meekness is a quality that makes a person always feel angry at the right time and never angry at the wrong time. Someone else has said a meek person feels angry on the right grounds, against the right persons, in the right manner, at the right moment, and for the right length of time.

Old Covenant Teaching

In Ps. 37.11, 22, 29, and 34, David taught:

But the humble will inherit the land, and will delight themselves in abundant prosperity.

For those blessed by Him will inherit the land; but those cursed by Him will be cut off.

The righteous will inherit the land, and dwell in it forever.

Wait for the Lord, and keep His way, And He will exalt you to inherit the land; when the wicked are cut off, you will see it.

In these passages, to "inherit the land" was to be victorious. It was the opposite of being cast out, conquered, and vanquished. From the very beginning (Deuteronomy 28-30), God had promised Israel that as long as they were faithful to him, they would be victorious. But when they renounced him, they would be driven out of the land.

In Zeph. 2.3, we find:

Seek the Lord, all you humble of the earth, who have carried out His ordinances; seek righteousness, seek humility. Perhaps you will be hidden in the day of the Lord's anger.

Jesus Taught Jews the Same as Old Covenant

Jesus taught in Mt. 11.29: "Take my yoke upon you, and learn of me: for I am meek and lowly in heart: and ye shall find rest unto your souls." Jesus was meek himself. Heb. 5.2 tells us he bore gently with the ignorant and erring. However, he was not weak. Tell that to the Jews he debated, and the ones he drove out of the temple.

New Covenant Teaching

We find that the New Covenant of Jesus taught the same thing that the Old Covenant taught on meekness. In Jas. 1.21, James said:

> Wherefore putting away all filthiness and overflowing of wickedness, receive with meekness the implanted word, which is able to save your souls.

Paul taught in II Tim. 2.24-25:

> And the Lord's servant must not strive, but be gentle towards all, apt to teach, forbearing, in meekness correcting them that oppose themselves; if peradventure God may give them repentance unto the knowledge of the truth...

Paul taught Christians to be meek toward God. For example, in Gal. 2.20, he said:

> I have been crucified with Christ: and it is no longer I that live, but Christ liveth in me: and that life which I now live in the flesh I live in faith, the faith which is in the Son of God, who loved me, and gave himself up for me.

In Rom. 6.19, he taught:

...for as ye presented your members as servants to uncleanness and to iniquity unto iniquity, even so also now present your members as servants to righteousness unto sanctification.

Likewise, God tells Christians to be meek toward men, toward civil authorities (Tit. 3.1, 2), and toward each other (I Pet. 5.5, Eph. 5.21). When we are contentious, quarrelsome, or overbearing, we do not violate the Law of Moses, but the New Covenant of Jesus Christ.

In Eph. 4.1-2, we are told:

I therefore, the prisoner in the Lord, beseech you to walk worthily of the calling wherewith ye were called, with all lowliness and meekness, with longsuffering, forbearing one another in love...

In Col. 3.12-13, we have:

Put on therefore, as God's elect, holy and beloved, a heart of compassion, kindness, lowliness, meekness, longsuffering; forbearing one another, and forgiving each other, if any man have a complaint against any; even as the Lord forgave you, so also do ye.

In Gal. 6.1, Paul commanded:

Brethren, even if a man be overtaken in any trespass, ye who are spiritual, restore such a one in a spirit of gentleness; looking to thyself, lest thou also be tempted.

Several times we have the example of Jesus himself commended to us. In I Pet. 2.23, Peter recalled how when Jesus was reviled, he didn't retaliate and rail on his abusers. In Lk. 23.34, Jesus prayed for the forgiveness of his enemies. Mt. 27.14 tells us that Jesus impressed Pilate with his lack of retaliation. Of course, Jesus' conduct was foretold in the Messianic text of Isa. 53.3:

He was despised and forsaken of men, a man of sorrows, and acquainted with grief; and like one from whom men hide their face, He was despised, and we did not esteem Him.

Conclusion

In this passage, Jesus taught that Israelites of his day, not Christians, would inherit the earth if they would but be faithful to God. He reiterated the same promise Moses had given them centuries before, as he virtually quoted Ps. 37.11. Christians are nowhere told that we'll inherit any land, like Israel did, and that we'll get to stay on a specific land. Israel had such a land promise, we do not. However, we are told that we'll be victorious if we're meek. We'll be overcomers, not cast out nor overcome. We reign with Christ. John saw a heavenly throng singing to Christ of the earthly reign of his faithful ones in Rev. 5.9-10:

Worthy art thou to take the book, and to open the seals thereof: for thou wast slain, and didst purchase unto God with thy blood men of every tribe, and tongue, and people, and nation, and madest them to be unto our God a kingdom and priests; and they reign upon the earth.

Paul taught the same thing in Rom. 8.35-37:

Who shall separate us from the love of Christ? shall tribulation, or anguish, or persecution, or famine, or nakedness, or peril, or sword?...Nay, in all these things we are more than conquerors through him that loved us.

Jesus taught in Rev. 3.21 that we overcome the same way he did, and that so doing, we reign with him!

He that overcometh, I will give to him to sit down with me in my throne, as I also overcame, and sat down with my Father in his throne.

Of course, the wisdom of this world taught us not to be humble, not to submit, but to assert ourselves, go out and get what we want. Napoleon, Hitler, and Nitzsche were aggressors, and were wealthy physically, but listen to James Tolle describe how poor they were when it came to true riches:

> They certainly possessed extensive earthly wealth, land, and power; but they were the poorest of the poor when it came to the true riches of life. Napoleon spent the last years of his life in vain regret on the lonely island of St. Helena, and Hitler died a miserable suicide on beholding the complete shattering of his earthly dreams in the death of the third Reich. The German philosopher Nietzsche preached the doctrine of aggression as the means to the mastery of life, but he ended his days hopelessly insane. (James Tolle, *The Beatitudes* [Fullerton, CA: Tolle Publications, Fullerton, CA: 1966], p. 43.)

The examples of these men reminds us of Prov. 16.32:

> He who is slow to anger is better than the mighty, and he who rules his spirit, than he who captures a city.

Tolle also quoted George MacDonald, who said:

> Which is more the possessor of the world—he who has a thousand houses, or he who, without one house to call his own, has ten in which his knock at the door would rouse instant jubilation? Which is the richer, the man who, his large money spent, would have no refuge; or he for whose necessity a hundred would sacrifice comfort? Which of the two possessed the earth, King Agrippa or the tent-maker Paul? Which is the real possessor of a book, the man who has its original and every following edition, and shows, to many an admiring and envying visitor, now this, now that, in binding characteristic, with possessor-pride, or the man who cherishes one little, hollow-backed, coverless, untitled, bethumbed copy, which he takes with him in his solitary walks and broods

over in his silent chamber, always finding in it some beauty of excellence or aid he had not found before, which is to him in truth as a live companion?" (George MacDonald, cited by James Tolle, *The Beatitudes* [Fullerton, CA: Tolle Publications, Fullerton, CA: 1966], p. 43.)

As we close our discussion of this beatitude, we see that Jesus' teaching here is not new, nor is it nobler than what Moses taught. It wasn't too high for the Israelites, nor is it too high for us. It was attainable for them, and it is for us. Yet from the example of many Israelites in Jesus' time, we see that we can be God's people and miss this principle completely!

v6: Blessed are they that hunger and thirst after righteousness: for they shall be filled.

To hunger and thirst after righteousness is to seek it, not thinking that you've already arrived as the standard of righteousness. Jesus encountered such an attitude of arrogant self-righteousness among many Israelites of his day.

Old Covenant Teaching

In Ps. 42.1, David wrote:

As the deer pants for the water brooks, so my soul pants for Thee, O God.

In Ps. 63.1, we read:

O God, Thou art my God; I shall seek Thee earnestly; My soul thirsts for Thee, my flesh yearns for Thee, in a dry and weary land where there is no water.

Isa. 55.1 tells us:

Ho! Every one who thirsts, come to the waters; And you who have no money come, buy and eat. Come, buy wine and milk without money and without cost.

Amos 8.11 said:

Behold days are coming, declares the Lord God, when I will send a famine on the land, not a famine for bread or a thirst for water, but rather for hearing the words of the Lord.

II Chron. 15.15 said:

And all Judah rejoiced concerning the oath, for they had sworn with their whole heart and had sought Him earnestly, and He let them find Him. So the Lord gave them rest on every side.

Jesus Taught Jews the Same as Old Covenant

Thus, Jesus taught Jews, who weren't hungering and thirsting after righteousness, exactly what Moses and the Old Testament prophets taught. He taught the same thing to the same people. In Lk. 18.9, we find that many of them "trusted in themselves that they were righteous." Such people don't feel the need to "hunger and thirst after righteousness," for they already have it. These were the same "know-it-alls" that wouldn't question Jesus as he taught them in parables (Mt. 13.10-13). They didn't know true righteousness, and they were too proud to ask a question and demonstrate that they did not know. An example of Jews who did hunger and thirst after righteousness was the Berean Jews of Ac. 17.11. Luke described them this way:

Now these were more noble than those in Thessalonica, in that they received the word with all readiness of mind, examining the scriptures daily, whether these things were so.

Their "readiness of mind" was the result of their "hungering and thirsting after righteousness." "Many of them therefore believed" that Jesus was the Christ they looked for. Jesus had no problem with Israelites who obeyed Moses in this regard.

Israelites of this caliber pleased and obeyed Moses, who commanded them in Dt. 6.6-7:

> And these words, which I am commanding you today, shall be on your heart; and you shall teach them diligently to your sons and shall talk of them when you sit in your house and when you walk by the way and when you lie down and when you rise up.

New Covenant Teaching

The New Covenant contains the same teaching. For example, in I Cor. 9.24, Paul said:

> Know ye not that they that run in a race run all, but one receiveth the prize? Even so run; that ye may attain.

In contrast to many of the Jews of his time, Paul said in Phil. 3.13-14:

> Brethren, I count not myself yet to have laid hold: but one thing I do, forgetting the things which are behind, and stretching forward to the things which are before, I press on toward the goal unto the prize of the high calling of God in Christ Jesus.

Conclusion

When Jesus taught Israelites to "hunger and thirst after righteousness," he didn't teach something newer, nobler, nor higher and more unattainable than the Mosaic Covenant taught. He taught the same thing that Moses taught to the same people. Hungering and thirsting after righteousness was attainable to them, and the New Covenant makes it clear that it is to us as well.

The example of the Jews shows us that we can be God's covenant people, and because of our lack of hungering and thirsting after righteousness, we can still miss the righteousness of God completely.

v7: Blessed are the merciful: for they shall obtain mercy.

This verse is self-explanatory. Jesus explained that unmerciful Jews would not receive mercy themselves.

Old Covenant Teaching

The Mosaic Covenant required Israelites to be merciful. In Ps. 18.25, David taught:

> With the kind Thou dost show Thyself kind; with the blameless Thou dost show Thyself blameless.

Another important Old Covenant passage is Hos. 6.6, where God said:

> For I delight in loyalty rather than sacrifice, and in the knowledge of God rather than burnt offerings.

In Mt. 9.13, Jesus pointedly quoted this passage to the Jews of his day:

> But go ye and learn what this meaneth, I desire mercy, and not sacrifice: for I came not to call the righteous, but sinners.

Jesus depreciated the emphasis of some Jews on religious ritual to the neglect of proper actions toward their fellowman. In II Sam. 22.26, we find:

> With the kind Thou dost show Thyself kind, with the blameless Thou dost show Thyself blameless.

In Mic. 6.8, we have:

> He has told you, O man, what is good; and what does the
> Lord require of you but to do justice, to love kindness,
> and to walk humbly with your God?

Jesus Taught Jews the Same as Old Covenant

When Jesus encountered Jews who weren't merciful, he taught them the same thing Moses taught. He taught the same thing to the same people. For example, in the parable of the good Samaritan in Luke 10, Jesus showed that the real neighbor was the one who showed compassion. He then told the Jews, "Go and do likewise," like Moses said!

In Mt. 9.10-13, Jesus quoted Hos. 6.6, noted above, and told the unmerciful Jews:

> But go ye and learn what this meaneth, I desire mercy,
> and not sacrifice.

In Mt. 23.23-24, Jesus told the religious leaders of the Jews:

> Woe unto you, scribes and Pharisees, hypocrites! for ye
> tithe mint and anise and cumin, and have left undone the
> weightier matters of the law, justice, and mercy and faith:
> but these ye ought to have done, and not to have left the
> other undone. Ye blind guides, that strain out the gnat,
> and swallow the camel!

Mt. 25.41-43 speaks of a judgment based in large part upon showing mercy:

> Then shall he say also unto them on the left hand, Depart
> from me, ye cursed, into the eternal fire which is prepared
> for the devil and his angels: for I was hungry, and ye did
> not give me to eat; I was thirsty, and ye gave me no drink;
> I was a stranger, and ye took me not in; naked, and ye
> clothed me not; sick, and in prison, and ye visited me not.

New Covenant Teaching

The New Covenant teaching of Christ taught the same thing about mercy. In Rom. 15.1, Paul said:

Now we that are strong ought to bear the infirmities of the weak, and not to please ourselves.

In I Thes. 5.14, Paul wrote:

And we exhort you, brethren, admonish the disorderly, encourage the fainthearted, support the weak, be long-suffering toward all.

In Eph. 4.32, we read:

...and be ye kind one to another, tenderhearted, forgiving each other, even as God also in Christ forgave you.

Conclusion

Again, Jesus' teaching concerning showing mercy in the Sermon on the Mount was not new, more noble, nor too high for the Jews of his day. He simply taught them exactly what Moses did. His New Covenant taught Christians now the same thing, and it's no less attainable for us than it was for the Jews under Moses.

v8: Blessed are the pure in heart: for they shall see God.

The word "pure" means "unalloyed," or unmixed. It comes from the figure of pure gold, for example, which doesn't contain any other materials. The Bible uses the term in the sense of "sincere," not hypocritical. The person who is pure in heart doesn't say one thing and do another.

Old Covenant Teaching

The Mosaic Covenant taught Jews to be pure in heart, unhypocritical, and sincere. For example, Isa. 29.13 (which Jesus quoted in Mt. 15.6-9) taught:

> ...Because this people draw near with their words and honor Me with their lip service, but they remove their hearts far from Me, and their reverence for Me consists of tradition learned by rote.

Solomon taught the same thing in Prov. 4.23:

> Watch over your heart with all diligence, for from it flow the springs of life.

David said in Ps. 24.3-4:

> Who may ascend into the hill of the Lord? And who may stand in His holy place? He who has clean hands and a pure heart, who has not lifted up his soul to falsehood, and has not sworn deceitfully.

The psalmist Asaph said in Ps. 73.1:

> Surely God is good to Israel, to those who are pure in heart!

Jesus Taught Jews the Same as Old Covenant

Thus, when Jesus taught the Jews of his day (many of whom were not pure in heart) in the Sermon on the Mount to be pure in heart, he simply brought them back to the Mosaic Covenant.

Additionally, throughout his ministry, Jesus taught the same people the same thing as Moses. In Mt. 23.25, 27-28, notice:

> Woe unto you, scribes and Pharisees, hypocrites! for ye cleanse the outside of the cup and of the platter, but

within they are full from extortion and excess....Woe
unto you, scribes and Pharisees, hypocrites! for ye are
like unto whited sepulchres, which outwardly appear
beautiful, but inwardly are full of dead men's bones, and
of all uncleanness. Even so ye also outwardly appear
righteous unto men, but inwardly ye are full of hypocrisy
and iniquity.

Whereas later in the Sermon on the Mount, in Mt. 6.22-24,
Jesus said:

The lamp of the body is the eye: if therefore thine eye be
single, thy whole body shall be full of light. But if thine
eye be evil, thy whole body shall be full of darkness. If
therefore the light that is in thee be darkness, how great
is the darkness! No man can serve two masters: for either
he will hate the one, and love the other; or else he will
hold to one, and despise the other. Ye cannot serve God
and mammon.

New Covenant Teaching

We find the doctrine of Christ for Christians obligates Christians to be unhypocritical as well. In II Cor. 7.1, Paul taught:

Having therefore these promises, beloved, let us cleanse
ourselves from all defilement of flesh and spirit, perfect-
ing holiness in the fear of God.

I Pet. 1.22 taught Christians:

Seeing ye have purified your souls in your obedience to
the truth unto unfeigned love of the brethren, love one
another from the heart fervently.

Paul said in I Tim. 1.5:

But the end of the charge is love out of a pure heart and a good conscience and faith unfeigned.

Paul in I Tim. 3.9 required deacons to be:

...holding the mystery of the faith in a pure conscience.

Paul said in II Tim. 2.22:

But flee youthful lusts, and follow after righteousness, faith, love, peace, with them that call on the Lord out of a pure heart.

James said in Jas. 4.8:

Draw nigh to God, and he will draw nigh to you. Cleanse your hands, ye sinners; and purify your hearts, ye doubleminded.

Heb. 10.22 taught us:

...let us draw near with a true heart in fullness of faith, having our hearts sprinkled from an evil conscience...

Conclusion

Jesus' teaching in the Sermon on the Mount concerning purity of heart was not new, more noble, nor unattainable for the Jews of his day. Moses had taught the same thing. Jesus' New Covenant taught Christians the same today, and it's still not new, too noble, nor too high for us. Again, we can be God's covenant people like the Jews of Jesus' time, and because of a lack of purity of heart, greatly miss fellowship with God.

v9: Blessed are the peacemakers: for they shall be called sons of God.

Here Jesus taught that those who produced peace instead of producing trouble would have the character of their heavenly father.

Old Covenant Teaching

In Prov. 12.20, Solomon wrote:

Deceit is in the heart of those who devise evil, but counselors of peace have joy.

Jesus Taught Jews the Same as Old Covenant

In the Sermon on the Mount, Jesus taught Jews who were anything but peacemakers, exactly what Moses taught. The approach of Jesus' Jewish enemies included: hypocritical judgment (Mt. 7.1-5, Mt. 23.1-4), accusations of fellowship with sinners (Mt. 9.10-12), and not keeping their traditions (Mt. 9.14, 12.2, 15.1-9). Their procedures advanced to name calling (Mt. 11.18, Lk. 11.15), trying to trap him (Mt. 12.10, 22.15, 35ff), and watching him (Lk. 14.1). Then they engaged in secret plotting (Mt. 12.14, Jn. 7.4), accused him of working by Satan (Mt. 12.24), intimidation (Mt. 13.54ff), indignation at his popularity with the common people (Mt.21.15), and refusing to come to the light (Mt. 22.16, Lk. 19.47-48, Jn. 7.4, 13, 26). They also asked many complicated questions that they weren't willing to answer themselves (Mt. 21.23ff, 22.23; Lk. 6.9, 20.1-8, 27-40), treated the Lord's servants shamefully (Mt. 22.6), preached many things they didn't practice (Mt. 23.1-4), and shut the kingdom to men (Mt. 23.13, Lk. 15, 19.7). Finally, they misrepresented him (Mt. 26.59), got mean when he crossed them (Lk. 4.29), were not willing to listen (Lk. 8.4ff), were self-righteous (Lk. 16.15, Lk. 18.9, where they "set all others at nought"), lied to defeat an enemy (Lk. 20.21, Jn. 8.33, Jn. 19.15), killed to defeat an enemy

(Lk. 22.2), kept others from hearing (Jn. 9.22, 11.47-40), and suppressed evidence (Jn. 12.10-11).

In Mk. 9.50, Jesus told the Jews:

> Salt is good: but if the salt have lost his saltiness, wherewith will ye season it? Have salt in yourselves, and have peace one with another.

Again, Jesus taught the same people (Israelites) the same thing that Moses had.

New Covenant Teaching

The New Covenant contains the same type of teaching about peacemakers. For example, in Rom. 14.19, Paul wrote:

> So then let us follow after things which make for peace, and things whereby we may edify one another.

In Heb. 12.14, we have:

> Follow after peace with all men, and the sanctification without which no man shall see the Lord:

Finally, in Jas. 3.14-18, we read:

> But if ye have bitter jealousy and faction in your heart, glory not and lie not against the truth. This wisdom is not a wisdom that cometh down from above, but is earthly, sensual, devilish. For where jealousy and faction are, there is confusion and every vile deed. But the wisdom that is from above is first pure, then peaceable, gentle, easy to be entreated, full of mercy and good fruits, without variance, without hypocrisy. And the fruit of righteousness is sown in peace for them that make peace.

Conclusion

Again, the teaching of Jesus in this beatitude, as well as all of the beatitudes, is not something new, more noble, and less attainable than what Moses taught. Jesus taught the Jews the same thing Moses taught them. It wasn't too noble for them, and the same teaching addressed to Christians under the New Covenant isn't too noble for us, either.

Persecution and Suffering—Mt. 5.10-12

In Mt. 5.10-12, Jesus said:

> Blessed are they that have been persecuted for righteousness' sake: for theirs is the kingdom of heaven. Blessed are ye when men shall reproach you, and persecute you, and say all manner of evil against you falsely, for my sake. Rejoice, and be exceeding glad: for great is your reward in heaven: for so persecuted they the prophets that were before you.

James Tolle gave a good explanation of why these verses are here:

> These beatitudes (which are right out of the Mosaic Law), run contrary to the wisdom of the world, thus provoking the enmity and opposition of evil men. Poverty in spirit runs counter to human pride; the spirit of mourning concerning one's deficiencies and shortcomings before God is resented by the callous, indifferent, self-satisfied world; a meek and quiet spirit is regarded as cowardly weakness; the craving for righteousness rebukes the cravings of the carnal man; the merciful spirit rebukes the hard-heartedness of the world; purity of heart contrasts painfully with the unclean hearts of worldly men; and the peacemakers cannot be endured by the persistently contentious and quarrelsome. Thus do the

possessors of righteousness come to be persecuted. (James Tolle, *The Beatitudes* [Fullerton, CA: Tolle Publications, 1966], pp. 75-76.)

The Sermon on the Mount, the Law of Moses, & the New Covenant (2)

MATTHEW 5:

v9: Peacemakers
OT: Prov. 12.20
JESUS TO JEWS: Mk. 9.50
NEW COVENANT: Rom. 14.19, Heb. 12.14, Jas. 3.18

vv10-12: PERSECUTION AND SUFFERING
OT: Heb. 11.32-40; Dan. 3.20, Est. 3.13
JESUS TO JEWS: Jn. 15.18
NEW COVENANT: Ac. 17.11, 13, Heb. 10.32-39, I Thes. 2.15-16, II Tim. 3.12, Ac. 5.41, Phil. 1.28, 29

vv13-16: SALT, LIGHT
OT: Isa. 43.10, Dt. 4.5-6, Ezk. 5.5-9, Mal. 3.12
JESUS TO JEWS: Mt. 5.13-16
NEW COVENANT: Phil. 2.15, Tit. 2.7, I Tim. 4.12

vv17-20: RELATION TO LAW OF MOSES
OT: Dt. 4.2, Prov. 30.6
JESUS TO JEWS: Mt. 5.17-20
NEW COVENANT: _____: (Rom. 7.4, 6, Gal. 5.18)

vv21-26: ANGER/HATE/MURDER
OT: Lev. 19.17, Isa. 1.11-17
JESUS TO JEWS: Mt. 19.10-13, Mt. 7.12, Mk. 12.32f
NEW COVENANT: Eph. 4.26, Rom. 13.9, I Jn. 3.15

vv27-30: LUST/ADULTERY
OT: Ex. 20.17, Dt. 5.21, Prov. 15.26, 12.2, 24.9
JESUS TO JEWS: Mt. 5.27-30
NEW COVENANT: Gal. 5.16-214, Col. 3.5-6

vv31-32: ADULTERY/BILL OF DIVORCEMENT
OT: Dt. 24.1-4
JESUS TO JEWS: Mt. 5.31-32, Mt. 19.3-9
NEW COVENANT: I Cor. 7.10-11

Figure 10

Old Covenant Teaching

To see where God's people could expect to be persecuted if they adhered to Old Covenant teaching, we have but to look at Heb. 11.32-40:

> And what shall I more say? for the time will fail me if I tell of Gideon, Barak, Samson, Jephthah; of David and Samuel and the prophets: who through faith subdued kingdoms, wrought righteousness, obtained promises, stopped the mouths of lions, quenched the power of fire, escaped the edge of the sword, from weakness were made strong, waxed mighty in war, turned to flight armies of aliens. Women received their dead by a resurrection: and others were tortured, not accepting their deliverance; that they might obtain a better resurrection: and others had trial of mockings and scourgings, yea, moreover of bonds and imprisonment: they were stoned, they were sawn asunder, they were slain with the sword: they went about in sheepskins, in goatskins; being destitute, afflicted, ill-treated (of whom the world was not worthy), wandering in deserts and mountains and caves, and the holes of the earth. And these all, having had witness borne to them through their faith, received not the promises, God having provided some better thing concerning us, that apart from us they should not be made perfect.

These heroes of faith were Jews every one. The Old Testament and the lives of the Old Covenant saints testified that if you had the character Moses desired, and depicted in the Beatitudes, you could expect to be persecuted for it! The life of Daniel shows it in Dan. 3.20:

> And he [Nebuchadnezzar—SGD] commanded certain valiant warriors who were in his army to tie up Shadrach, Meshach and Abednego, in order to cast them into the furnace of blazing fire.

As does the life of Esther in Esth. 3.13:

> And letters were sent by couriers to all the king's prov-
> inces to destroy, to kill, and to annihilate all the Jews,
> both young and old, women and children, in one day, the
> thirteenth day of the twelfth month, which is the month
> Adar, and to seize their possessions as plunder.

Jesus Taught Jews the Same as Old Covenant

The Jews could expect persecution and suffering because they
wouldn't worship the Persian idols! Thus, in the Sermon on the
Mount, Jesus' teaching about persecution was the same as that
contained in the Old Covenant. Likewise, in Jn. 15.18-20, Jesus
taught his Jewish apostles the same thing:

> If the world hateth you, ye know that it hath hated me
> before it hated you. If ye were of the world, the world
> would love its own: but because ye are not of the world
> therefore the world hateth you. Remember the word that
> I said unto you, A servant is not greater than his lord. If
> they persecuted me, they will also persecute you: if they
> kept my word, they will keep yours also.

New Covenant Teaching

In Ac. 17.11, 13, we see faithful Jews persecuted by the
unfaithful:

> Now these were more noble than those in Thessalonica,
> in that they received the word with all readiness of mind,
> examining the scriptures daily, whether these things
> were so. But when the Jews of Thessalonica had knowl-
> edge that the word of God was proclaimed of Paul at
> Berea also, they came thither likewise, stirring up and
> troubling the multitudes.

In Heb. 10.32-35, we have the same thing:

But call to remembrance the former days, in which, after ye were enlightened, ye endured a great conflict of sufferings; partly, being made a gazingstock both by reproaches and afflictions; and partly, becoming partakers with them that were so used. For ye both had compassion on them that were in bonds, and took joyfully the spoiling of your possessions, knowing that ye have for yourselves a better possession and an abiding one.

So in I Thes. 2.14-16, we read:

For ye, brethren, became imitators of the churches of God which are in Judea in Christ Jesus: for ye also suffered the same things of your own countrymen, even as they did of the Jews; who both killed the Lord Jesus and the prophets, and drove out us, and please not God, and are contrary to all men: forbidding us to speak to the Gentiles that they may be saved; to fill up their sins always: but the wrath is come upon them to the uttermost.

In II Tim. 3.12, Paul said:

Yea, and all that would live godly in Christ Jesus shall suffer persecution.

In I Cor. 4.10-13, we read:

We are fools for Christ's sake, but ye are wise in Christ; we are weak, but ye are strong; ye have glory, but we have dishonor. Even unto this present hour we both hunger, and thirst, and are naked, and are buffeted, and have no certain dwelling-place; and we toil, working with our own hands; being reviled, we bless; being persecuted, we endure; being defamed, we entreat: we are made as the filth of the world, the offscouring of all things, even until now.

In Ac. 5.41, Luke told us:

They therefore departed from the presence of the council, rejoicing that they were counted worthy to suffer dishonor for the Name.

In II Cor. 11.23, we have:

Are they ministers of Christ? I more; in labors more abundantly, in prisons more abundantly, in stripes above measure, in deaths oft. Of the Jews five times received I forty stripes save one. Thrice was I beaten with rods, once was I stoned, thrice I suffered shipwreck, a night and a day have I been in the deep; in journeyings often, in perils of rivers, in perils of robbers, in perils from my countrymen, in perils from the Gentiles, in perils in the city, in perils in the wilderness, in perils in the sea, in perils among false brethren; in labor and travail, in watchings often, in hunger and thirst, in fastings often, in cold and nakedness.

Finally, in Phil. 1.28-29, we read:

...and in nothing affrighted by the adversaries: which is for them an evident token of perdition, but of your salvation, and that from God; because to you it hath been granted in the behalf of Christ, not only to believe on him, but also to suffer in his behalf.

Tolle said concerning persecution:

The persecution the faithful Christian endures for the sake of Christ is in fact the finest compliment that can be given him. We persecute a person because we take him seriously, considering him as a real threat to us. No one will persecute a person whom he feels to be inadept and ineffective. Men like Paul were persecuted because their sincerity, zeal, and righteousness plainly threatened the way of life of Christ's enemies. Can it be that the alleged Christianity of so many is so tepid that the wicked do not persecute it, but simply ignore it? A time-serving, com-

[Fullerton, CA: Tolle Publications, 1966], pp. 75-

Thus, James told Christians in Jas. 5.10:

Take, brethren, for an example of suffering and of patience, the prophets who spake in the name of the Lord.

In II Cor. 1.7, Paul mentioned the sufferings of the Corinthian Christians:

...and our hope for you is stedfast; knowing that, as ye are partakers of the sufferings, so also are ye of the comfort.

Paul, in Rom. 8.16-18, told Christians about another aspect of their suffering with Christ:

The Spirit himself beareth witness with our spirit, that we are children of God: and if children, then heirs; heirs of God, and joint-heirs with Christ; if so be that we suffer with him, that we may be also glorified with him.

Paul, in II Cor. 4.16-17, told his attitude toward his own sufferings:

Wherefore we faint not; but though our outward man is decaying, yet our inward man is renewed day by day. For our light affliction, which is for the moment, worketh for us more and more exceedingly an eternal weight of glory.

Peter taught the same thing in I Pet. 1.6-7:

Wherein ye greatly rejoice, though now for a little while, if need be, ye have been put to grief in manifold trials, that the proof of your faith, being more precious than gold that perisheth though it is proved by fire, may be found unto praise and glory and honor at the revelation of Jesus Christ...

Conclusion

Again, Jesus' teaching in this section is not newer, nobler, nor less attainable than the teaching of the Old Covenant. Likewise, neither is his teaching to Christians in the New Covenant!

Salt and Light—Mt. 5.13-16

In Mt. 5.13-16, Jesus told the Jews of his day:

Ye are the salt of the earth: but if the salt have lost its savor, wherewith shall it be salted? It is thenceforth good for nothing, but to be cast out and trodden under foot of men. Ye are the light of the world. A city set on a hill cannot be hid. Neither do men light a lamp, and put it under the bushel, but on the stand; and it shineth unto all that are in the house. Even so let your light shine before men; that they may see your good works, and glorify your Father who is in heaven.

Salt and light are symbols of influence. While many use these verses to say that Christians should be influential, Jesus was teaching Israelites on this occasion. We next see that he taught them exactly what God had taught them in the Old Covenant.

Old Covenant Teaching

In Isa. 43.10, God said:

You are My witnesses, declares the Lord, and My servant
whom I have chosen.

This verse doesn't speak of the so-called "Jehovah's Witnesses" in Brooklyn, but of the solemn responsibility of Israel to
be as preserving salt, and a shining light to the world around them.
In Dt. 4.5-6, Moses told Israel:

See, I have taught you statutes and judgments just as the
Lord my God commanded me, that you should do thus
in the land where you are entering to possess it. So keep
and do them, for that is your wisdom and your understanding in the sight of the peoples who will hear all these
statutes and say, Surely this great nation is a wise and
understanding people.

In Ezek. 5.5-8, we have much the same teaching:

Thus says the Lord God, This is Jerusalem; I have set her
at the center of the nations, with lands around her. But
she has rebelled against my ordinances more wickedly
than the nations and against my statutes more than the
lands which surround her; for they have ordinances and
have not walked in my statutes. Therefore, thus says the
Lord God, Because you have more turmoil than the
nations which surround you, and have not walked in My
statutes, nor observed My ordinances, nor observed the
ordinances of the nations which surround you, therefore,
thus says the Lord God, Behold, I, even I, am against you,
and I will execute judgments among you in the sight of
the nations.

In Mal. 3.12, God told Israel:

And all the nations will call you blessed, for you shall be
a delightful land, says the Lord of hosts.

Jesus Taught Jews the Same as Old Covenant

Thus, Jesus taught Jews, who were anything but salt and light, exactly what Moses taught about being a good example and influence on others.

New Covenant Teaching

Jesus, in his New Covenant, taught Christians the same thing. For example, in Phil. 2.14-15, Paul said:

> Do all things without murmurings and questionings; that ye may become blameless and harmless, children of God without blemish in the midst of a crooked and perverse generation, among whom ye are seen as lights in the world.

Paul, in Tit. 2.7-8, told Titus to instruct young men:

> ...in all things showing thyself an ensample of good works; in thy doctrine showing uncorruptness, gravity, sound speech, that cannot be condemned; that he that is of the contrary part may be ashamed, having no evil thing to say of us.

In I Tim. 4.12, Paul said:

> Let no man despise thy youth; but be thou an ensample to them that believe, in word, in manner of life, in love, in faith, in purity.

In Eph. 5.8, Christians are commanded:

> ...for ye were once darkness, but are now light in the Lord: walk as children of light.

Conclusion

Obviously, Jesus teaching Jews to be salt and light was not new, more noble, nor too high or unattainable. Nor is his similar teaching to us in the New Covenant asking too much of Christians.

Law of Moses—Mt. 5.17-20

In this section, Jesus said:

Think not that I came to destroy the law or the prophets: I came not to destroy, but to fulfil. For verily I say unto you, Till heaven and earth pass away, one jot or one tittle shall in no wise pass away from the law, till all things be accomplished. Whosoever therefore shall break one of these least commandments, and shall teach men so, shall be called least in the kingdom of heaven: but whosoever shall do and teach them, he shall be called great in the kingdom of heaven. For I say unto you, that except your righteousness shall exceed the righteousness of the scribes and Pharisees, ye shall in no wise enter into the kingdom of heaven.

In contrast to many of his time who thought that Jesus came on the scene and began to dismantle the Mosaic Law, throw it down, and destroy it, Jesus insisted that was not what he came for. The word *destroy* means "to throw down, to destroy utterly." It is used in Mt. 24.2 where Jesus, speaking of the destruction of the temple, said, "There shall not be left here one stone upon another, that shall not be *thrown down*." Jesus didn't do to the law what he said he would do to the temple, that is, destroy it. Rather, he lived according to the law, taught it, and exhorted others to do the same. This is the thrust of this section of the Sermon on the Mount.

Old Covenant Teaching

When Jesus taught strict obedience to the Law of Moses, he taught exactly what the Old Covenant taught. For example, in Dt. 4.2, Moses said:

> You shall not add to the word which I am commanding you, nor take away from it, that you may keep the commandments of the Lord your God which I command you.

Likewise, in Prov. 30.6, Solomon wrote:

> Do not add to His words lest He reprove you, and you be proved a liar.

Jesus Taught Jews the Same as Old Covenant

Thus, when Jesus said that anyone who broke the least precept of the Law of Moses, and taught others to do the same, was the least in the kingdom of heaven, he taught exactly like Moses. He taught it to the same people. If in the Sermon on the Mount Jesus contradicted Moses, he also contradicted himself.

New Covenant Teaching

Of course, no teaching like this exists in the New Covenant. We don't dare teach "Whosoever therefore shall break one of these least commandments (of the Law of Moses), and shall teach men so, shall be called least in the kingdom of heaven" to men now, either Jews or Greeks. Neither would we teach men today what Jesus taught Jews in Mt. 23.23: "For ye tithe mint and anise and cumin, and have left undone the weightier matters of the law, justice, and mercy, and faith: but these ye ought to have done, and not to have left the other undone." Rather, we teach men today that they are "dead to the law" (Rom. 7.4), "discharged from it" (Rom. 7.6, if they were ever under Moses' law), and that if they're led by the Spirit, they are not under the law (Gal. 5.18).

Jesus' teaching in Mt. 5.17-20 was limited strictly to Jews, just as were Dt. 4.2 and Prov. 30.6.

Conclusion

This is one section of the Sermon on the Mount that applied exclusively to Israelites, and taught some things we are not to teach Christians. Yet Jesus taught Israelites exactly like Moses did: nothing new, nothing more noble, nothing unattainable. The Jews could keep the law. They just didn't.

In verse 20, the expression "except your righteousness exceed the righteousness of the scribes and Pharisees" is much abused. Often, preachers use these verses to teach that Christians should contribute financially to their collective work to a greater extent than the Jews tithed. Rather, Jesus told Jews of his day that their righteousness must exceed that of the traditionalists of their day. Note that he did not say that their righteousness had to exceed that of Abraham and David. The righteousness of Abraham and David was the result of their perfect faith (Rom. 4.1-12). This was the righteousness of Noah (Heb. 11.7). It was the righteousness of faith available to all Israelites (Rom. 9.32). But it was not a righteousness based upon law-works, or upon a supercilious, hypocritical pretension of faithful conformity to law with little allegiance to God that the scribes and Pharisees had. The Jews to who Jesus spoke could be saved the same way Abraham and David were, but their righteousness would have to be of an entirely different nature!

"Ye Have Heard but I Say unto You"

We now begin a section of the Sermon on the Mount, where six times Jesus drew a contrast between something they'd heard and what Jesus said. As suggested in the introduction to our study of the Sermon on the Mount, many take these statements as a contrast between the Law of Moses and the Law of Christ. However, we'll see in this section that Jesus didn't contrast the New Covenant with the Mosaic Covenant. He contrasted what the Jews had made out of the Mosaic Covenant with Moses! Thus, in each of these six statements, Jesus taught exactly what Moses taught; again to the same people!

Sometimes, as Jesus showed in this first case (Mt. 5.21-26), the Jews merely oversimplified what Moses taught. Surely, Moses taught "thou shalt not kill," but that's not nearly all Moses taught concerning relations with brethren. Suppose I were to ask you how your family gets along, and you said, "Fine, we haven't had any murders in our family this week!" I'm glad that's true, but a family with no murders in one week might still have much hate, despicable attitudes, mistreatment, etc. Thus, Jesus emphasized additional teaching from Moses, which the Jews of his day greatly neglected.

The same is true with the section on adultery vs. lust (Mt. 5.27-30). To say that one hadn't committed adultery didn't mean that he pleased God in the sexual realm. Even Moses taught that there were other sexual sins that one might readily violate, and still not be an adulterer. Jesus taught exactly like Moses to the Israelites of his day.

Likewise, the Jews of Jesus' day thought the critical part of divorce was the bill of divorcement. In Mt. 5.31-32, Jesus taught exactly like Moses on this subject, and exposed the laxity of Jewish attitudes toward divorce in his day.

When Jesus dealt with oaths (Mt. 5.33-37), he didn't contrast his New Covenant teaching concerning oaths with Moses. He contrasted Moses' teaching with the slack attitude the Jews of his day had developed toward oaths. He taught the same people Moses taught the same thing Moses taught.

The same thing is true with vengeance (Mt. 5.38-42) and love of enemies (Mt. 5.43-48). However, in the case of love of enemies, Jesus exposed the Jews for doing something Moses never said: "Hate thine enemies." Keep these introductory remarks in mind as we consider each of these six contrasting points.

Murder vs. Hate—Mt. 5.21-26

It was said to them of old time, Thou shalt not kill; and whosoever shall kill shall be in danger of the judgment:

but I say unto you, that every one who is angry with his brother shall be in danger of the judgment; and whosoever shall say to his brother, Raca, shall be in danger of the council; and whosoever shall say, Thou fool, shall be in danger of the hell of fire. If therefore thou art offering thy gift at the altar, and there rememberest that thy brother hath aught against thee, leave there thy gift before the altar, and go thy way, first be reconciled to thy brother, and then come and offer thy gift. Agree with thine adversary quickly, while thou art with him in the way; lest haply the adversary deliver thee to the judge, and the judge deliver thee to the officer, and thou be cast into prison. Verily I say unto thee, Thou shalt by no means come out thence, till thou have paid the last farthing.

Jesus showed that just not killing doesn't mean you're dealing with your fellowman correctly. One might not kill someone, but may still have despicable attitudes toward his fellowman that make him highly displeasing to God.

Old Covenant Teaching

The Mosaic Law taught the same thing. For example, in Lev. 19.17, Moses taught:

You shall not hate your fellow-countryman in your heart; you may surely reprove your neighbor, but shall not incur sin because of him.

Jesus Taught Jews the Same as Old Covenant

Thus, Jesus taught Jews, some of whom thought "anything goes" in mistreating your fellowman, and indeed, did it all to Jesus, exactly what Moses taught. He taught the same thing to the same people. It appears that the whole of the Sermon on the Mount is to contrast the outward religion of many of the Jews of his day with the inward religion of the heart. This is especially noticeable in verse 23, where Jesus showed the priority of treating people right over religious ritual. This, again, is exactly what Moses (and other inspired Old Covenant prophets) taught. For example, in Isa. 1.11-17, God chastised Israel, though they offered sacrifices God had commanded:

> What are your multiplied sacrifices to Me? says the Lord. I have had enough of burnt offerings of rams, and the fat of fed cattle, And I take no pleasure in the blood of bulls, lambs, or goats. When you come to appear before Me, who requires of you this trampling of My courts? Bring your worthless offerings no longer, their incense is an abomination to Me. New moon and sabbath, the calling of assemblies—I cannot endure iniquity and the solemn assembly. I hate your new moon festivals and your appointed feasts, they have become a burden to Me. I am weary of bearing them. So when you spread out your hands in prayer, I will hide my eyes from you, yes, even though you multiply prayers, I will not listen. Your hands are full of bloodshed. Wash yourselves, make yourselves clean; remove the evil of your deeds from My sight. Cease to do evil, learn to do good; seek justice, reprove the ruthless; defend the orphan, plead for the widow.

This is the whole point of Hos. 6.6, which Jesus quoted in Mt. 9.10-13, when he told the Jews of his day to "go and learn what this means":

> For I delight in loyalty rather than sacrifice, and in the knowledge of God rather than burnt offerings.

In Mt. 7.12, Jesus showed this emphasis in the Old Covenant on the proper treatment of the Jews' fellowmen:

> All things therefore whatsoever ye would that men should do unto you, even so do ye also unto them: for this is the law and the prophets.

Indeed, he said in Mk. 12.32-34:

And the scribe said unto him, Of a truth, Teacher, thou
hast well said that he is one; and there is none other but
he: and to love him with all the heart, and with all the
understanding, and with all the strength, and to love his
neighbor as himself, is much more than all whole burnt
offerings and sacrifices. And when Jesus saw that he
answered discreetly, he said unto him, Thou art not far
from the kingdom of God.

Thus, Jesus' teaching concerning murder vs. hate is exactly
the same as that given by Moses and the prophets of old. When
Jews, who heard Jesus in Matthew 5, hated their brethren and
cursed and mistreated them, they didn't just reject Christ. They
rejected Moses, who taught them how to treat their fellowman.

New Covenant Teaching

Of course, the New Covenant taught Christians how to treat
our fellowman as well. In Eph. 4.31, Paul said:

Let all bitterness, and wrath, and anger, and clamor, and
railing, be put away from you, with all malice: and be ye
kind one to another, tenderhearted, forgiving each other,
even as God also in Christ forgave you.

In Rom. 13.9, Paul said to Christians:

...and if there be any other commandment, it is summed
up in this word, namely, Thou shalt love thy neighbor as
thyself.

In I Jn. 3.14-15, the apostle John said:

We know that we have passed out of death into life,
because we love the brethren. He that loveth not abideth
in death. Whosoever hateth his brother is a murderer: and
ye know that no murderer hath eternal life abiding in him.

The Christian who hates his brother often strives to kill him spiritually, and usually does so!

Conclusion

Again, in the matter of murder vs. hate, Jesus didn't teach something new. He didn't destroy the law; he upheld it. He didn't teach anything more noble or less attainable than what Moses taught, especially in a context where he taught strict adherence to what Moses taught! What he taught here was not too high for the Jews, and similar teaching in the New Covenant is not too high for Christians. Christians should contemplate the example of the self-righteous Jews, who thought as long as they didn't murder each other, they pleased God, and anything else was permissible. One can be in covenant relationship with God, think thusly, and be entirely wrong.

Adultery vs. Lust—Mt. 5.27-30

Ye have heard that it was said, Thou shalt not commit adultery: but I say unto you, that every one that looketh on a woman to lust after her hath committed adultery with her already in his heart. And if thy right eye causeth thee to stumble, pluck it out, and cast it from thee: for it is profitable for thee that one of thy members should perish, and not thy whole body be cast into hell. And if thy right hand causeth thee to stumble, cut it off, and cast it from thee: for it is profitable for thee that one of thy members should perish, and not thy whole body go into hell.

Old Covenant Teaching

We often take the statements of Jesus to show that he drew the line on sexual sins much higher than did Moses. "Jesus drew the line at lust, while Moses drew it at adultery." Not so! Moses drew the line at the point of lust, as well. Notice in Ex. 20.17, where in the Ten Commandments, Moses said:

> Thou shalt not covet your neighbor's house; you shall not covet your neighbor's wife or his male servant or his female servant or his ox or his donkey or anything that belongs to your neighbor.

In Prov. 15.26, Solomon said:

> Evil plans are an abomination to the Lord, but pleasant words are pure.

In Prov. 12.2, he said:

> A good man will obtain favor from the Lord, but He will condemn a man who devises evil.

In Prov. 24.9, he said:

> The devising of folly is sin, and the scoffer is an abomination to men.

Jesus Taught Jews the Same as Old Covenant

Certainly, Jesus didn't destroy the Mosaic Law, but upheld it. He didn't teach anything new or more noble than Moses. He taught an everyday code of ethics for Jews, just as Moses had done. Like Moses, he placed the emphasis on the condition of the heart. The Jews of his day placed the emphasis on physical sexual sins, rather than the condition of their hearts.

New Covenant Teaching

The New Covenant of Jesus taught Christians the same thing. In Gal. 5.16-24, Paul said:

But I say, Walk by the Spirit, and ye shall not fulfil the lust of the flesh. For the flesh lusteth against the Spirit, and the Spirit against the flesh; for these are contrary the one to the other; that ye may not do the things that ye would. But if ye are led by the Spirit, ye are not under the law. Now the works of the flesh are manifest, which are these: fornication, uncleanness, lasciviousnessAnd they that are of Christ Jesus have crucified their flesh with the passions and the lusts thereof.

Notice particularly Paul's teaching on self-control, the lusts and passions of the flesh, lasciviousness, etc. Then notice Col. 3.5-6, where Paul mentioned "evil desire":

Put to death therefore your members which are upon the earth: fornication, uncleanness, passion, evil desire, and covetousness, which is idolatry.

Conclusion

Both Moses and Jesus taught Jews the same thing Paul taught Christians. Just because one doesn't commit overt illicit sexual acts, doesn't mean he pleases God. God looks on the person's heart and sees the lust therein.

Adultery vs. Bill of Divorcement—Mt. 5.31-32

This section will be covered in Chapter 5, "Jesus on Divorce Under Moses."

Oaths—Mt. 5.33-37

In these verses, Jesus said:

Again, ye have heard that it was said to them of old time, Thou shalt not forswear thyself, but shalt perform unto

The Sermon on the Mount, the Law of Moses, & the New Covenant (3)

MATTHEW 5:

vv33-37: OATHS
OT: Dt 6.13, 10.10
JESUS TO JEWS: Mt. 23.16-22
NEW COVENANT: Jas. 5.12, Gal. 1.20, II Cor. 1.23, Rom. 1.9,
Phil. 1.8, I Thes. 5.27, Heb. 6.16

vv38-42: VENGEANCE
OT: Ex. 21.24-25, Dt. 19.21, Lev. 19.18
JESUS TO JEWS: Mt. 5.38-42
NEW COVENANT: Rom. 12.19, I Pet. 2.12-13

vv43-48: LOVE OF ENEMIES
OT: Ex. 23.4-6, Lev. 19.18, Prov. 25.21
JESUS TO JEWS: MT 5.43-48
NEW COVENANT: Rom. 12.20

MATTHEW 6:

vv1-18: HYPOCRISY
OT: Isa. 29.13, Prov. 4.23, Ps. 24.3-4
JESUS TO JEWS: Mt. 23.25, 27, 28, Jn. 5.44, Jn. 12.43
NEW COVENANT: Gal. 1.10

vv19-34: IMPROPER PHYSICAL PRIORITIES
OT: Dt. 28.2-12
JESUS TO JEWS: Mt. 6.33
NEW COVENANT: Phil. 4.6, 7, 19, Heb. 13.5, 6

MATTHEW 7:

vv1-5: HYPOCRITICAL JUDGMENT
OT: Same as 6.1-18 - didn't forbid judgment
JESUS TO JEWS: Jn. 7.24
NEW COVENANT: I Cor. 5.9-13, I Tim. 5.19-20

Figure 11

the Lord thine oaths: but I say unto you, Swear not at all; neither by the heaven, for it is the throne of God; nor by the earth, for it is the footstool of his feet; nor by Jerusalem, for it is the city of the great King. Neither shalt thou swear by thy head, for thou canst not make one hair

white or black. But let your speech be, Yea, yea; Nay,
nay: and whatsoever is more than these is of the evil one.

Thayer said the word translated "swear" means "to swear,
affirm, promise with an oath, to call a person or thing as a
witness." Sometimes we hear that someone (including at least
one President of the United States) will not swear that something
is true, but he will affirm that it is. Thayer said there is no
difference. We often confuse "swearing" with profanity. Profanity is speaking of special or sacred things in a common manner.
Swearing or taking an oath is the calling upon someone as a
witness that one will do what he has promised to do.

Before the Law of Moses, Abraham swore and made others
do the same. In Gen. 14.22-23 Abram swore to the king of Sodom:

And Abraham said to the king of Sodom, I have sworn
to the Lord God Most High, possessor of heaven and
earth, that I will not take a thread or a sandal thong or
anything that is yours, lest you should say, I have made
Abram rich.

In Gen. 21.23-24, Abimelech requested that Abraham swear
to him:

...now therefore swear to me here by God that you will
not deal falsely with me, or with my offspring, or with
my posterity; but according to the kindness that I have
shown to you, you shall show to me, and to the land in
which you have sojourned. And Abraham said, I swear
it.

In Gen. 24.3, Abraham made his servant take an oath:

I will make you swear by the Lord, the God of heaven
and the God of earth, that you shall not take a wife for
my son from the daughters of the Canaanites, among
whom I live...

Old Covenant Teaching

It will surprise some, but God commanded Jews under Moses to take oaths or swear by his name, and he felt honored when they did so. Notice in Dt. 6.13, where God told Israel:

> You shall fear only the Lord your God; and you shall worship Him, and swear by His name.

Similarly, in Dt. 10.20, Moses commanded:

> You shall fear the Lord your God; you shall serve Him and cling to Him, and you shall swear by His name.

Jesus Taught Jews the Same as Old Covenant

Jesus taught Jews who had a careless attitude toward oaths exactly what Moses had taught them. He didn't forbid oath taking, but, like Moses, he forbade trivial oaths and violating oaths by perjury. To see the attitude of many Jews toward oaths, notice Mt. 23.16-22:

> Woe unto you, ye blind guides, that say, Whosoever shall swear by the temple, it is nothing; but whosoever shall swear by the gold of the temple, he is a debtor. Ye fools and blind: for which is greater, the gold, or the temple that hath sanctified the gold? And, Whosoever shall swear by the altar, it is nothing; but whosoever shall by the gift that is upon it, he is a debtor. Ye blind: for which is greater, the gift, or the altar that sanctifieth the gift? He therefore that sweareth by the altar, sweareth by it, and by all things thereon. And he that sweareth by the temple, sweareth by it, and by him that dwelleth therein. And he that sweareth by the heaven, sweareth by the throne of God, and by him that sitteth thereon.

Here we see their outward concern for the wording of an oath, with no concern for their verbal integrity.

Jesus himself took oaths, as we see in Mt. 26.63, as the high priest questioned him:

> But Jesus held his peace. And the high priest said unto him, I adjure thee by the living God, that thou tell us whether thou art the Christ, the Son of God. Jesus saith unto him, Thou hast said:

The term "adjure" here means "to place under oath."

New Covenant Teaching

In Jas. 5.12, God commanded Christians:

> But above all things, my brethren, swear not, neither by the heaven, nor by the earth, nor by any other oath: but let your yea be yea, and your nay, nay; that ye fall not under judgment.

At first glance, this passage seems to forbid all oath taking, but several facts convince us otherwise. First, the word "other" James used is one of two words translated "other" in the New Testament. One is *heteros*, "another of a different kind," that Paul used in Gal. 1.8 ("If anyone preacheth *another* gospel"—another of a different kind). The other is *allos*, "another of the same kind," that is used in Jn. 14.16 ("I will send *another* comforter"). The oaths James forbade are *those of the same kind* as he enumerated: by heaven, by earth, or by any other of this same kind. Thus, James forbade the same trivial oaths Jesus forbade of the Jews.

We also see this to be true when we notice the examples of oaths in the New Testament by persons we are to imitate. For example, in Gal. 1.20, Paul swore, or made an oath, and called God for a witness, when he said:

> Before God, I lie not.

He did it again in II Cor. 1.23:

I call God for a witness upon my soul.

Also in Rom. 1.9, we find:

For God is my witness.

Finally, he did it in I Thes. 5.27:

I adjure you.

In other words, Paul said, "I place you under oath." In Heb. 6.16, where the author of Hebrews said:

> For men swear by the greater: and in every dispute of theirs the oath is final for confirmation. Wherein God, being minded to show more abundantly unto the heirs of the promise the immutability of his counsel, interposed with an oath; that by two immutable things, in which it is impossible for God to lie.

Thus, men take oaths, and God follows men's examples.

Conclusion

Jesus' teaching on oaths in the Sermon on the Mount is not new. He didn't destroy the law, as the Jews thought, but he upheld it. He didn't teach anything about oaths more noble than Moses did. He taught the same thing, which was attainable by the Jews, and the same teaching in the New Covenant is attainable by us.

Personal Vengeance—Mt. 5.38-42

In these verses, Jesus said:

> Ye have heard that it was said, An eye for an eye, and a tooth for a tooth: but I say unto you, Resist not him that is evil: but whosoever smiteth thee on thy right cheek,

turn to him the other also. And if any man would go to law with thee, and take away thy coat, let him have thy cloak also. And whosoever shall compel thee to go one mile, go with him two. Give to him that asketh thee, and from him that would borrow of thee turn not thou away.

Old Covenant Teaching

In Lev. 19.18, Moses said:

You shall not take vengeance, nor bear any grudge against the sons of your people, but you shall love your neighbor as yourself; I am the Lord.

Thus, Moses forbade retaliation. Personal vengeance didn't belong to the Jews, either. In Ex. 21.22-25, we see how the judges decided how punishment was to be meted out:

And if men struggle with each other and strike a woman with child so that she has a miscarriage, yet there is no further injury, he shall surely be fined as the woman's husband may demand of him; and he shall pay as the judges decide. But if there is any further injury, then you shall appoint as a penalty life for life, eye for eye, tooth for tooth, hand for hand, foot for foot, burn for burn, wound for wound, bruise for bruise.

Dt. 19.18-21 also shows how the judges of Israel were to mete out punishment:

And the judges shall investigate thoroughly life for life, eye for eye, tooth for tooth, hand for hand, foot for foot.

Finally, notice Lev. 24.14 in this regard:

Bring the one who has cursed outside the camp, and let all who heard him lay their hands on his head; then let all the congregation stone him.

Moses addressed all these passages to the judges of Israel. They were restrictive; they didn't permit the judges to overdo the punishment.

Jesus Taught Jews the Same as Old Covenant

On the subject of personal vengeance, Jesus taught the same thing Moses did to the same people. Many Israelites he taught thought they could take personal vengeance. People now often misapply this teaching to self-defense, capital punishment, and passive non-resistance of all evil. Whatever Jesus taught in either the Old Covenant or the New Covenant, he didn't teach on that subject in these passages, for they deal with personal vengeance.

New Covenant Teaching

The apostle Paul taught the same thing to New Covenant people. For example in Rom. 12.19, Paul said:

> Avenge not yourselves, beloved, but give place unto the wrath of God: for it is written, Vengeance belongeth unto me; I will recompense, saith the Lord.

Peter, in I Pet. 2.21-23, taught the same thing:

> For hereunto were ye called: because Christ also suffered for you, leaving you an example, that ye should follow his steps: who did no sin, neither was guile found in his mouth: who, when he was reviled, reviled not again; when he suffered, threatened not; but committed himself to him that judgeth righteously.

Just as Christ, living and teaching the Law of Moses, didn't exercise personal retaliation, neither should we who live and teach the Law of Christ. God never permitted his covenant people, under Moses or Christ, to take the law into their own hands!

Conclusion

Again, the teaching of Jesus in the Sermon on the Mount regarding personal vengeance is not new, nor is it higher than the teaching of Moses. The same teaching to Christians is just as attainable for them as was Moses' teaching to the Jews.

Hate vs. Love of Enemies—Mt. 5.43-48

In Mt. 5.43-48, Jesus said:

> Ye have heard that it was said, Thou shalt love thy neighbor, and hate thine enemy: but I say unto you, Love your enemies, and pray for them that persecute you; that ye may be sons of your Father who is in heaven: for he maketh his sun to rise on the evil and the good, and sendeth rain on the just and the unjust. For if ye love them that love you, what reward have ye? do not even the publicans the same? And if ye salute your brethren only, what do ye more than others? do not even the Gentiles the same? Ye therefore shall be perfect, as your heavenly Father is perfect.

This is the sixth and final of the contrasting statements Jesus made. So far, the Jews' statements have been shallow interpretations of Moses' teaching. Here, though, we have an outright misrepresentation. Moses never said, "Hate thine enemy." Thus, Jesus here corrected their misrepresentation, striving to bring the Jews of his day back to the Mosaic code.

Old Covenant Teaching

Rather than telling Jews to "hate thine enemy," here is what Moses actually told the Jews about their conduct toward their enemies. See Ex. 23.4-5, where Moses commanded:

If you meet your enemy's ox or his donkey wandering away, you shall surely return it to him. If you see the donkey of one who hates you lying helpless under its load, you shall refrain from leaving it to him, you shall surely release it with him.

The key passage is Lev. 19.18:

You shall not take vengeance, nor bear any grudge against the sons of your people, but you shall love your neighbor as yourself; I am the Lord.

Here, of course, is the so-called "golden rule." However, the golden rule didn't come from Christ, but from Moses. Notice the same teaching in Prov. 25.21, which Paul quoted in Rom. 12.20:

But if thine enemy hunger, feed him; if he thirst, give him to drink: for in so doing thou shalt heap coals of fire upon his head.

Jesus Taught Jews the Same as Old Covenant

In the gospels, Jesus told the Jews that the tax collectors and Gentiles knew this principle. It's hard to imagine the effect this teaching would have had on Jews. In effect, he told them that the dogs beat them at their own game!

New Covenant Teaching

We've just noticed where Paul quoted Solomon in Rom. 12.20, where he said:

But if thine enemy hunger, feed him; if he thirst, give him to drink: for in so doing thou shalt heap coals of fire upon his head.

Conclusion

Jesus' teaching on one's attitude toward one's enemies in the Sermon on the Mount is not new. He didn't destroy the law, as the Jews thought, but he upheld it. He didn't teach anything about love of enemies more noble than Moses did. He taught the same thing, which was attainable by the Jews, and the same teaching in the New Covenant is attainable by us.

Conclusion on Matthew 5

We see that everything in Matthew 5 is out of the Law of Moses. Rather than Jesus contrasting his New Covenant with the Mosaic one, he contrasted the Mosaic one with the shallow, hypocritical, outward shell many Jews of his day had made out of Moses.

Matthew 6-7

The reader is urged to examine Figures 11 and 12 comparing Matthew 6-7 with the teaching of the Old Covenant to see that they are essentially Old Testament teaching as well. Certainly, every precept of the Sermon on the Mount is Old Covenant teaching. The contrast was between the Law of Moses and Judaism, or outward vs. inward religion. Jesus' teaching was no higher, no different, no more noble, no more unattainable than was the teaching of Moses.

In the Sermon on the Mount, Jesus drew the same distinction Paul did in Rom. 2.28-29:

> For he is not a Jew who is one outwardly; neither is that circumcision which is outward in the flesh: but he is a Jew who is one inwardly; and circumcision is that of the heart, in the spirit not in the letter; whose praise is not of men, but of God.

Realizing that Jesus didn't teach anything here that Moses hadn't already taught Israel, why should the Israelites have any problem at all with what Jesus taught? Without doubt, Jesus said

The Sermon on the Mount, the Law of Moses, & the New Covenant (4)

MATTHEW 7:

vv6-12: BENEVOLENCE
OT: Dt. 15.7-12, Prov. 28.27
JESUS TO JEWS: Lk. 10, Mt. 9.13, 23.23, 24, 25.41-46
NEW COVENANT: Jas. 1.27, Eph. 4.28

vv13-14: TWO WAYS
OT: Dt. 30.19, 20
JESUS TO JEWS: Mt. 7.13-14
NEW COVENANT: Rom. 6.15-23

vv15-20: FALSE TEACHERS
OT: Dt. 13.5, 18.22
JESUS TO JEWS: Mt. 24.4, 5, 11
NEW COVENANT: II Pet. 2.1-2

vv21-23: FAITH IN CHRIST
OT: Dt. 18.18, 30.30
JESUS TO JEWS: Jn. 8.24, Lk. 6.36, Jn. 5.36
NEW COVENANT: Mk. 16.16, Ac. 3.23

Shouldn't Apply Mt. 5.31-32 or

Mt. 19.3-9 to anyone but Jews, any more than:

Mt. 8.1-4: "Go show yourself to the priest as Moses commanded"

Mt. 19.16, 17: "Keep the commandments"

Figure 12

this very thing in Jn. 5.45-47:

Think not that I will accuse you to the Father: there is
one that accuseth you, even Moses, on whom ye have set
your hope. For if ye believed Moses, you would believe
me; for he wrote of me. But if ye believe not his writings,
how shall ye believe my words?

Jesus had no problem with inward Jews. Neither did Paul, nor
do Christians today. Jesus was an inward Jew. The apostles were
all inward Jews. All the early Christians were. But Jesus had
definite conflicts with outward Jews, as did the apostles, and the
early Christians. Had Moses still been alive, he would have, too!

Conclusion

Over and over in our study of the Sermon on the Mount we've
seen that Jesus did not contrast his teaching with that of Moses'.
Instead, Jesus correctly interpreted Moses' teaching to the Jews
of his day. Jesus gave strong admonitions to the Jews to try to
turn them back to full obedience of Moses' words. While most
of these teachings are contained in the New Covenant for Christians, to take any of the Sermon on the Mount and try to bind it
on Christians is to completely ignore its context and Jesus'
purpose in preaching the sermon.

Chapter 5

Jesus on Divorce Under Moses

Highlights

- *Jesus taught same as Moses in Mt. 5.32, Mt. 19.9.*
- *God didn't permit loose divorce for Jews because they rebelled against him.*
- *Hardness of heart wasn't rebellion toward God, but lack of receptiveness of unfaithful wives.*
- *Joseph's options with Mary.*

In the previous chapter, we looked at the Sermon on the Mount and ascertained that, rather than being New Covenant teaching, Jesus' teaching was that of a faithful Jewish rabbi faithfully interpreting Moses' teaching to his Jewish audience. In that chapter we covered every verse of Matthew 5, except for Mt. 5.31-32. We now discuss those verses, along with Mt. 19.3-9, in which Jesus correctly interpreted Moses' teaching on divorce and remarriage in Dt. 24.1-4 for his Jewish audience.

Adultery vs. Bill of Divorcement—Mt. 5.31-32

The Teaching of Jesus

> It was said also, Whosoever shall put away his wife, let him give her a writing of divorcement: but I say unto you, that every one that putteth away his wife, saving for the

cause of fornication, maketh her an adulteress: and whosoever shall marry her when she is put away committeth
adultery.

The Teaching of the Old Covenant

As we studied in Chapter 3, the cardinal passage dealing with
divorce in the Old Covenant is Dt. 24.1-4 where Moses said:

> When a man takes a wife and marries her, and it happens
> that she finds no favor in his eyes because he has found
> some indecency in her, and he writes her a certificate of
> divorce and puts it in her hand and sends her out from
> his house, and she leaves his house and goes and becomes
> another man's wife, and if the latter husband turns
> against her and writes her a certificate of divorce and puts
> it in her hand and sends her out of his house, or if the
> latter husband dies who took her to be his wife, then her
> former husband who sent her away is not allowed to take
> her again to be his wife, since she has been defiled; for
> that is abomination before the Lord, and you shall not
> bring sin on the land which the Lord your God gives you
> as an inheritance.

As we established in Chapter 3 through a word study of
"indecency" or "unseemliness," the unseemly thing of Deuteronomy 24 was illicit sexual intercourse or activity not punishable
by death. It included both adultery, with insufficient witnesses to
carry out the death penalty, and lasciviousness, unchaste handling
of members of the opposite sex. It included all illicit sexual
intercourse or activity not punishable by death. What did Moses
permit in cases where a man's wife was guilty of illicit sexual
intercourse (fornication) which was not punishable by death? He
permitted the man to put her away. And he was to give her a bill
of divorcement in such cases.

Jesus Taught Jews the Same as Moses in Mt. 5.32 and Mt. 19.9

We now establish that Moses' teaching is exactly what Jesus taught, both in Mt. 5.31-32 and Mt. 19.3-9. When Jesus finished both of these passages, the only grounds on which one could put away his spouse and remarry, were on the grounds of illicit sexual intercourse! Jesus taught Jews in Matthew 5 and Matthew 19 exactly what Moses taught the same people. In particular, Mt. 5.31-32 comes only twelve verses after Jesus pronounced a woe on those who would do and teach differently than the Law of Moses. Notice his statement in Mt. 5.17-19:

> Think not that I came to destroy the law or the prophets: I came not to destroy, but to fulfil. For verily I say unto you, Till heaven and earth pass away, one jot or one tittle shall in no wise pass away from the law, till all things be accomplished. Whosoever therefore shall break one of these least commandments, and shall teach men so, shall be called least in the kingdom of heaven: but whosoever shall do and teach them, he shall be called great in the kingdom of heaven.

As we commented before in Chapter 3, the Jews were convinced that Jesus came to discard Moses' teaching, and he was denying that very thing. When Jesus said, "Whosoever therefore shall break one of these least commandments, *and shall teach men so*, shall be called least in the kingdom of heaven," he pronounced a woe on the teacher who would so teach the Jews.

Did Jesus then turn right around and teach them something different from Moses on divorce and remarriage? The context demands that the answer is, "Obviously not!" However, in both Mt. 5.31-32 and Mt. 19.3-9, Jesus used the Greek word *porneia*, translated fornication, "illicit sexual intercourse in general." Thus, since Jesus correctly interpreted Moses for these Jews, he irrefutably set forth the meaning of "indecency" or "unseemliness" in Dt. 24.1, which agrees with our word study in Chapter 3 of how the word was used throughout the Old Testament. Moses only authorized divorce for fornication in Deuteronomy 24, and authorized the remarriage of the put-away fornicator.

Jesus' Teaching in Mt. 19.3-9

Having seen that Jesus' teaching to Jews in Mt. 5.31-32 was addressed to Jews, and taught the same thing as Moses' teaching to the same people in Deuteronomy 24, we now turn our attention to Mt. 19.3-9.

> v3: And there came unto him Pharisees, trying him, and saying, Is it lawful for a man to put away his wife for every cause?

The fact that these Pharisees were "trying" Jesus shows that they were not really sincere in their question; that is, they weren't really asking to seek the truth, but rather testing Jesus, hoping to get Jesus to contradict Moses. When these Pharisees asked if divorce for every cause was lawful, what law do you suppose they referred to? The Law of Christ, which wouldn't be effective for some time yet, and which they didn't know anything about, or the law under which they and Jesus lived, the Mosaic Law? Of course, they asked with reference to the Law of Moses, which they were attempting at this very time to get him to contradict. Everybody in this account lived under the Mosaic Law. Additionally, although they asked about "every cause," they were not really interested in the case of verified adultery, for John 8 shows they knew what to do in the case of a woman taken in the act of adultery: "Moses said we ought to stone such," they correctly said.

The causes the Jews were asking about were cases other than adultery verified. At the time the Jews questioned Jesus, rabbis of various schools were involved in a raging controversy about the teaching of Moses. Conservative rabbis of the school of Hillel taught that the "unseemliness" or "indecency" of Dt. 24.1 was fornication. Liberal rabbis of the school of Shammai taught that Moses permitted divorce for just about any reason. They said that if a man found a prettier wife, he could, with Moses' blessing, treacherously put away his wife and marry the prettier one. If one "spun [yarn—SGD] in the streets," he could do the same. These Jews were "trying" Jesus to see what side he would take in their inflamed controversy. In verses 4-6, Jesus replied:

> And he answered and said, Have ye not read, that he who made them from the beginning made them male and female, and said, For this cause shall a man leave his father and mother, and shall cleave to his wife; and the two shall become one flesh? So that they are no more two, but one flesh. What therefore God hath joined together, let not man put asunder.

Jesus quoted from Gen. 2.24 recording the origin of marriage. On the phrase, "let not man put asunder," please see more comments on I Cor. 7.15 in the next chapter, "Divorce Under Christ—I Cor. 7.1-16." For now, we merely remark that Jesus made marriage sound pretty permanent, much more permanent than many of the rabbis taught. Man was not to put asunder what God had joined. So his answer was, "No, you can't get rid of your wives for any old reason."

The Jews took his answer to be siding with the conservative rabbis, so they asked more about Dt. 24.1-4 in verses 7-8. Their quotation from Moses again shows they were questioning Jesus with reference to the Law of Moses when they began their question with, "Is it lawful?" They did not like Jesus' answer and asked him another question:

> They say unto him, Why then did Moses command to give a bill of divorcement, and to put her away? He saith unto them, Moses for your hardness of heart suffered you to put away your wives: but from the beginning it hath not been so.

Moses Suffered Jews to Put Away Their Wives

Many times, we're tempted to understand the word "suffered" to mean something like this: God *tolerated* the Jews putting away their wives in the Old Testament, but it was something he really didn't want to do. Many view God as "caving in" to the rebellious Jews, and so he permitted treacherous divorce. Normally, they're thinking that God permitted divorce for less than fornication. Of course, we demonstrated in Chapter 3 that Moses didn't permit divorce for anything less than fornication. So did God really not think the Jews should divorce, but he caved in to them and let them do it anyway?

We wouldn't permit a preacher today to do what many think God did in the Old Testament, would we? If a preacher backed off from the Bible's teaching concerning baptism because, "The people were so rebellious, I knew they wouldn't obey the truth, so I just gave in," would we tolerate such? We daresay not for a minute! If a preacher permitted immoral divorce and remarriage because he knew the people were going to divorce and remarry anyway, would we tolerate such a quisling for a preacher? Not for a minute! He'd be fired within the week. Yet many think that God did those very things in the Old Testament. We hold modern preachers to a higher standard than we think God kept in the Bible. Who can believe it? No, God didn't cave in to rebellious Jews and tolerate teaching we wouldn't now. Are we more holy than God? There's something wrong with that picture, isn't there?

In Ex. 15:11, Moses and the children of Israel sang praise to God for delivering them from Egypt:

> Who is like Thee among the gods, O Lord? Who is like Thee, majestic in holiness, awesome in praises, working wonders?

To the question, "Who is like God, majestic in holiness?" can we now answer, "Modern-day preachers and Christians, because they take stands now that God didn't have the courage to take in the Old Testament?" Surely, we're thinking wrong if we think we take more stalwart moral stands than God did, aren't we?

In Job 4:17, Job's friend Eliphaz rebuked some of Job's charges that he was more righteous than God with the question:

Can mankind be just before God? Can a man be pure before his maker?

Plainly, if we hold our preachers and ourselves to a higher standard than God held himself in Deuteronomy 24, we're making the same mistake Job did, aren't we? If we think that God permitted loose divorce for sixteen hundred years then finally got his courage together when Jesus came back and really stood for the truth, perhaps we're thinking more highly of ourselves than we ought to think.

In Rom. 12.2, Paul told Christians not to be conformed to this world. Was God in Deuteronomy 24? If the common view is correct, that God really didn't want the Jews to divorce for less than fornication, but he allowed it anyway, he was conformed to this world for sixteen centuries! Do you believe it?

In II Tim. 2:12-13, Paul compared the faithfulness of God and man:

...if we endure, we shall also reign with him: if we shall deny him, he also will deny us: if we are faithless, he abideth faithful; for he cannot deny himself.

If the common view of God in the Old Testament is correct, that God really didn't want the Jews to divorce for less than fornication but had to cave in because of their rebelliousness, then God denied himself throughout the whole Mosaic period! He should have done better, shouldn't he? He should have been as stalwart as we are! Believe it, who can?

No, the word "suffered" doesn't mean that God caved in, or merely tolerated the Jews putting away their wives.

Figure 13 demonstrates the true meaning of the word "suffered." The word is translated from the Greek word *apitrepo*, which Thayer says means "to permit, allow, give leave." In other words, when Jesus said Moses "suffered" divorce [we understand it to be for fornication—SGD], Moses was permitting it, authorizing it. In the figure we see how the word is used in the New Testament. In Mt. 8.21, the disciple, who really didn't want to serve his Lord, said, "Lord, suffer me [*apitrepo*] first to go and bury my father." He was asking for permission or authority,

Jesus: "Moses suffered you to put away your wives"

Suffered: "to permit, allow, give leave" (Thayer, p. 245.)

Mt. 8.21: "SUFFER me first to go and bury my father"

Lk. 9.61 - "I will follow thee; but LET me first go and bid them
farewell"

Ac. 21.39 - "I beseech thee, SUFFER me to speak unto the people"

Ac. 21.40 - "and when he had GIVEN HIM LICENSE, Paul spake..."

I Tim. 2.12 - "I SUFFER not a woman to teach nor to usurp
authority..."

Jn. 19.38 - "Joseph of Arimathea besought Pilate . . . and Pilate
GAVE HIM LEAVE"

I Cor. 16.7 - "I trust to tarry a while with you, if the Lord PERMIT"

Heb. 6.3 - "And this will we do, if God PERMIT"

Ac. 26.1 - "Thou art PERMITTED to speak for thyself. Then Paul
Paul . . . answered for himself"

I Cor., 14.34 - "Let your women keep silence . . . it is not
PERMITTED unto them to speak"

**Moses Permitted or Authorized Divorce for
Indecency**

Figure 13

wasn't he? In Lk. 9.61, a similar servant said, "I will follow thee:
but let [*apitrepo*] me first go and bid them farewell," again asking
for permission or authority to do a thing. In Ac. 21.39, when the
newly-arrested Paul asked the centurion for permission to speak
to the crowd, the record says, "And when he had given him
license [*apitrepo*], Paul spake unto them." Paul was given license
or authority to speak to the crowd. Similarly, in Jn. 19.38, Joseph
of Arimathea sought the body of Jesus "and Pilate gave him leave
[*apitrepo*]." Pilate didn't tolerate Joseph or cave in to him, he

authorized him to take the body of Jesus. The word is also translated "permit" or "permitted" in I Cor. 16.7, Heb. 6.3, and I Cor. 14.34 where Paul said, "Let your women keep silence, for it is not permitted unto them to speak." In this case Paul discussed that there is no license or authority for such.

Thus, Jesus affirmed that Moses permitted, or authorized, men to put away their wives for fornication, and they could go and become another man's wife with nary so much as a fine or the offering of a turtledove.

What Did Jesus Mean by Hardness of Heart?

"But," some may ask, "didn't Moses grant that permission because of the hardness of their hearts? (Mt. 19.8)" Certainly, but hardness toward whom? Many often assume "hardness of heart toward God." In other words, many have the idea that although God didn't want them to, because the Jews were so stubborn and didn't want to obey God, God gave them the liberty of divorcing their wives for illicit sexual activity.

First, that assumption flies in the face of God's pattern of dealing with his people. As one reads the Old Testament, he finds that when God's people were rebellious, God generally restricted them. He didn't give them even more liberty, just as we discipline our own children.

Second, let's look at the term "hardness" just a little closer. The word means "impervious," like rock. It indicates a lack of receptiveness or penetration. This lack of reception may be either as a result of rebellion toward God (as in Pharaoh's case), or it may be just a lack of understanding. For example, Mark used the word in this second sense of the apostles in Mk. 16.14:

And afterward he was manifested unto the eleven themselves as they sat at meat; and he upbraided them with
their unbelief and hardness of heart, because they believed not them that had seen him after he was risen.

Jesus' apostles were not rebellious, they were just not recep-
tive to the resurrection, at that point. Some hard-hearted people

are rebellious, but not all of them are. Suppose that the hardness
of heart spoken of in Mt. 19.8 is lack of receptiveness to the
spouse, the one guilty of illicit sexual activity—the unseemly
thing of Deuteronomy 24. We have all heard some men say that
if their spouse was ever unfaithful to them, they would divorce
them in a minute. Sometimes it happens that their spouse becomes unfaithful, and they don't do that at all. Many will take
her back if she will just repudiate her sin. Some will take her back
whether she repudiates it or not. But some cannot take her back
because they can't work the problem of their spouse being with
another man. In such cases, what did Moses permit? In Dt. 24.1,
he said:

> When a man takes a wife and marries her, and it happens
> that she finds no favor in his eyes because he has found
> some indecency in her, and he writes her a certificate of
> divorce and puts it in her hand and sends her out from
> his house...

In other words, Moses said that if a man's wife committed
fornication not punishable by death, and he couldn't work the
problem, he could put her away. The "she finds no favor in his
eyes" of Deuteronomy 24 is the same as "hardness of heart" in
Matthew 19. She can't find any favor in his eyes because of her
fornication, either because she won't repent of it, or even if she
will, her husband still can't accept her back into the marriage bed.
That is exactly what Jesus implied in Mt. 5.31-32 and Mt. 19.3-9.
Again, Jesus taught the same people the same thing that Moses
taught. Neither Jesus nor Moses granted liberty because Israel
was rebellious, but because some men couldn't live with a spouse
who had been unfaithful to them.

"Doesn't the Whosoever Refer to More Than Just Jews?"

Many times, when someone begins to realize that in Matthew
5 and 19, all the participants are Jews, quoting and living under
the Mosaic Law, they then wonder if Jesus' statement that "Who-

soever puts away his wife" couldn't be referring to more than just Jews? First, there's no one other than Jews in the context. There's no law other than the law the Jews lived under in the context. Second, the term "whosoever" must always be interpreted by its context, for "whosoever" never means everyone without qualification.

In Figure 14, we see how the word "whosoever" is used, and that it must always be interpreted by its context. For instance, in Ex. 31.15, Moses said, "*Whosoever* works on the sabbath shall be put to death." Did that mean that Gentiles or Christians who work on the sabbath shall be put to death? Not at all. Just Jews, the people to whom this legislation was addressed, were under such a penalty, and it's falsely applied outside that context. No one outside that context was included in "whosoever." Likewise, in Ex. 12.15, Moses said, "*Whosoever* eats anything leavened shall be cut off from the congregation of Israel." Even though Moses said "whosoever," since there is no one other than Jews in the context, the passage applies only to Jews. Anyone, who applies this passage outside that context, does so falsely. In I Jn. 4.15, John, opposing the Gnostics of his time who denied the deity of Christ, said, "*Whosoever* shall confess that Jesus is the Son of God is in fellowship with God." Does this include the Pope or Jehovah's Witnesses, both of whom affirm that Jesus is the Son of God? They're not in the context, and the passage is falsely applied outside the context of John's teaching on Gnosticism. In Mk. 11.23, Jesus said, "*Whosoever* shall say to this mountain, Be thou taken up and cast into the sea; and shall not doubt in his heart, but shall believe that what he saith cometh to pass; he shall have it." If you try this with your nearest mountain thinking it will happen, you're sure to be disappointed. Even though Jesus said "whosoever," you are not in the context, and you're falsely applying the passage to yourself.

Figure 15 illustrates this point further. Mt. 5.19, speaking of the teaching of the Old Testament law and prophets, says, "*Whosoever* therefore shall break one of these least commandments, and shall teach men so, shall be called least in the kingdom of heaven." Does this mean that Gentiles and Christians, who don't keep all the teaching of the Old Testament law and prophets, are doomed? Of course not. To use "whosoever" thusly is to use it

"Whosoever" Shall Put Away

Must Be Interpreted By Context:

Ex. 31.15 - WHOSOEVER works on the sabbath shall be put to death

Falsely applied outside the context!

Ex. 12.15 - WHOSOEVER eats anything leavened shall be cut off from the congregation of Israel

Falsely applied outside the context!

I Jn. 5.1 - WHOSOEVER believeth Jesus is the Christ is begotten of God

Falsely applied outside the context!

I Jn. 4.15 - WHOSOEVER shall confess that Jesus is the Son of God is in fellowship with God

Falsely applied outside the context!

Mk. 11.23 - WHOSOEVER says to this mountain

Falsely applied outside the context!

Figure 14

falsely. So with Mt. 5.31-32 and Mt. 19.9. When Jesus said "whosoever," he spoke only to whom the teaching was addressed. As we've noticed, Jesus was a Jew, his audience was Jewish, and the passage they discussed was the Mosaic Law in Dt. 24.1-4. There isn't a Christian or a Gentile in the account. To apply these passages outside the Jewish context is to apply them falsely.

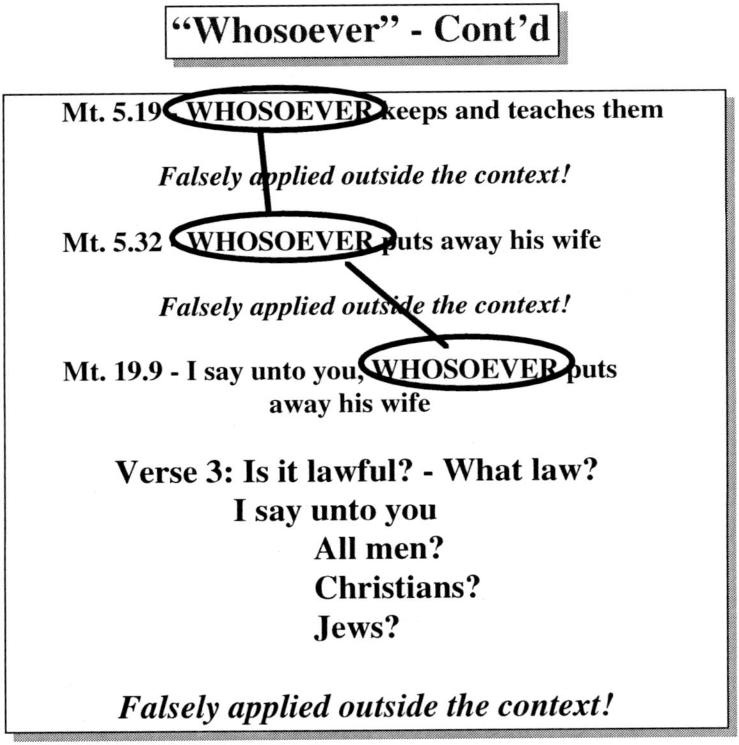

"Whosoever" - Cont'd

Mt. 5.19 ⟨WHOSOEVER⟩ keeps and teaches them

Falsely applied outside the context!

Mt. 5.32 ⟨WHOSOEVER⟩ puts away his wife

Falsely applied outside the context!

Mt. 19.9 - I say unto you, ⟨WHOSOEVER⟩ puts away his wife

Verse 3: Is it lawful? - What law?
I say unto you
All men?
Christians?
Jews?

Falsely applied outside the context!

Figure 15

Conclusion

We see that Mt. 5.31-32 and Mt. 19.3-9 apply to Jews, not Christians. We should view it just like Mt. 8.4, given immediately after Jesus concluded the Sermon on the Mount, and he came down, said:

And Jesus saith unto him, See thou tell no man; but go, show thyself to the priest, and offer the gift that Moses commanded, for a testimony unto them.

The Gospels & The Law of Moses

Gal. 4.4 - born under the law
Mt. 15.24 - not sent but to lost sheep of house of
          Israel
Jn. 3.3-5 - born of water and the Spirit
Lk. 4.16 - Jesus in synagogue on sabbath
Mt. 5.5 - the meek shall inherit the land
Mt. 5.19, 20 - faithful teacher of the law
Mt. 8.4 - go, show yourself to the priest as Moses
          commanded
Mk. 2.27 - the sabbath was made for man
Mk. 6.17-18 - it is not lawful for you to have her
Mt. 15.4 - if dishonor parents, you die
Mt. 19.3 - is it lawful to put away your wife?
Mt. 22.36 - what is the great commandment of
          law?
Mt. 23.23 - tithe mint, anise, and cummin
Mt. 26.18 - Jesus keeping the Passover

Where do Mt. 5.32, 19.3-9 fit in?

Figure 16

We don't think of applying this verse to Christians, yet it came from the same context. Mt. 19.3-9 applied to Jews also, not Christians. Just like the teaching of Mt. 19.16, containing the Ten Commandments, given to the rich young ruler applied to Jews, not Christians. We should no more apply these passages to anyone other than Jews than we would apply the sabbath commandment to anyone other than Jews.

Figure 16 contains a number of passages throughout the gospels to demonstrate the prevalence of Old Covenant teaching throughout. The list begins with Gal. 4.4 (not in the gospels, of course, but introductory to the work of Christ), where Paul said, "Jesus was born under the law." In Mt. 15.24, Jesus said, "I was not sent but to the lost sheep of the house of Israel," so the vast, vast, majority of his teaching was addressed to Jews. In Jn. 3.3, 5, Nicodemus talked to Jesus about being born of water, certainly talking about baptism, but which baptism? The gospels tell us that at the time this conversation took place, John the Baptist was preaching in Judea and having stupendous success. All Jerusalem went out to hear him, and all Judea, even the publicans. As Nicodemus and Jesus talked about baptism, which baptism was it? Was it the one they were all hearing about that day, John's baptism, or was it baptism in the name of Christ, which no one would hear a word about for three more years in Ac. 2.38? Nicodemus couldn't have possibly understood Christ's words to refer to baptism in the name of Christ. Had we been standing beside him, we couldn't have, either. Likewise, Nicodemus couldn't have been "buried with Christ" in baptism because Christ hadn't died and been buried yet. Neither could he have been "raised with Christ" in baptism because Christ hadn't been raised yet. He couldn't have been "baptized into Christ's body" because his body, the church, didn't yet exist. None of these truths so commonly held by Christians now applied to Nicodemus then.

In Lk. 4.16, Jesus was in the synagogue on the sabbath. In Mt. 5.5, in the Sermon on the Mount, in which every syllable is out of the Mosaic Law, Jesus said, "The meek shall inherit the land." As we've demonstrated, this is essentially an Old Covenant land promise to Israel, not a land promise to Christians. In Mt. 5.19-20, Jesus promised to be a faithful teacher of the Mosaic Law and the prophets. In Mt. 8.4, immediately after the Sermon on the Mount, Jesus healed a leper and told him, "Go, show yourself to the priest as Moses commanded." In Mk. 2.27, Jesus pointed out to his Pharisaic critics that "the sabbath was made for man, not man for the sabbath," showing how they were abusing the Mosaic Law under which they lived. In Mk. 6.17-18, John the Baptist told Herod that it was not "lawful" for him to have his brother Philip's wife. According to what law? Every person in the story was living under the Mosaic Law.

In Mt. 19.3, the Pharisees asked Jesus, "Is it lawful for a man to put away his wife for every cause?" Lawful according to what law? Again, every person in the chapter was a Jew living under the Mosaic Law. In Mt. 22.36, the Jews asked Jesus, "What is the greatest commandment of the law?" Again, what law? The only law these Jews knew about was the Mosaic Law, and Jesus' answer quoted Moses directly. In Mt. 23.23, Jesus said, "Ye tithe mint, anise, and cumin, and leave undone the weightier matters

Marriage, Divorce, & Remarriage

of the law." What law? Again, the Mosaic Law. In Mt. 26.19, Jesus, on the last night of his life, kept the Passover feast. By what law did he so do? Again, according to Moses.

In short, the gospels are a Jewish story, not a Christian story. They contain the account of John the Baptist and Jesus urgently thrusting the Jewish nation up against the wall, demanding re-

Plan of Study

Old Testament

Not for fornication	*For fornication*
No, Mt. 5.32, 19.9	Yes, Dt. 24.1-4
Neither party can remarry without committing adultery	Both parties could remarry

New Testament

Not for fornication	*For fornication*

Figure 17

pentance lest the nation be imminently destroyed. Notice where Matthew 5 and 19 fit in: right in the middle of this Jewish story.

Our conclusions on Jesus' and Moses' Old Testament teaching on divorce is shown in Figure 17, where we see our "plan of study" again. On the subject of divorce and remarriage in the Old Covenant, we have seen (1) In the not-for-fornication case, divorce was not authorized (Mt. 5.31-32, Mt. 19.3-9), and those who unscripturally divorced and remarried committed adultery. (2) In the for-fornication case, divorce was authorized (Dt. 24.1-4), and both parties were authorized to remarry.

Example: Joseph's Options with Mary

The case of Joseph and Mary, both of whom were Jews who lived under the Old Covenant, demonstrates what we've just been studying. Figure 18 delineates Joseph's options when he was confronted with Mary's "obvious" adultery. (1) He couldn't accuse her of committing fornication before marriage, because they were already married. (2) He couldn't pursue the adultery-verified option and have her put to death, because there were no witnesses. (3) Since he suspected her of adultery, he could have

Joseph's Options

Adultery verified - death
No Witnesses

Adultery suspected - law of jealousy

Fornication before Marriage
They were already married!

Divorce for Unseemliness, Dt. 24.1-4
Mt. 1.19 - being a righteous man

Figure 18

pursued the law of jealousy of Numbers 5, taken her before the priest, and had her go through that humiliating experience. Had he done so, evidently God would have been Mary's witness that she hadn't committed adultery. Rather than mortifying her, Matthew said, "And Joseph her husband, being a righteous man, and not willing to make her a public example, was minded to put her away privily." The passage Joseph was basing the divorce on was none other than Dt. 24.1-4.

Chapter 6

Divorce Under Christ—I Cor. 7.1-16

Highlights

- *Celibacy is not refraining from sex, but refraining from marriage.*
- *Paul applied Moses' and Jesus' teaching to Gentile Christians for the first time.*
- *Paul addressed mixed marriages, which Jesus and Moses didn't, then taught something neither Moses nor Jesus taught, yet contradicted neither Moses nor Jesus.*

So far in our study, we've covered Moses' teaching on divorce to Jews in Deuteronomy 24, and seen that Moses permitted divorce only for fornication. We've also seen that Jesus, correctly interpreting Moses for Jews, taught the same thing. Jesus essentially clarified Moses' teaching, saying that when Jews divorced for other than fornication and remarried, they committed adultery, i.e., fornication involving another's spouse.

In this chapter, we now consider for the first time teaching on the subject directed toward Christians. Rather than appeal to Jesus' interpretation of Moses in Matthew 5 and 19, as we saw in the previous chapter, we come to the first teaching in the scriptures not addressed to Jews under Moses' law, but to both Jew and Gentile Christians under law to Christ, I Cor. 7.1-16. After we study Paul's references to Jesus' teaching in this chapter, we'll know better what use Christians should make of the teaching of Christ on this subject.

The first six chapters of I Corinthians contain Paul's answers to questions forwarded to him by Chloe, a Christian woman in Corinth who had informed Paul concerning certain problems in the Corinthian church. I Corinthians 7 deals with additional questions the Corinthian church had written Paul. We will discuss this section verse by verse.

v1: Introduction

v1: Now concerning the things whereof ye wrote: It is good for a man not to touch a woman.

To "touch a woman" is not mere contact, but sexual contact or intercourse with a woman. We first saw this in Gen. 20.6, where Abimelech nearly had intercourse with Sarah, Abraham's wife, but God intervened, and said to him, "I did not let you touch her."

Since Paul said that it's not good for a man to have intercourse with a woman, it ought to sound strange to us, for God said in Gen. 2.18 that it is "not good for man to be alone." This is the ordinary truth, to which Paul's statement is extraordinary.

Not understanding the reason for this strange statement, Roman Catholics use this verse to substantiate their practice of priestly celibacy (the Greek word in the New Testament means literally "not to marry," *not* "to refrain from sexual intercourse"; renegade Roman Catholic priests who commit fornication are still celibate, because they don't have spouses), saying celibacy is better spiritually than being married.

Paul, in verse 26, made it clear that he made such statements as this because of a "present distress" that the Corinthians faced, not because celibacy was better. They faced problems in which it would be easier for single Christians than for married ones to remain faithful to God. In a time of persecution or physical danger, single people have fewer concerns than those with spouses or children.

Paul didn't say celibacy was better, he merely said it was good, at least in the extraordinary circumstance presented here. If one man says he's not going to marry in such a circumstance, that's good. If another man says he will marry, that's good as well, for Heb. 13.4 teaches, "Let marriage be had in honor among all, and let the bed be undefiled: for fornicators and adulterers God will judge."

vv2-7: Normal Marriages

In the next section, Paul spoke of normal marriages, those that function the way God would have them to:

v2: But, because of fornications, let each man have his own wife, and let each woman have her own husband.

Notice the plural form of "fornication" here. Paul said that the way for men and women to avoid each and every type of illicit sexual intercourse, or activity, whether it be bestiality, homosexuality, adultery, incest, illicit sexual intercourse between two single people, etc., is for each person to have their own spouse. This is general authorization for every person to be married to his own spouse, and there were former adulterers, homosexuals, and divorced persons in the Corinthian church (I Cor. 6.11, 7.27-28). It's never right for a person to be married to another person's spouse, but it's always right for a person to have his own spouse, unless there's a person in a specific situation who is specifically prohibited from having a spouse. Of course, some readers have some prohibitions already in mind, and we're not arguing those points presently. We're merely noting that in absence of specific prohibitions against marriage, this passage authorizes every person to have his own spouse.

Such a prohibition would be doubly necessary because of Paul's characterization of the false teachers of I Tim. 4.3, who were "forbidding to marry." We're pretty handy about applying such teaching to Roman Catholics of our time for "forbidding priests to marry." For now, we just need to keep in mind that if we forbid someone to marry when God has given general authority for marriage of everyone with no specific prohibition forthcoming, then Paul's condemnation would apply just as well to us. This is important to keep in mind because in certain divorce and remarriage situations, some will say, "It's always safe to take the more conservative position." Mark it well, it's never safe to prohibit marriage where God did not. Paul affirmed that everyone who needs to avoid fornications needs to have his own spouse. In verses 7-9, Paul will affirm that all men cannot contain their sexual desires outside of marriage. Before we prohibit such people the right of marriage, we'd better be certain God was the author of the prohibition, especially when God made some so that they cannot contain their sexual desires without marriage. God's advice to such people was not to "take lots of cold showers." God's advice was for every person to have his own spouse.

>   v3: Let the husband render unto the wife her due: and likewise also the wife unto the husband.

In a normal marriage, each partner renders their due to the other, i.e., that which is due them in the sexual realm. A wife is obligated to her husband in the sexual realm, and vice versa, for both to "avoid fornications."

>   v4: The wife hath not power over her own body, but the husband: and likewise also the husband hath not power over his own body, but the wife.

To appreciate fully Paul's teaching, we must understand a figure of speech, called "ellipsis," which he used here as well as many times elsewhere in his writings. "Ellipsis" simply means "words left out," which the writer wants the reader to supply. All people in all languages use ellipsises. When we tell Junior, "Shut the door," we omit the subject, but he understands that we are speaking to him.

The particular type of ellipsis in this verse is identifiable by the occurrence of "not" and "but" as initial words in dependent clauses that modify a common verb. If we don't recognize this figure of speech the hundreds of times it occurs in the New Testament, we will teach false doctrine about each one of them. The most basic example we find in the New Testament is I Pet. 3.3-4, where Peter instructed Christian women:

>   Whose adorning *let it not* be the outward adorning of braiding the hair, and of wearing jewels of gold, or of

putting on apparel; *but let it* be the hidden man of the heart, in the incorruptible apparel of a meek and quiet spirit, which is in the sight of God of great price.

Some of our Pentecostal friends, who don't recognize this figure of speech, use this verse to prohibit their women from wearing gold jewelry and having their hair done. They claim, "The Bible plainly says, let it not be the outward adorning of braiding the hair, and of wearing jewels of gold." They are not so hard on Peter's next phrase, though, "or putting on of apparel." Was Peter also plainly prohibiting women from wearing apparel? Of course not! And they shouldn't bind an interpretation on others, which they refuse to obey themselves. If they don't believe their argument enough to obey it consistently by leaving off clothes along with gold and braided hair, why should we?

Note that the "not" clause and the "but" clause both modify the verb "to let." Peter, in effect, said, "not only, but also," with emphasis on the "also" phrase. In other words, "let your apparel be not *only* the outward, but *also* the inward, and *especially* the inward." Christian women should put more emphasis on their inward clothing of a meek and quiet spirit than they put on their physical clothing.

We find a similar basic example in Jn. 6.27, where Jesus told his listeners:

Work not for the food which perisheth, but for the food which abideth unto eternal life.

Notice again the "not-but " construction with the common verb "to work." One who doesn't spot this ellipsis could say, "The Bible plainly says not to work for physical food." His interpretation would conflict with other passages: "If any will not work, neither let him eat" (II Thes. 3.10). If one recognizes the figure of speech Jesus used, he'll not make an absolute prohibition out of the "not" phrase. Then he can correctly understand that Jesus taught that we should work for both physical and spiritual food, and put the emphasis on the spiritual.

Thus, when Paul said, "The wife hath not power over her own body, but the husband: and likewise also the husband hath not power over his own body, but the wife," he was not teaching that the wife has total absolute power over her husband's body. Likewise, he was not teaching that the husband has total absolute power over his wife's body, so that he can command her to have sexual relations, for instance. Paul said that in the sexual realm of the context, both have power over the other's body. The wife doesn't have the power to say an absolute yea or nay about sexual relations, and neither does the husband. Both the husband and wife have a certain power over their own sexual natures, but the spouse has even more power. The power of the spouse over the other is not to demand that the other make love, but to recognize that the spouse depends on them for sexual satisfaction. When either party needs sexual relations, the other one has the responsibility of fulfilling the other's needs. Again, this is to enable them to avoid fornications. The passage emphasizes the husband's power to satisfy his wife's desires in comparison to her ability to satisfy herself. The reverse is true for the wife's power over the husband. This is not a verse of authorizing demanding satisfaction from the other, but rather it is a verse commanding the mate to satisfy the other who is so dependent on him or her so that you don't deprive that mate because of fornications.

> v5: Defraud ye not one the other, except it be by consent for a season, that ye may give yourselves unto prayer, and may be together again, that Satan tempt you not because of your incontinency.

To defraud means to take something that belongs to another, or to cheat someone. Thus, neither a wife nor a husband should cheat or withhold their sexual obligation to the other, with one exception: by consent for a season, a "limited period of time." A couple may refrain from sexual relations temporarily, when both are agreeable. Again, the reason for the strict limitations is to avoid fornications, so that Satan cannot tempt them because of their inability to suppress their sexual desires.

> v6: But this I say by way of concession, not of commandment.

Paul affirmed that he was permitting temporary abstinence from sexual relations, but he was not commanding it. No couple has to refrain, but with mutual consent, they may do it.

> v7: Yet I would that all men were even as I myself. Howbeit each man hath his own gift from God, one after this manner, and another after that.

Evidently, from I Cor. 9.5 ("have we no right to lead about a wife that is a believer, as Cephas?"), Paul was not married at this time. However, Paul wasn't wishing that all men were unmarried, so that his generation in such a case would have been the last one, but that all men had the same ability that Paul had. His gift was that he could control his sexual desires outside marriage. In this verse and in verse 9, he pointed out that all men don't have that ability. In Exodus 4, God told Moses that he makes men with certain abilities, to speak, to see, etc. Paul here affirmed that God also gives certain men the ability to abstain from sexual relations without temptation, although this is not the general rule.

vv8-9: To the Unmarried and Widows

Paul continued by taking up the case of the unmarried in general and widows in particular:

> v8: But I say to the unmarried and to widows, It is good for them if they abide even as I.

Still referring to the "present distress" of verse 26, Paul recommended that unmarried men stay unmarried. This is unusual and abnormal, according to Gen. 2.18. This is the only recommendation for celibacy (not to have a spouse—SGD) in the New Testament, conditioned upon the present distress and the following verse:

> v9: But if they have not continency, let them marry: for it is better to marry than to burn.

Here is how unmarried people are to deal with incontinency, their inability to control their sexual desires. They are to marry rather than burn in their sexual desires., this verse gives general authorization for any unmarried person to marry if they cannot contain their sexual desires. To bind celibacy (again, lack of marriage, not lack of sexual intercourse) in any case, we need a specific prohibition in that case. Our Roman Catholic friends' contention that it's better to burn than to marry, for priests or anyone else, is just the opposite of what Paul taught.

vv10-11: The Unhappily Married

Next, Paul took up the case of the unhappily married:

> v10: But unto the married I give charge, yea not I, but the Lord, That the wife depart not from her husband.

"Give charge" is from *parangello*, meaning literally "to pass along," like a military command. The NASB rendering of "give instruction" is weak. The KJV use of "command" is better. The thirty times that this word is used in the New Testament demonstrate that it always carries the idea of "command." In Ac. 4.18, members of the Sanhedrin "*charged*" Peter and John not to speak any more in the name of Christ. When Peter and John didn't obey that command, in Ac. 5.28, the High Priest said, "We *strictly charged* you not to teach in this name: and behold, ye have filled Jerusalem with your teaching, and intend to bring this man's blood upon us." In Ac. 17.30, we have the same word in "The times of ignorance therefore God overlooked; but now he *commandeth* men that they should all everywhere repent."

The command is for a Christian not to *depart* from the mate. "Depart" is a standard word for divorce, or put asunder, from *chorizo*. This is the word Jesus used in Mt. 19.6 when he said, "What therefore God hath joined together, let not man *put asunder*."

This charge was from Paul, yet not Paul, but from the Lord. The careful reader will notice that this is another elliptical construction meaning words are left out for emphasis. Paul's point was not that he didn't give the command, for he just did! It was that Jesus also gave it, and that's what gives the command it's power. Both Jesus and Paul commanded unhappy Christians not to divorce, but the command received its real power from Jesus! Now, where did Jesus give the command not to divorce? It had to be in passages like Mt. 5.32 and Mt. 19.9, where in another form, Jesus proclaimed that if people did divorce not for fornication, and remarried, they would commit adultery. Of course, we saw in Chapter 5 that Jesus was teaching Jews what Moses taught on the subject. In I Corinthians 7, Paul applied that teaching for the first time to Gentile Christians. Thus, Moses, Jesus, and Paul taught identically the same thing on the subject of divorce and remarriage. Paul continued:

> v11: But should she depart, let her remain unmarried, or else be reconciled to her husband; and that the husband leave not his wife.

"Depart" here is *chorizo* again. Despite the Lord's military command, one partner divorces anyway. Paul then said for him or her to remain unmarried. Jesus said that if the divorced remarry, they will commit adultery.

"Unmarried" refers to anyone other than his wife who divorced him. This woman has a spouse and he's identified as the "husband" to whom she must be reconciled. It's because this woman has a spouse that she will commit adultery if she remarries another man.

Many times it's thought that since Paul gave a military command against divorce (no fornication is considered here), and then legislated no remarriage if they did, that no sin was committed in the divorce itself. Nothing could be further from the truth. It's true that no adultery would be committed in such a divorce, but first, isn't sin committed when one breaks a direct formal military command from the Lord? Second, Christians who divorce (with no fornication involved) are covenant breakers. In Rom. 1.31, Paul spoke of the ungodly Gentiles who, among other sins, were covenant breakers, and pronounced them worthy of death. Covenant breaking is a serious sin.

This matter of a clear prohibition with further legislation which some take to be license to violate the prohibition may be cleared up when we realize that God many times prohibited a certain behavior, then pronounced further restrictions on the person who violated the prohibition. For example, in the Ten Commandments, God prohibited stealing. However, in Ex. 4.22, he said that if someone stole a sheep and was caught with the sheep in his possession, he was to make a double restitution. Since God made provision for a fine if the person was caught, did that mean it was all right for him to steal the sheep in the first place? Not at all, but since the person had violated God's prohibition against stealing, God pronounced a fine to further restrict such behavior, to minimize the sin. In Ex. 22.1, Moses provided that if the thief sold or slaughtered the purloined sheep, he had to pay four times as much! This was not saying it was alright to steal the sheep in the first place, but that the more one persisted in the sin, the more it would be punished.

So here there are several levels of sin. If a Christian treacherously divorces his mate, he has violated a plain commandment from God. If he never remarries, he's still guilty of that. If he goes ahead and remarries, he's now an adulterer as well as a covenant breaker.

In summary, in I Cor. 7.10-11, Paul taught Christians for the first time the same thing that Moses and Jesus taught Jews.

vv12-16: Mixed Marriages

v12: But to the rest say I, not the Lord: If any brother hath an unbelieving wife, and she is content to dwell with him, let him not leave her.

v13: And the woman that hath an unbelieving husband, and he is content to dwell with her, let her not leave her husband.

Now Paul turned to divorce and remarriage matters concerning "the rest," that is, those remaining after he has discussed the happily married Christians, unhappily married Christians, the unmarried, and the widows. To those Christians married to non-Christians, Paul gave instruction, unlike vv10-11, that the Lord did not give while he was on the earth. In other words, Jesus didn't address mixed marriages in his earthly teaching.

Many times we fail to appreciate what a timely topic this was for new Christians at Corinth. Under the Mosaic Law, Jews were strictly prohibited from intermarrying with people of certain nations occupying the land of Canaan (Ex. 34.14-16, Dt. 7.3, Josh. 23.12-13). In Neh. 10.29-30 and 13.23-30, Nehemiah issued similar prohibitions to Israelites after their restoration from Babylonian captivity. In certain cases these marriages were broken up. In Ezra 9.1-2, Ezra realized the people were highly displeasing to God for violating these prohibitions. The remedy was that such marriages were to be broken up. In Ezra 9, 10, and 13, God commanded the Jews to divorce these foreign wives.

Since the Jews looked down on Gentiles, no doubt, the early Christians were familiar with the Old Testament's prohibition of Jews intermarrying with certain Gentiles. Naturally, these first Christians would wonder if they needed to break up their own marriages with non-covenant people under Christ. If marriage to unbelievers made Jews unholy, did marriage to non-Christians make their marriages likewise unholy? Since Jesus taught only Jews while he was on earth, and the problem didn't arise until after the apostles carried the gospel to the Gentiles, Jesus didn't deal with this subject.

Therefore, whatever Paul taught on this subject cannot be a contradiction with Jesus' teaching, since Jesus didn't even address the subject of mixed marriages. Paul didn't contradict Jesus any more than Jesus and Moses contradicted God's original marriage law in Gen. 2.24, when there was no divorce (and no death, for that matter). Moses gave additional revelations from those in Genesis 2 to different people (Jews) in different circumstances (those married to unfaithful wives). Likewise, Paul gave an additional revelation to those in Deuteronomy 24 and Matthew 5 and 19 to different people (Christians) in different circumstances (mixed marriages).

The subject of forgiveness of sin serves as a good example of contradiction versus additional teaching. We read in the first gospel sermon in Acts 2 where Peter convinced his Jewish audience that rather than killing a blasphemer as they proudly thought they had done, they had killed the Messiah they were looking for. They asked, "Men and brethren, what shall we do?" For the first time, Peter told what to do to rid themselves of the guilt of sin: "Repent ye, and be baptized in the name of Jesus Christ for the remission of your sins, and you shall receive the gift of the Holy Spirit." However, in Ac. 8.20-24, when Simon sought to buy the gift of God with money, Peter said unto him:

Thy silver perish with thee, because thou hast thought to obtain the gift of God with money. Thou hast neither part nor lot in this matter: for thy heart is not right before God. Repent therefore of this thy wickedness, and pray the Lord, if perhaps the thought of thy heart shall be forgiven thee. For I see that thou art in the gall of bitterness and in the bond of iniquity. And Simon answered and said, Pray ye for me to the Lord, that none of the things which ye have spoken come upon me.

Now, did Peter contradict his own teaching from Acts 2? In both passages, he told people what to do for the forgiveness of their sins. One audience he told to repent and be baptized, the other he told to repent and pray for forgiveness. Is this a contradiction? Not at all! Peter's audience in Acts 2 was non-Christians. Simon, in Acts 8, was already a Christian. So Peter gave a new teaching to a different audience which was in a different circumstance. Likewise with Paul, Jesus, and Moses on divorce in a mixed marriage. Jesus and Moses taught nothing to Jews on the subject. Paul gave a new teaching to a different audience (Christians) which was in a different circumstance (mixed marriage).

While on earth, Jesus told the apostles in Jn. 16.12-13:

I have yet many things to say unto you, but ye cannot bear them now. Howbeit when he, the Spirit of truth, is come, he shall guide you into all the truth: for he shall not speak from himself; but what things he shall hear, these shall he speak: and he shall declare unto you the things that are to come.

Certainly, one of the things the apostles were not ready for while Jesus was with them was a lot of teaching concerning Gentile Christians married to non-Christians. At that time, they had no concept that the Gospel was even going to be carried to the Gentiles. Even though Peter preached the first gospel sermon affirming the promise was to both Jews and Gentiles in Ac. 2.39, later, when Peter was sent by God to preach to the Gentile Cornelius in Acts 10, Peter thought God was mistaken. God performed miracles to convince Peter to preach to Gentiles as he had prophesied years before. Men of the caliber of Peter and Paul were not ready to deal with mixed marriages among Gentiles for years after the resurrection of Christ. However, truth that was revealed to them later in no way contradicted anything God had revealed earlier.

To the believer in a mixed marriage where the unbeliever is content to dwell with the Christian, Paul said, "Let him not leave her." He again used the word *chorizo*, translated "put asunder" in Mt. 19.6. So Paul said that believers in such a favorable situation don't have to divorce their "alien" mates like the Jews of Ezra's and Nehemiah's day did. If the unbeliever is content to dwell with you as a Christian, not a principle-compromising Christian, but a committed, faithful one, stay with him, don't divorce him.

> v14: For the unbelieving husband is sanctified in the wife, and the unbelieving wife is sanctified in the brother: else were your children unclean; but now are they holy.

"Sanctified" means "set apart" or "special." Although the word is usually used of Christians, here it's used of unbelievers. It doesn't mean that the unbeliever is sinless, or that he's pleasing to God, but that he's "special." This unbeliever, content to dwell with a faithful Christian (many unbelievers aren't) is in a situation where he has the opportunity and privilege of hearing the word of God, and seeing it in action in the life of his spouse. In the Northwest United States, where logging is a prevalent industry, we might say that loggers probably don't have the best reputation for spirituality. However, if some loggers work for a faithful

Christian who owns a sawmill, they're in a special situation that most loggers don't have the benefit of. They're in a circumstance where they will have opportunities for new attitudes, insights, etc.

So with unbelievers married to faithful Christians at Corinth. If a Christian was married to a worshipper of Zeus, and wondered if she should leave him, Paul's answer was, "If he's content to live with you while you're faithful, don't break up the marriage." The unbeliever was in a special situation where she might be able to influence him. Even her children were in a special situation where one parent was a faithful Christian, and the other, while not a Christian, was at least tolerant of the other's spirituality. Even they were set apart from other children. This is parallel teaching to that of Peter in I Pet. 3.1-2, where Peter said:

> In like manner, ye wives, be in subjection to your own husbands; that, even if any obey not the word, they may without the word be gained by the behavior of their wives; beholding your chaste behavior coupled with fear.

Then, Paul dealt with the case where the unbeliever is not so magnanimous:

> v15: Yet if the unbelieving departeth, let him depart: the brother or the sister is not under bondage in such cases: but God hath called us in peace.

"Depart" here is *chorizo* again, also translated leave (verse 10), and put asunder (Mt. 19.6). Paul, addressing a situation that neither Jesus nor Moses even addressed, to people neither Jesus nor Moses ever addressed, said, let him do the thing Jesus said no man can do in Mt. 19.6. Let him put the marriage asunder in such cases, that is, not in the marriage of two non-Christians or two Christians, but in the willful divorce initiated by the unbeliever.

There is great controversy over Paul's meaning when he said, "The brother or sister is not under bondage in such cases." The dispute arises because Paul used a different word for bondage (*doulos,* obligation) than the word he usually used for bound (*deo,* to tie or bind together). Thus, some claim that two entirely different concepts are involved in these two words. It's customary to present a blizzard of quotations and argumentation from linguistic scholars that, whether by design or not, wears down the reader so that he doesn't know what Paul meant.

Briefly, this author believes the argument is more academic than practical. First, just because the two words are different doesn't mean they're talking about two different concepts. In Rom. 3.30, Paul said that God "shall justify the circumcision by (*ek*) faith, and the uncircumcision through (*dia*) faith," but no one believes that because Paul used two different words Jews are justified any differently than are Gentiles. The words *deo* and *doulos* share a common history. Scholars agree that *doulos* probably came from *deo*. I believe in this case that one has obligation (*doulos*) precisely because he is bound (*deo*).

However, I believe Paul spoke of the breaking of the marriage bond mainly because he said (in essence), "Let him do the very thing that Jesus said in Mt. 19.6 no man can do—put the marriage asunder." Of course, this is different teaching than Paul gave to unhappily married Christians in I Cor. 7.10-11. There he said, (1) don't depart, but if you do (2) don't marry or else be reconciled. To those in mixed marriages he said in I Cor. 7.15, (1) don't depart, but if the unbeliever does put the marriage asunder, (2) the believer is not under bondage. It seems apparent that the bondage of which Paul spoke is of two parts. If the unbeliever departs, the believer is not under bondage (1) to remain unmarried (2) or else to be reconciled. As John Murray, renowned Presbyterian commentator said:

> If freedom from obligation to bed and board is all that Paul has in mind in verse 15, we should expect him to say virtually the same thing as in v11. But that is precisely what he does not say. (John Murray, *Divorce* [Philadelphia, PA: The Presbyterian and Reformed Publishing Co., 1961], p. 74.)

There are two additional practical observations we offer in this case: In 99 percent of such cases as this, we know what the unbeliever is going to do after he departs. If he's so ungodly he doesn't appreciate what a special situation he's in, living with a godly woman, and he can't tolerate her godly life, when he abandons her, he's going to seek out someone who will support him in his sin and he'll commit fornication with her. The one percent of the cases where the person is abnormal and doesn't get sexually involved with someone else, we'll not deal with yet. However, in the practical case, he'll commit fornication, and we deal with the case of an innocent party being treacherously divorced by a fornicating spouse in chapter 9: "The Rights of One Unjustly Put Away." There we will argue that the actions of an ungodly spouse living under an ungodly government do not affect the rights of the spouse to put away a fornicating spouse. We do not regard that as proved yet, but point the reader in that direction in this case.

The second practical observation on this passage is, just how would a spouse abandoned by a person so ungodly that he didn't want to live with a faithful Christian go about being in obligation to the unbeliever? He's not even there! A wife couldn't be in subjection to such a man at all! Just how do you obey a deserter? That's like God telling me how to be a good mother, or to be sure and wear boots when I'm flapping my arms and flying! I couldn't do it with all my might!

A number of legendary gospel preachers of the past commented on this very point. For example, G. C. Brewer wrote:

> But someone suggests that he means that the Christian is not bound to live with and to give the marriage privilege to such a deserting partner. That would be a wise statement from an inspired man!...He had already told them to live with these heathen spouses if they can. It would be absurd to tell them that they are under no obligation to live with those who have deserted them, and refused their companionship. How could they live with such a person?...Then, someone is ready to say, according to that, Paul allowed divorce for desertion, whereas Christ made fornication the only ground for divorce. There is no conflict there. Desertion by a heathen includes or presupposed unfaithfulness to the partner, of course. Could anyone suppose that such a heathen, with no ideas

of Christian morality, but who because of opposition to such Christian ideals deserts his partner, would live a chaste and celibate life henceforth? (G. C. Brewer, *Contending for the Faith*, pp. 100-101, reprinted from the *Gospel Advocate*, August 3, 1933, p. 722.)

R. L Whiteside said:

The passage seems plain enough; yet opinions differ as to its application. This difference of opinion grows out of the notion that its plain meaning does not seem to harmonize with Matt. 19:9. If a person did not already have his mind made up, he would have no trouble in understanding this verse. It can refer to nothing else than the marriage bonds, or vows. If either husband or wife becomes a Christian and the other is so bitter against Christianity as to refuse to live with the believer, the believer is not under bondage in such cases—is completely released from the marriage vows, and as if no marriage had ever taken place. If this is not so, the believer is still under bondage. But does this contradict Matt. 19:9? It does not, any more than Matt. 19:9 contradicts God's original marriage law.

In the beginning God made a male and a female. The one female was suited to the needs of the one male (Gen. 2:24). This is evidently the original law of marriage for the whole human family, and would have continued to be the law with no exceptions had not sin entered the world.

The first and permanent marriage law is found in Gen. 1:27, 28; 2:24. This law made no provision for divorce— not even for a separation. But the authority that makes a law can abolish it, or he can amend it, as circumstances or occasions demand. It will appear plain from what Jesus said that the original law made no provision for any separation for any cause; yet the Law of Moses suffered a man to put away his wife, but commanded him to give her a bill of divorcement when he did so. That bill of divorcement was required when the separation took place (Deut. 24:1). Because God added this amendment to his own marriage law, will someone accuse him of contradicting his own law? And when Jesus gave fornication as grounds for divorce and remarriage, will someone accuse him of contradicting God's marriage law? And when the inspired apostle Paul gave another cause for the complete annulment of the marriage vows, he did not contradict that law.

...The two passages deal with different angles of the matter. Jesus speaks of the man who shall put away his wife for other reasons than adultery; Paul speaks of a man or woman who has been forsaken by the wife or the husband. The man must not put away his wife and marry another, except for fornication; but if an unbelieving husband or wife leaves the believer, what then? "The brother or sister is not under bondage in such cases." As long as the unbeliever was content to dwell with the believer, the believer was still under bondage (verse 12, 13). The believer must not put the unbeliever away. "Yet if the unbelieving depart, let him depart: the brother or sister is not under bondage in such cases." If his future actions are in any way limited by his former marriage, then he is still bound by that marriage—is still under bondage.

OBJECTION: If the unbeliever departs, then the believer is no longer under bondage to live with the unbeliever. But, although they are permitted to live separately, they are not permitted to marry someone else.

REPLY: Indeed! Permitted to live separately! Read the verse, and you will discover that it is not a question of permitting them to live separately—the unbeliever refuses to live with the believer, permission or no permission.

Paul's instruction is to the brother or the sister who has been deserted by the unbelieving companion. Their living separately from such companions is not a matter of permission, but of necessity, and Paul said: "The brother or the sister is not under bondage in such cases." How any one can figure out how a person can be free from bondage, and yet the marriage bonds will not permit him to marry again, is beyond me. The fact is, such persons would be under a sort of double bondage—circumstances would bind them to live separately from the unbeliever who ran off, and their former marriage bonds would bind them not to marry again! The fact is, if such a person is not as free as he was before he married, he is still under bondage; and no amount of talk can make it otherwise. In marriage God does the uniting, and he alone can dissolve the marriage bonds. A couple who separate without a scriptural cause are still under bondage. Let us not affirm that the brother or sister is not bound to live with the unbeliever who runs off! Such would imply that if both were believers, and one ran away, the other would be bound to live with the runaway spouse! How would a person go about living with one who runs off? Let us not charge Paul with the folly of saying to the believer: "You are not bound to live with the unbeliever who will not live with you." It would be just too bad if the Lord did require a believer to live with his runaway spouse!

Marriage was intended to be permanent. But when one party breaks the marriage bonds by immoral conduct, Jesus gives the innocent party the right to marry again. Later, when the gospel began to be preached, bitter enmity against it arose. A husband or wife obeyed the gospel; the other did not. The unbeliever might be so bitter against Christianity as to refuse to live with the believer. This was a new development. What should be done about it? Paul tells us. Jesus didn't deal with this eventuality while he was on the earth. (R. L. Whiteside,

Reflections [Denton, TX: Inys Whiteside, 1965], pp.
411-427.)

When Paul said that the deserted believer "is not under
bondage in such cases, but God hath called us unto peace," what
does the "peace" refer to? Jay Adams wrote:

> Too often Christians, on bad advice, have settled for the
> in-between. Let me describe it. Believing (wrongly) that
> she must remain married to her unbelieving husband, no
> matter what, a Christian woman holds on even when her
> husband wants to end their marriage. He, then, may begin
> running around with other women (if he hasn't been
> doing so already) and at length may even desert her. Yet,
> urged on by bad counsel, she will not agree to a divorce.
> He may stay away from home for six-month periods at a
> time, occasionally show up for a week or so. This upsets
> the kids and the life of the home (hopes are aroused and
> shattered). His wife may get pregnant (if married, she
> must agree to sex if he seeks it), and so it goes on and on.
> She is always hoping against hope, yet there is no evi-
> dence at all of a desire on his part to consent to marriage.
> She may hang on for years, for life!

> There is nothing peaceful about that! Everything is con-
> stantly being upset; nothing is settled. There is nothing
> but loose ends. God wants the matter to be concluded so
> that (in one way or the other) there will be peace—reso-
> lution of the matter. This is an important principle. (Jay
> Adams, *Marriage, Divorce, and Remarriage in the Bible*
> [Phillipsburg, NJ: Presbyterian and Reformed Publish-
> ing Company, 1980], p. 49.)

Paul then said:

> v16: For how knowest thou, O wife, whether thou shalt
> save thy husband? Or how knowest thou, O husband,
> whether thou shalt save thy wife?

This verse is generally understood to mean that even though the unbeliever has deserted the believer, she is still to live with him, because "Who knows, you might save him." I rather think that it more practically teaches her to go ahead and let him depart, because why would anybody think she's going to save him? What makes a wife think she's going to save such a husband? If he's not content to dwell with a godly wife, carouses around, drinking

Plan of Study

Old Testament

Not for fornication	For fornication
No, Mt. 5.32, 19.9	Yes, Dt. 24.1-4
Neither party can remarry without committing adultery	Both parties could remarry

Mixed Marriages Not Considered: Ex. 34.14-16, Dt. 7.3, Josh. 23.12-13, Neh. 10.29-30, 13.23-30

New Testament

Not for fornication	For fornication
No, I Cor. 7.10-11	
↓	
Mt. 5.32, 19.9 Mk. 10.11 Lk. 16.18	

Mixed Marriages: I Cor. 7.12-16

Figure 19

and dancing with other women, what makes anyone think she's going to influence him? So let him go, because God has called Christians unto peace.

With our discussion of these first sixteen verses of I Corinthians 7, we now present our conclusions thus far in Figure 19. Our conclusions about not-for-fornication divorce under Christ's teaching for Christians is that it's not permitted (I Cor. 7.10-11), just like Jesus and Moses taught Jews. When it happens, both Christians are to (1) not enter any other marriage, or (2) be reconciled to their spouse. In the case of a believer married to a non-Christian, the believer is to stay with the unbeliever if he's content to dwell with her or him in that condition. If the unbeliever puts the marriage asunder, the believer is to let him do it, and is not obligated to (1) not enter any other marriage, or (2) be reconciled to the spouse. Paul said he was taking up a case Jesus didn't discuss while on earth, to different people, so we ought not to be surprised if Paul's instruction was different.

Chapter 7

Unscriptural Divorce:
The Problem Presented

Highlights

- *Jesus discussed three ways of committing adultery.*
- *God didn't permit treacherous divorce "in the beginning."*

Thus far in our study of divorce and remarriage, we've covered Dt. 24.1-4 to ascertain Moses' teaching to Jews on the subject. We then came to Matthew 5 and 19 and obtained Jesus' clarification, again to Jews, of Moses' teaching. We then went to I Corinthians 7 to get our first look at New Covenant teaching. There we noted that Paul incorporated Jesus' (and therefore Moses') teaching into his own and applied it to both Jew and Gentile Christians for the first time. In addition, Paul added teaching to Christians in mixed marriages, which neither Moses nor Jesus had given.

Since we now understand that Paul bound Jesus' teaching to Jews on Christians, we want to examine in more detail Jesus' teaching on unscriptural divorce in Matthew 5 and 19. As we do, we'll notice "the problem" of teaching the gospel to people today who have undergone unscriptural divorce. In the following chapter, we'll consider a number of positions advanced to address the problem by prominent brethren.

Mt. 5.27-32

v27: Ye have heard that it was said, Thou shalt not commit adultery:

v28: but I say unto you, that every one that looketh on a woman to lust after her hath committed adultery with her already in his heart.

v29: And if thy right eye causeth thee to stumble, pluck it out, and cast it from thee: for it is profitable for thee that one of thy members should perish, and not thy whole body be cast into hell.

v30: And if thy right hand causeth thee to stumble, cut it off, and cast it from thee: for it is profitable for thee that one of thy members should perish, and not thy whole body go into hell.

v31: It was said also, Whosoever shall put away his wife, let him give her a writing of divorcement:

v32: but I say unto you, that every one that putteth away his wife, saving for the cause of fornication, maketh her an adulteress: and whosoever shall marry her when she is put away committeth adultery.

As we noted in chapter 4, in the Sermon on the Mount, there are six statements of the form, "Ye have heard that it was said, but I say unto you." In each of these six statements, Jesus showed that the shallow interpretation that the Jews applied to Moses' teaching still caused them problems. For instance, on the subject of brotherly relations, what if I ask, "Have any members of your congregation murdered any other members lately?" and you reply, "No, we've never had a case of murder in our church" Does that mean there are no problems between brethren there? No, it doesn't mean that at all. When you've got brethren hating each other, whispering about each other, maligning each other's motives, and otherwise mistreating each other, you've still got lots of brotherly problems, don't you? In other words, it's just not as simple as counting the number of murderers in a local church.

Likewise, on the subject of sexual sins, what if I ask, "Is anybody committing adultery in the congregation of which you're a member," and you say, "No, sir. Nobody's ever committed adultery in our congregation." Does that mean that your church is free of sexual sin? No, it might just be that you have a bunch of people who lust sexually in their hearts for one another. Again, it's just not as simple as counting the number of overt adulterers, is it?

Jesus corrected these shallow misconceptions in the Sermon on the Mount, particularly with regard to sexual matters here in Mt. 5.27-32. Notice the comparison Jesus made between the three ways to commit adultery: (1) the overt act of just committing sexual intercourse or activity with another's wife, (2) lusting after another's wife, and (3) unscriptural or treacherous divorce and remarriage.

Suppose there's a woman who lives across the street with whom a man wants to commit an overt act of adultery. He sees her, walks across the street, talks her into it, and they commit adultery. That's the overt act.

But Jesus taught that there are two other ways the man can do exactly the same thing. Suppose the lady's husband is a big burly guy, and he's afraid to do the overt sin. Instead, he just stares out the window at her, imagining how he would like to commit adultery with her, and what techniques he would use. Jesus affirmed that the man commits the same sin in his mind. He has the heart of an adulterer, just as much as if he had walked over there and done the sin overtly. He just doesn't have the courage of an overt adulterer. Notice that the "wife" is in the context because of the reference to the overt act of adultery. Jesus didn't discuss a single man lusting after a single woman. There isn't a single woman in the context. Failure to realize this led to one Papal announcement that this verse teaches that it is a sin for a man to lust after his own wife!

Once we realize the fellow is committing the same physical act in his mind as he contemplates what he would like to do to her, we can understand Jesus' statement, "He that looketh on a woman to lust after her hath committed adultery with her in his heart." Men have struggled with this passage for centuries, wondering if they've violated it. When I was a young man, I thought if a fellow just happened to notice an attractive woman, how she wasn't built like a running back for the Dallas Cowboys football team, he had committed adultery with her in his heart. No, that's not what Jesus said. Jesus explained *how* you commit adultery in your heart: you do it by committing the physical act in your mind. When you go beyond noticing that she doesn't look like a football player, and imagine what you would do if you could, and all the techniques you would use, you're committing the physical act in your mind, and you're guilty of adultery. You have the heart of an adulterer, even if you might not have the courage of one.

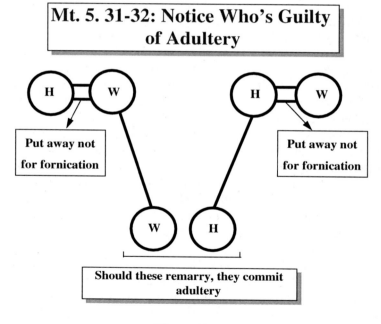

Mt. 5. 31-32: Notice Who's Guilty of Adultery

Put away not for fornication

Put away not for fornication

Should these remarry, they commit adultery

Figure 20

In this passage, Jesus taught a third way to commit exactly the same sin. Suppose the man doesn't either walk over there with his feet and commit the overt physical act, and he doesn't just stay there imagining the physical act, but he detours down to the court house and unscripturally divorces his wife. Next he talks the lady across the street into doing the same thing with her husband, and then they marry each other and move in together. What is the man doing? He's doing the same thing, committing adultery, just as though he had walked over there with his feet, or done it in his mind, the only difference is that he's using the legal system to accomplish the same end. It's important to notice that exactly the same act is being committed, one with the feet, one with the mind, and one with an ungodly court in an ungodly nation that permits such a treacherous act. The end result is the same: The man ends up with another man's wife.

With this in mind, consider whether a husband who habitually uses pornography (pictures which exhibit sexual body parts) is also committing adultery. According to Jesus' use of the word adultery, is the man not guilty of adultery? If he entertains himself by frequenting strip shows, again, is he not guilty of adultery? One might say, "Oh, but it's mental adultery." These terms were foreign to Jesus, who said the man was committing exactly and identically the same sin whether he did it with his eyes, his feet, or the courts.

Now let's look at Figure 20. Pictured are two couples. In each marriage, one of the spouses puts the other away not for fornication, but treacherously, for some trivial reason. One partner from each of those first marriages then marries each other. Jesus said that the couple in the second marriage commits adultery. He specifically identified one man and one woman who commit adultery.

In Figure 21, we draw some inescapable conclusions from Jesus' statement about this second couple that commits adultery. Recall that in Chapter 2, "Violations of Marriage," we developed the definition of adultery, and demonstrated that it is a very specific type of sexual sin. Adultery is illicit sexual intercourse or activity with the spouse of another. We pointed out that two single people cannot commit adultery, trying as hard as they can. Neither can a man commit adultery with his own wife.

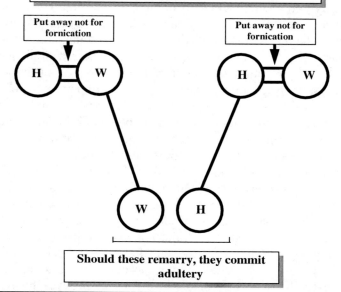

Figure 21

Thus, when Jesus said that if these two people from treacherous divorces marry that they then commit adultery, we draw these two conclusions, by the definition of adultery:

1. This second couple is not a husband and wife, because a husband and wife cannot commit adultery together.

2. Since they commit adultery in this second union, they're still spouses, though not the spouse of each other.

Those two conclusions are true, or our definition of adultery is not true. We'll take up attempts at new, until lately never-heard-of, definitions of adultery in the next chapter. For now, we'll recall that God himself defined adultery in Rom. 7.2-3: when a woman who has a husband joins herself to another man, she shall be called an adulteress.

If these two people are spouses, but not each others' spouses, it means that they're still bound to their original spouses. It means that their unscriptural divorces had no effect on their marriage bonds to each other at all. For example, suppose a man tires of his wife, gets out the salt shaker, tells her, "I'm going to show you!" Then he shakes salt on their marriage license, and walks out. What has he done to their marriage bond? Nothing. What will happen if he joins himself to another woman? He commits adultery, doesn't he? Unless his marriage bond is broken by death or by a putting away for fornication, he's still married, and if he joins himself to another woman, he's an adulterer, regardless of how much salt he sprinkles on his marriage license!

Jesus here taught that unscriptural divorce has the same effect as the salt shaker, which is none at all. We next notice Jesus' teaching in Mt. 19.3-12, which is similar to this in Mt. 5.31-32.

Mt. 19.3-12

We've already made a few comments concerning these verses in Chapter 5. Then in Chapter 6 we learned that Jesus' teaching, while originally addressed to Jews, was incorporated by Paul into his teaching to Christians. We now wish to notice a few more details about Jesus' teaching.

> v3: And there came unto him Pharisees, trying him, and saying, Is it lawful for a man to put away his wife for every cause?

As we've demonstrated all through this study, keep in mind that everyone involved in this account was a Jew, living under

Moses' law. When they asked, "Is it lawful?" the only law these Jews knew was Moses' law. They were under it, and Jesus had claimed to be a faithful teacher of it (Mt. 5.19-20). Momentarily, both Jesus and the Pharisees would refer to Dt. 24.1-4. Thus, they're asking based on Moses' law. Also, if Jesus didn't answer the question based on Moses' law, they didn't get an answer to their question. Jesus changed the subject and didn't tell them he was going to.

We've already alluded to the fact that at that time, several schools of rabbis and their disciples were involved in quite a dispute about the grounds for divorce under Moses. However, they were not in disagreement about the effect of divorce, i.e., all sides understood that divorce based on Moses' teaching freed both parties to remarry. In this dispute, Rabbi Hillel held that Moses allowed divorce for numerous trivial causes. Rabbi Shammai insisted it could be only for a moral cause.

Although the Pharisees asked about divorce "for every cause," they did not disagree on divorce for fornication. Essentially, they asked about divorce for every reason *other than fornication*. In other words, they asked, "Can we get rid of our wives for any old reason?"

> v4: And he answered and said, Have ye not read, that he who made them from the beginning made them male and female,

> v5: and said, For this cause shall a man leave his father and mother, and shall cleave to his wife; and the two shall become one flesh?

Jesus' answer contained a quotation from Gen. 1.27 in verse 4 and a quotation from Gen. 2.24 in verse 5; both are references back to the origin of marriage. Note Jesus' use of the word "beginning" here. Many times in commenting on Matthew 19, preachers will make a pronouncement (the author has done it himself, but never again—SGD) saying, "In this passage, Jesus said that God allowed loose divorce for the Jews, but Jesus restored the law back to its state at the beginning." The following quotation from J. D. Thomas, well-known preacher and professor at Abilene Christian University, is typical:

> Divorce was never planned for or intended by God in his purpose for marriage, as Jesus declares in Mt. 19.7, 8...The teaching of Jesus relative to marriage and divorce restored the original principle of marriage which was "from the beginning," namely, "one man for one woman," and divorce was henceforth allowed only for the cause of fornication (Mt. 19.8, 9). (J. D. Thomas, *Divorce and Remarriage* [Abilene, TX: Biblical Research Press, 1977], p. 7.)

Now look carefully at Jesus' use of "beginning" in the verse. Did Jesus say he was restoring God's law to what it was in the beginning? Not at all. Of course, the word "beginning" is in the verse, but that's not what it says. Not only is that not what he said, but it's just not true. When Jesus gets through with Mt. 19.3-12, most of us will agree that only death and putting away for fornication will break a marriage bond. Was that God's marriage law "in the beginning"? In Genesis 1 and 2, which Jesus quoted from, *neither death nor divorce for fornication broke the marriage bond*, for neither one existed at that time. The doom of death was not even pronounced upon mankind until Genesis 3! In the beginning, God contemplated marriage bonds broken by neither death nor divorce for fornication; Jesus' teaching allowed for both.

> v6: So that they are no more two, but one flesh. What therefore God hath joined together, let not man put asunder.

Notice here that the things joined together in marriage are a man and a woman, not a man and God, or a woman and God, or a man and a woman with God. As we've seen, in marriage God binds a husband to a wife. To the Jews, this was beginning to sound like God didn't think they could "get rid of their wives for any old reason," wasn't it? So they rebut Jesus with:

v7: They say unto him, Why then did Moses command
to give a bill of divorcement, and to put her away?

The passage they were thinking of here could only have been
Dt. 24.1-4, where "put away," to them at least, included fornication, and both parties were free to remarry. This was how they
used the word. If Jesus used "put away" in some different sense
without telling them, he deceived them.

v8: He saith unto them, Moses for your hardness of heart
suffered you to put away your wives: but from the
beginning it hath not been so.

We've talked about "hardness of heart" in Chapter 5, noting
that it meant lack of receptiveness toward the offending wife,
which makes Jesus' teaching square perfectly with Moses' statement that "she finds no favor in his eyes" because of her fornication. It wasn't that God really didn't want them to divorce loosely,
but he caved in and let them do it until Jesus came and straightened everything out. God had it straightened out in Deuteronomy
24. The Jews went astray from that, and now Jesus correctly
interpreted Moses for these Pharisees.
    "From the beginning" refers back to Genesis 1 and 2, where
neither death nor divorce for fornication existed. Originally, God
didn't give provision for either to break the marriage bond. When
Jesus finished his teaching in this passage, provision existed for
both. This verse doesn't teach that Jesus restored the marriage
law to what it was in the beginning, and in fact, if we think about
it, none of us believe that he did.

v9: And I say unto you, Whosoever shall put away his
wife, except for fornication [*porneia*—Greek], and shall
marry another, committeth adultery: and he that marrieth
her when she is put away committeth adultery.

When Jesus said, "you," to whom was he speaking? Christians? Gentiles? No, only Jews, in reference to Moses. This was
Jewish teaching that was to remain so until Paul brought it in and
made it Christian teaching in I Corinthians 7.

For "fornication," the NASV Bible gives "immorality," not even sexual immorality, just immorality. This is a poor translation for *porneia*, "illicit sexual intercourse in general." When Hitler gassed six million Jews, that was abysmally immoral, but it wasn't fornication. When some crackpot goes to the drug store and contaminates over-the-counter medicine with cyanide, that's immoral, but it's not fornication.

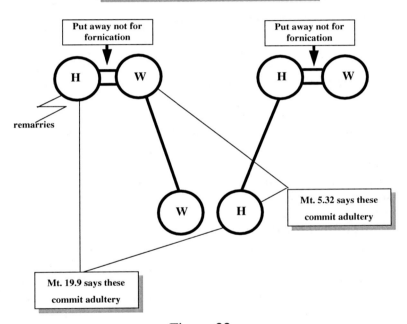

Figure 22

Jesus then proceeded to teach that in a not-for-fornication divorce, those who remarry are going to be involved in adultery, similar to Mt. 5.32. Figure 22 shows who's guilty and what they're guilty of. It's important to notice that although Mt. 19.9 is quite similar to Mt. 5.32, there are differences. Matthew 5.32

says that a woman (the treacherously put-away one) and a man (the man who marries her) commit adultery. Matthew 19.9 says that two men (both the treacherous divorcer and the man who marries his put-away wife) commit adultery. We understand that all three commit adultery, because as we saw in Mt. 5.32, the definition of adultery drives us to conclude that a putting away not for fornication didn't break the marriage bonds. Thus, the new relationships result in adultery being committed. Adultery is not just an ugly word. It's a very specific sin: someone is living with someone else's spouse!

> v10: The disciples say unto him, If the case of the man
> is so with his wife, it is not expedient to marry.

These disciples were used to the teaching of some rabbis who sanctioned divorce for trivial reasons and reacted to Jesus' teaching: if what he taught was true, it was better not to marry. Many in our society say the same thing. Not wanting to go through a divorce, they just live together and avoid marriage. Likewise, if someone has a casual view of marriage, thinking he can divorce in a year or two if things don't work out, they might think they'd probably be better off not marrying, as well, unless they're determined not to commit fornication. Better for the man, the woman, and God.

> v11: But he said unto them, Not all men can receive this
> saying, but they to whom it is given.

"This saying" is "it is not expedient to marry." Not all men can live without marriage. Paul could, but Paul said all men didn't have the ability he had, to live with controlled sexual desires without marriage.

> v12: For there are eunuchs, that were so born from their
> mother's womb: and there are eunuchs, that were made
> eunuchs by men: and there are eunuchs, that made them-
> selves eunuchs for the kingdom of heaven's sake. He that
> is able to receive it, let him receive it.

"Eunuchs" are men who are unable to engage in sexual intercourse. Eunuchs could certainly live without marriage. Jesus listed three types of eunuchs, those born eunuchs, that is, born deformed. Other eunuchs became so involuntarily. Perhaps some ruler mutilated them to use them around their daughters, harem, etc. Other eunuchs mutilated themselves for the kingdom of heaven's sake, that is, so they could devote themselves to God's service without being encumbered by the responsibilities and desires of marriage. At any rate, Jesus used eunuchs as an example of someone who could live without marriage.

In summary on Matthew 19, Jesus correctly interpreted Moses' teaching for these Jews living under Moses, and agreed with Moses entirely. The reader is encouraged to note Mark's record of a similar discussion in Mk. 10.2-12 and Lk. 16.18 in which divorce for fornication is not contemplated. The resultant adulterous relationships are the same, however.

The Problem Presented

We're now ready to present the problem that many recognize in divorce and remarriage situations: Jesus (and hence Paul) taught that both Jews and Christians who unscripturally divorced and remarried, and those who married those coming from such situations, commit adultery. This presents a real problem for us to know what to tell people we're trying to teach the Gospel to who are involved in unscriptural divorces and remarriages.

How long does that adultery last? By definition, as long as someone is having sexual intercourse or activity with another's spouse, that is, until the previous bonds are scripturally broken (if possible), and new bonds are scripturally made (if possible). We notice that it is possible to continuously live in adultery. In Rom. 6.1-2, Paul said:

What shall we say then? Shall we continue in sin, that grace may abound? God forbid. We who died to sin, how shall we any longer live therein?

So it is possible to live in sin. More specifically, it's possible to live in fornication and adultery. Notice Paul's teaching in Col. 3.5-7:

> Put to death therefore your members which are upon the earth: fornication, uncleanness, passion, evil desire, and covetousness, which is idolatry; for which things' sake cometh the wrath of God upon the sons of disobedience: wherein ye also once walked, when ye lived in these things;

Paul recognized that the Colossians had lived in fornication and sexual uncleanness before they became Christians. As we saw in Chapter 2, "Violations of Marriage," the consequences of living in fornication or adultery are serious: none who do "shall inherit the kingdom of God."

A couple realizing that they are cohabiting with another's spouse unawares can be a highly emotional situation, particularly if they thought they were honorably married for twenty-five years, and have a number of children. Those who bring them the sad news are often met with charges of, "Who do you think you are, breaking up a husband and his wife?" Of course, no one ought to break up a husband and his wife, for every one is entitled to his own wife. However, no one is entitled to another person's spouse.

Conclusion

As these first seven chapters illustrate, God intended for marriage to be lifelong. Short of death, marriage bonds are broken only by putting away for fornication, or, in mixed marriages, abandonment by the non-believer. When couples divorce without fornication, and remarriages take place, adultery is the result. As far as controversies on this subject go, there is little disagreement thus far. In Chapter 8, "Unscriptural Divorce & Remarriage: A Variety of Answers," we will examine a number of solutions which, over the decades, have been proposed to answer this problem.

Chapter 8

Unscriptural Divorce & Remarriage:
A Variety of Answers

Highlights

- *Two problems that have to be worked to resolve any unscriptural divorce and remarriage situation.*
- *God doesn't hate all divorce, at least equally.*
- *Must one divorce an impenitent fornicating spouse?*
- *Every exception clause in the Bible contains a necessary implication.*
- *Alien sinners are not amenable to all the law of God, but all are under sophisticated moral law to God.*

The previous chapter presented "the problem," essentially what to advise people who have gotten involved with unscriptural marriage and divorce situations to remedy their problem. We pointed out that in not-for-fornication divorce and remarriage situations, people often find themselves living with someone else's spouse, and are themselves still the spouse of someone they thought they had broken the marriage bond with years ago. As we begin to contemplate solving such problems as these, this chapter considers a number of prominent answers that have been proposed and embraced by many teachers in previous decades.

AUTHOR'S NOTE: To the person reading these words who might be realizing that they've been involved in a not-for-fornication divorce and remarriage: if you're beginning to recognize that there are questions and complications you've not contemplated before, you should take the matter seriously, but not be

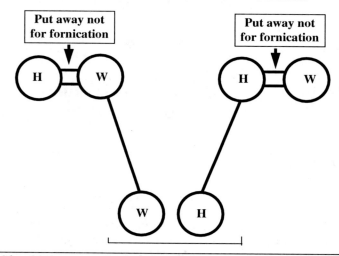

Unscriptural Divorce & Remarriage: The Problem Presented

Should these ever be scripturally bound to each other, two things would have to happen:

Previous bonds would have to be scripturally broken

New bonds would have to be scripturally made

Every position on divorce and remarriage must and does deal with these two problems:

Can the previous bonds now be scripturally broken?

Can new bonds then be scripturally made?

Figure 23

panicky. We advise you not to do anything rashly, for you probably don't know enough for yourself yet to make rational, scriptural decisions. Keep reading and keep studying for yourself.

By the time we get to the last chapters, you should have enough tools at hand to sort out your marital situation for yourself and determine what God would have you to do.

Figure 23 illustrates what has to happen for such a situation to be resolved, if it can be. As the chart illustrates, the common situation is that unscriptural divorces have taken place, and then remarriages occurred which resulted in adultery. The two problems that produced this situation were (1) unscriptural, not-for-fornication divorces that should not have taken place originally, and (2) adulterous unions were entered into which shouldn't have taken place, either.

As we've noted before, scriptural authority exists for every person to have his own spouse. No one is ever entitled to the spouse of another, and not everyone may have the spouse they would like. However, in order for the couple at the bottom of the chart to ever be bound scripturally to each other (and we're by no means guaranteeing that they can) two things would have to happen. The first bonds would have to be scripturally broken, either by means of death or by putting away for fornication. The second bonds would have to be scripturally made. *These two problems are always addressed by every proposed solution to the problem of what to tell people in unscriptural divorce and remarriage.* Every proposed answer deals with these two problems in one way or another.

In this chapter, we're going to briefly study a number of positions that arose in the twentieth century. Before divorce was so prevalent in our society, and when divorcees were so stigmatized (much more than now), the issue really didn't attract much attention. However, now religious groups of every stripe are either dealing with it, have already summarily dealt with it, or are still hiding their head in the sand, hoping it will go away.

It is important to understand that every proposed answer must deal with these two questions. All those proposed in the future will, as well. Many times, people read or attend religious debates that deal with these two problems without understanding why those particular debate propositions were arrived at, or what the relation of the propositions are to the real-life issues at hand. It is hoped that as we go through these various answers, it will

become apparent how each position deals with these two problems and why it is necessary for them to do so.

The following are the positions we'll discuss in this chapter:

Olan Hicks Position—Adultery Consists of Two Things

No Divorce at All, Even for Fornication

God Hates Divorce

Divorce for Fornication Allowed, No Remarriage for
Either Party

Baptism Washes Away Sin

E. C. Fuqua Position—Alien Sinners Only Amenable to
Civil Law

Lloyd Moyer Position—First Act of Fornication Breaks
One Marriage Bond, Second Act Creates Another One

J. T. Smith Positions—(1) One Unjustly Put Away Cannot
Put Away a Fornicating Spouse, and (2) The Put-Away
Fornicator Cannot Remarry

Although there are other positions that are held, this selection
of positions has had and still has significant influence in the
religious world, and they will serve to illustrate most of the
controversial aspects of this subject. It will be worth our time to
understand them, and how they relate to what we've learned thus
far.

Olan Hicks Position—Adultery Consists of Two Things

One of the most recent positions to attract attention on the
divorce and remarriage front is that of Olan Hicks. Hicks is a
long-time gospel preacher, who has written and spoken extensively on this subject. While his position is not the most popular

at the present time, since it's new, it's probably attracting more attention than any other position presently. Therefore, it's worthy of the reader's attention. The writer has met with brother Hicks, spent about five hours visiting with him on this subject, was treated very courteously by him; and frankly, personally likes him and his wife a great deal. I appreciate his being open to study, and his courage at trying to get brethren to open their minds and study the subject.

While we have emphasized the importance of accurate definitions of fornication and adultery, Hicks would agree, then say that our definition is not accurate at all. From Mt. 5.32 and 19.9, Hicks argues that adultery is not just illicit sexual intercourse involving a spouse, but that it also includes other forms of covenant treachery or unfaithfulness to the marriage covenant other than illicit sexual intercourse. A typical statement of Hicks' position is:

> If one looks at Mt. 19.9 without prior misconceptions, it says very simply that a man who puts away his wife without fornication as the cause, and marries another, commits adultery. Why would anyone not accept the idea that it is committed in the doing of those two things? (Olan Hicks, *Divorce and Remarriage, The Issues Made Clear* [Searcy, AR: Gospel Enterprises, 1990], p. 38.)

Hicks' basic point is extremely simple. Here Jesus said that by doing just two things, putting away and remarrying, this man commits adultery. It doesn't say anything about sexual intercourse.

Of course, all agree that adultery is never right, and that to please God, adultery must stop. If the standard definition of adultery, which we hold, is right, for adultery to stop, sexual intercourse or activity with another's spouse must stop, and the marriage must be forfeited. If Hicks is correct, and putting away and remarrying constitute adultery, then as he says, putting away and remarrying must stop, but sexual intercourse may continue, and the couple must continue in the marriage. In other words, divorce, even treacherous (without scriptural cause), breaks the previous marriage bond, and remarriage makes the new one. This is the way Hicks works the two problems that must be worked in order for the couple to stay together.

Hicks has two basic lines of argument to sustain the concept of sexless adultery: (1) scriptures where adultery apparently doesn't refer to sexual intercourse, and (2) declaring that we must add to the text to sustain the standard definition of adultery as involving illicit sexual intercourse or activity.

Scriptures Where Hicks Affirms that Adultery Apparently Doesn't Include Illicit Sexual Intercourse

Jer. 3.9

In Jer. 3.9 Israel is said to commit adultery with stumps and stones. God spoke in the prophets many times of Israel's idol worship as adultery, or spiritual unfaithfulness to him, as God's bride abandoning him and running to foreign gods. Stumps and stones refer to the carved idols themselves. So surely, there was no physical sexual intercourse involved. Thus, Hicks affirms this is a case of adultery with no sexual intercourse involved.

So we ask, is this a valid definition of adultery, or is it a figurative reference to the close involvement and companionship between Israel and other gods? Fornication is used figuratively the same way. In Ezek. 16.26, Ezekiel said of Israel's military alliances with Egypt, that she "played the harlot with the Egyptians." As far as I know, no one, including Hicks, has proposed modifying the standard definition for fornication to include military alliances, saying that illicit sexual intercourse is unnecessary for fornication to be committed. Does the United States commit literal fornication with the nations with whom we have military alliances? Thayer (*Thayer's Greek-English Lexicon of the New Testament*, p. 417) and Vine (*Vine's Expository Dictionary of New Testament Words*) admit to a figurative use of adultery in this sense and refer to this very passage, but Thayer still defines adultery as "illicit sexual intercourse involving a spouse." He doesn't allow a figurative use of the word to force him to modify his basic definition. E. W. Bullinger, in his famous work, *Figures of Speech Used in the Bible,* has this to say about those who neglect a figurative aspect to much of Biblical language:

> From non-attention to these figures, translators have made blunders as serious as they are foolish. Sometimes they have translated the figure literally, totally ignoring its existence; sometimes they have taken it fully into account, and have translated, not according to the letter, but according to the spirit; sometimes they have taken literal words and translated them figuratively. Commentators and interpreters, from inattention to the figures, have been led astray from the real meaning of many important passages of God's Word; while ignorance of them has been the fruitful parent of error and false doctrine. It may be truly said that most of the gigantic errors of Rome, as well as the erroneous and conflicting views of the Lord's People, have their root and source, either in figuratively explaining away passages which should be taken literally, or in taking literally what has been thrown into a peculiar form or Figure of language: thus, not only falling into error, but losing the express teaching, and missing the special emphasis which the particular Figure was designed to impart to them. (E. W. Bullinger, *Figures of Speech Used in the Bible* [Grand Rapids: Baker Book House, 1898], p. xvi.)

Thus, scholars say that when Bible students such as Hicks disregard figurative language in the Bible and start modifying standard definitions of basic Bible words on that basis, they're falling into grievous error. We could just as well take Jesus' pronouncement of Herod as a fox, and demand that our dictionaries modify their definitions of fox to include a wicked Jewish king, if we neglect the fact that Jesus was speaking figuratively. No, a fox is not a wicked Jewish king; a fox is a figure of a wicked Jewish king. Likewise, when Jesus said, "I am the door," figuratively describing his being the access to fellowship with God, he wasn't expecting us to rewrite the definition of the word "door" and say that one of the meanings of the word is "the Christ." A door is merely a figure for Christ.

Mt. 5.28

One of Hicks' chief examples of adultery not including sexual intercourse is Mt. 5.28, where Jesus said, "He that looks on a woman to lust after her has committed adultery with her in his heart." Hicks affirms there is no sexual activity in this passage. I disagree. As we pointed out in the previous chapter in our discussion of this passage, Jesus described three ways that exactly the same sin of adultery is committed: with the feet (overtly), with the mind (by imagining the actual physical sexual act in the mind), and using the courts (by unscriptural divorce and remarriage) to accomplish the same physical sexual act with the same woman. Hicks misses Jesus' point in Mt. 5.27-32. Jesus used the word adultery to show that the same sin is being committed in all three cases. He's not a modern-day Jehovah's Witness—using the word three different ways in the same paragraph!

Mt. 12.39

In Mt. 12.39, Jesus spoke of the Jews of his day as "an evil and adulterous generation" seeking after a sign. Hicks says of this passage that there's no sexual infidelity involved. Oh? First, what makes him think so? Invariably, when a nation goes away from God, they become ever more involved in immorality in general, and certainly, physical sexual immorality was prevalent in Jesus' time. They were sexually adulterous if they were (1) doing it with their feet, (2) doing it with their eyes, or (3) doing it with the courts, and they were doing all three! Second, Jesus could have been speaking figuratively, as we saw in Jeremiah and Ezekiel. There is no necessary ground for Hicks to assume that our definition is wrong based on this passage.

Jas. 4.4

James, speaking of the apostate Jews of the first century shortly before the destruction of Jerusalem, said, "Ye adulteresses, friendship with the world is enmity with God." Hicks again affirms that there's no sexual intercourse involved, but he has no grounds to make that assumption. Isn't it just possible that friendship with the world includes illicit sexual activity? Isn't it just possible that those who are friends with the world are committing adultery with their feet, eyes, and the courts? And, of course, adultery could be used here figuratively as in the passages in Jeremiah and Ezekiel.

Mt. 19.9

Hicks uses Jesus' statement that "whosoever puts away his wife and marries another commits adultery" to argue that adultery doesn't necessarily involve sexual intercourse. He says that "whoever does two things, put away and remarry, commits adultery." However, actual, physical illicit sexual intercourse is involved in this passage just like it is in Mt. 5.32. This is adultery accomplished using the courts. Although Hicks merely assumes no physical adultery here, this is the basis of his definition of adultery as "covenant treachery," since one is treacherously violating a marriage covenant.

If covenant treachery is adultery, treacherous divorce alone is covenant treachery, isn't it? Having an affair with just a divorce and no remarriage is covenant treachery, isn't it? Remarrying one treacherously divorced is covenant treachery, isn't it? Imagining an affair with one not divorced nor remarried is covenant treachery, to be sure. Lying to your wife is certainly covenant treachery. Defrauding her sexually is covenant treachery. Slapping your wife, economically abusing her, verbally abusing her, and sexually abusing her are all covenant treachery, aren't they? Are all these adultery as well? Sounds like we've got quite a few definitions we'd better change if we follow Hicks' logic consistently, doesn't it?

Hicks Says We Must Otherwise Add to the Text

In addition to passages that he affirms do not permit physical sexual intercourse when speaking of adultery, Hicks also says we must add extraneous sexual intercourse to passages which do not include it. His favorite illustration is Mt. 19.9, of which he says:

> If one looks at Mat 19:9 without prior misconceptions it says very simply that a man who puts away his wife without fornication as the cause, and marries another, commits adultery. Why would anyone not accept the idea that it is committed in the doing of those two things? If someone says "Whosoever aims the gun and pulls the trigger commits murder," it conveys to us the idea that murder is committed in the doing of those two things. Why is it any less simple in the reading of this passage?" (Olan Hicks, *Divorce and Remarriage, The Issues Made Clear* [Searcy, AR: Gospel Enterprises, 1990], p. 38.)

Hicks says "without prior misconceptions" we will conclude that adultery consists of two things, divorcing and remarrying. I suggest that reading it without prior misconception includes not ripping verse 9 out of the context of Jesus' teaching about committing actual physical sexual adultery (1) with the feet, (2) with the eyes, and (3) with the courts. I'm afraid if someone reads Mt. 19.9 and concludes that sexual adultery is not involved, he is the one who's approaching the passage with a prior misconception.

I actually like Hicks' example, "Whosoever aims the gun and pulls the trigger commits murder," perhaps more than I should. Let me ask our readers a question, "Have you ever aimed a gun and pulled the trigger?" If so, Hicks says you've committed murder! By Hicks' newfound definition of murder, you are guilty! How many murderers are reading these words? Are you one of them? You are, according to Hicks' example, if you've ever gone target shooting. I suggest otherwise. Even if a victim is involved, Hicks' definition has fatal errors. Unless there is intent, there's no murder. If the cartridge misfires, there's no murder. If the gun isn't loaded, there's no murder. If the bullet doesn't hit the victim, there's no murder. If the bullet doesn't fatally wound the victim, there's no murder. It appears Hicks needs to add quite a few things to his own definition of murder, most of which are subsequent to aiming and pulling the trigger.

So it is with Mt. 19.9. After putting away and remarrying, there will be no adultery without subsequent sexual intercourse or activity, which wasn't added by me, nor by the lexicographers who gave us the definitions. God placed sexual intercourse exclusively in marriage in the first book of the Bible. With the standard definition of adultery, we don't have to add sexual intercourse to Jesus' teaching on divorce and remarriage. It's already in (1) adultery with the feet, (2) adultery with the eyes, and (3) adultery with the courts.

What Other Definitions Do We Need to Change?

Hicks' attempt to change the definition of adultery "without adding anything to the text" makes us wonder about the definitions of some other Bible words. Speaking of incest, Moses wrote in Lev. 18.8, "You shall not lie with your mother." Do we need to adjust our concept of incest? Should we follow Hicks' admonition and not add any more thoughts? Does just lying on a bed with your mother constitute incest?

How about our definition of homosexuality? In Lev. 18.22, Moses said, "You shall not lie with a male as one lies with a female." Don't add any more thoughts! If Hicks is right and sexual intercourse isn't necessary to commit adultery, then why would sexual intercourse or activity be necessary to commit an act of homosexuality? Our definition of fornication would be questionable, because many times in Leviticus, we've already seen that it was called "uncovering the nakedness" of someone. If we follow Hicks and don't add any thoughts to the text, we need to redefine that word, too.

Following Hicks' lead, we could conceivably have to change the definition of every word in the Bible. The safest course is to use God's definition of adultery in Rom. 7.2-3 ("a spouse who joins to another"), which agrees with all the scholars on the subject, rather than using a definition no one on earth heard of until the 1980s.

In conclusion on Hicks' position, I believe it is simplistic in that it ignores the power and purpose of figurative language. It also ignores the context of most of the passages it relies on to get sexual intercourse out of passages where God included it. The end result is, if illicit sexual intercourse or activity is truly involved in adultery, and adultery is never right, the sexual intercourse must stop in those divorce and remarriage situations that cannot be remedied.

No Divorce at All, Even for Fornication

The second answer to the problem of unscriptural divorce and remarriage is the position of some that there should be no divorce at all, even for fornication. In such a case, of course, there would be no question of remarriage of a treacherously put-away person. As we stated early in this chapter, every answer proposed to the problem of the unscripturally divorced and remarried couple of Figure 23 has to deal with two questions: (1) Can the previous bond now be scripturally broken, and (2) Can the new bond be scripturally made? This position answers the two questions this way: (1) the original bond can never be scripturally broken, except by death, and (2) no new bond may be scripturally made.

God Hates Divorce

This position arises out of an utter abhorrence of divorce. It's based on Mal. 2:14-16, where God said:

> The Lord has been a witness between you and the wife of your youth, against whom you have dealt treacherously, though she is your companion and your wife by covenant. But not one has done so who has a remnant of the Spirit. Take heed then, to your spirit, and let no one deal treacherously against the wife of your youth. For I hate divorce," says the Lord, the God of Israel. So take heed to your spirit, that you do not deal treacherously.

As we've already seen, this passage refers to Jewish men after the Babylonian captivity who were treacherously divorcing their Jewish wives to marry foreign wives. In that case, we would have hated it as well, and would have said that there should have been no such divorce at all, because there was no fornication involved. As some sin is inevitably involved in any divorce, whether it's committed by a fornicator who is being put-away, or by a treacherous spouse putting away another not for fornication, God probably hates every divorce to some degree, and so should we. Is it possible to hate divorce too much? Just here perhaps we should appreciate that there are two types of divorce: (1) treacherous, or not for fornication, and (2) punitive, where one is divorced for impenitent adultery. This second kind of divorce is the kind God did with Israel, isn't it? When Israel became idolatrous and made military alliances with other nations in place of relying on God for protection, God taught Israel that such behavior wasn't right. When Israel would not repent, God sent drought, pestilence, and enemy nations to try to turn Israel around. After patiently working with Israel for hundreds of years, when she became a harlot with a forehead of flint, God finally divorced her, righteously, in Jer. 3.8:

> And I saw that for all the adulteries of faithless Israel, I had sent her away and given her a writ of divorce, yet her treacherous sister Judah did not fear; but she went and was a harlot also.

Of course, when God put-away faithless Israel, he was absolutely righteous in doing so. As he explained, God could no more be in fellowship with Israel's impenitent idolatry than he could be in fellowship with the Canaanites when they were guilty of the same behavior. Surely, there was a lot about that divorce that God hated, but it was still the righteous thing for him to do. Punitive divorce worked in that case, because eventually Israel repented and came back to God.

Another example of punitive divorce is what Joseph was going to do to Mary by following Dt. 24.1-4, which permitted putting away an impenitent adulterous wife. Matthew said Joseph was a righteous man. The only mistake he was making was that Mary wasn't a fornicator, but he was righteous in thinking he had the right to put away an impenitent adulterous wife.

In Ez. 10.1-5, God commanded the Israelites to put away their foreign wives. Even if God hated that divorce, it was still right for them to do it.

Thus, just because God hates divorce doesn't mean that it's not authorized, or the righteous thing to do in certain circumstances, nor that it can't take place. It is altogether true that God hates divorce, but he neither hates all divorces the same way, nor does he hate every aspect of divorce, even when he divorced Israel. Even so, God doesn't condemn divorce *per se*.

Before we leave the concept of punitive divorce, consider I Cor. 6.15, where in exhorting Corinthian Christians about sexual sins, Paul said:

> v15: Do you not know that your bodies are members of Christ? Shall I then take away the members of Christ and make them members of a harlot? May it never be!

The word "harlot" here is from *porneia*, meaning a fornicator. Suppose the harlot in this case is not a prostitute, but one's spouse. Suppose further that the fornicating spouse is impenitent. Can the innocent Christian be one body with such a harlot? God's answer is, "God forbid!" Evidently, God demands punitive divorce in this case, just like he did with Israel, and what Joseph intended to do with Mary.

Many times in discussing divorce and remarriage, we hear men say, "Boy, if my wife was unfaithful to me, I'd put her away in a minute." Is that what God wants? Is that what God did with his wife, Israel? No, he loved Israel, and he wasn't looking for an excuse to "let the hammer down on her." So he worked with her, trying to get her to repent, and it was only after tremendous effort on God's part, and his seeing that Israel simply wasn't going to repent, that God put Israel away. God's righteousness demanded that he do so.

The principle of "treating someone the way you would want to be treated" also demands that if one's spouse is unfaithful, we shouldn't divorce him as soon as possible, unless of course that's what we want for ourselves. If someone is unfaithful to his wife, he probably doesn't want her to immediately "let the hammer down on him," does he? Can he put himself in her place, and see that if she is the guilty party, that she would probably like to be forgiven if she repents? The example of God's patience, and yet his determination not to be in fellowship with his wife's sin, should serve modern husbands and wives well. We ought to work with an unfaithful spouse, and in the case of impenitence, punitive divorce might be the very thing God intends to happen. Hopefully, in such cases, the divorce will bring about repentance as it did in the case of God and his wife.

This Position Negates the Exception Clause

We will have a lot to say about the exception clauses of Mt. 5.32 and Mt. 19.9 in a future chapter, but suffice it to say that the position that there is no divorce at all, even for fornication, makes the exception clause in these passages meaningless. We agree that if one puts away his wife *not for fornication* and remarries, he commits adultery. Do we also agree that if one puts away his wife *for fornication* and remarries, he also commits adultery? If we do, then the exception clause means nothing at all. We may as well rip it out of our Bibles.

No Remarriage for Either Party

TheRoman Catholic position on divorce and remarriage is essentially that divorce for fornication is permitted, but no remarriage is allowed for either party Nowadays, Catholics depend much more on "annulling" marriages to break marriages than divorce. Historically, when a couple undertook a marriage, and it was found out that someone had misrepresented himself as eligible for marriage when he was not, the Roman Catholic church would declare the marriage null and void, as though it had never taken place. Now, prominent people particularly can have their marriages annulled even when they've been married for decades and have quite a number of children, saying they "didn't understand something about the vows." One of the attractive things to Catholics about annulment is that both parties are free to remarry. According to Canon law expert Edward N. Peters, author of *100 Answers to Your Questions on Annulments* (Necedah, WI: Basilica Press, 1997), each year Catholic Church tribunals declare over 80,000 annulments worldwide, with 50,000 of these coming from America.

It's easy to see how the Roman Catholic position on divorce deals with the two parts of the problem. It says the previous bond can be scripturally broken for fornication, which is correct, but that no new marriage can be made.

This position has several major problems. First, it ignores the effect of divorce in Mt. 19.3, 7, and 8. As we saw in Chapter Five, Jesus and the Pharisees discussed these verses in Dt. 24.1-4, where divorce for fornication resulted in both parties being free to remarry. If divorce for fornication meant something different than that in Mt. 19.9, Jesus fooled the Pharisees. If Roman Catholic scholars think the effect of divorce in Mt. 19.9 is different than that in Mt. 19.3, 7, and 8, then they're fooling themselves.

Second, this position also ignores the power of the exception clause. Jesus taught, and Roman Catholics and we agree, that whosoever puts away his wife *not for fornication* and remarries, commits adultery. Roman Catholics also teach that whosoever puts away his wife *for fornication* and remarries, commits adultery, which makes the exception clause mean absolutely nothing at all. Perhaps this is why Roman Catholics prefer to use Lk. 16.18 as their proof text on divorce and remarriage, as it does not include the exception clause.

Exception clauses are not meaningless. As a matter of fact, *every single exception clause in the Bible contains a necessary implication*, teaching which is inescapably implied, though it's not explicitly stated. Let's notice a few examples. In Mk. 7.3, Jesus said, "All the Jews, except they wash their hands diligently, eat not." Does this mean they don't eat even when they wash? Not at all. The exception clause necessarily implies, though the direct statement is never made, that when the Jews do wash their hands diligently, they do eat. Stated another way, *when the exception is taken, the end result is exactly the opposite to that stated.*

In Ac. 8.1, Luke said, "All scattered except the apostles." Does this mean even the apostles were scattered? No. The exception clause necessarily implies, though the direct statement is never made, that the apostles were not scattered. When *the exception is taken, the end result is exactly the opposite.*

In Jn. 6.44, Jesus said, "No man can come unto me except the father draw him." Does this mean that he can't come even when the father draws him? No, the exception clause necessarily implies that when the father draws you, you can come to Christ. *The end result is the opposite to what is stated, because the exception has been taken.*

In II Tim. 2.5, Paul said, "One is not crowned, except he have contended lawfully." Does this mean he's not crowned even when he contends lawfully? Similarly, no. In Mt. 19.9, when Jesus said, "Whosoever shall put-away his wife, except for fornication, and shall marry another, committeth adultery." Does this mean that he commits adultery even if he puts her away for fornication and remarries? *Not unless the exception clause means absolutely nothing at all.*

Baptism Washes Away Sin

The most popular approach to the problem of unscriptural divorce and remarriage is probably this one, that baptism washes away sin, so you don't have to worry about unscriptural divorce and remarriage problems encountered before you became a Christian.

Certainly, baptism washes away sin, for Jesus told Saul on the road to Damascus, "And now why tarriest thou, Arise, and be baptized, and wash away thy sins." If we believe the Bible, we believe baptism puts one into Christ (Gal. 3.27), that it saves a penitent believer (Ac. 2.38), and that it's necessary in order for one to be called a Christian (I Cor. 1.13). All these we can be confident of because the scriptures so teach.

It's easy to see how this position deals with the two problems that must be solved for the couple involved in unscriptural divorce and remarriage. For this position, baptism is the act that breaks the previous marriage bond, and makes the new one. But where would we go to show that baptism washes away wives? What passage teaches that baptism breaks old marriage bonds not properly broken, and makes new marriage bonds that were not properly made?

How far does this approach go? Would the baptism of a man living in open harlotry with a prostitute marry him to the harlot? If a heathen is living with twenty-five wives, does his baptism marry him to all twenty-five of his wives? Surely, we can see that the Bible teaches many things about baptism, but divorcing and remarrying is not part of that teaching.

E. C. Fuqua Position—Alien Sinners Only Amenable to Civil Law

This highly popular position, was strongly advanced by a preacher in the 1950s named E. C. Fuqua. The basis of Fuqua's position is that alien sinners are only under civil law. The appeal of this position for solving the typical unscriptural divorce and remarriage problem is that civil law says the previous bonds are broken by not-for-fornication divorce, and the new bonds are valid since civil law licensed them to be made!

Following are some representative quotations from Fuqua's writings:

> While in the World, people cannot be with or without "a scriptural cause" for anything, seeing they are not under Christian law, but under Civil Law exclusively. (*The Vindicator*, Oct. 1951, p. 6.)

> All his law and legislation are exerted in the church, and over its members exclusively; so that the World is in no sense under any law of Christ. (*Ibid.*, Oct. 1951, p. 5.)

> God has placed the World as such under Civil Law exclusively. (*Ibid.*, Oct. 1951, p. 5.)

> Nor do I find where those in the World are given any law from God on any subject. Gentiles or other aliens are without law to God. (*Ibid.*, May 1950, p. 6.)

Thus if a man marries a woman, then leaves her in
destitution for another, he sins against Civil Law—
God's only law in the world. (*Ibid.*, Feb. 1952, p. 6.)

Worldly people are judged solely by the law of the world.
(*Ibid.*, Dec. 1951, p. 2.)

Baptism is the dividing line between the World and the
Church (I Cor. 12.13). Up till then, Civil laws control.
After baptism, Christ's law takes over. (*Ibid.*, Dec. 1951,
p. 2.)

That being true, nothing done in the world was looked
upon as a sin, for it transgressed no law from Him. (*Ibid.*,
Oct. 1951, p. 4.)

Therefore, no specific sins, like fornication, could be
levied against people in the world. (*Ibid.*, Oct. 1951, p.
4.)

They were not "living in adultery" in the world, because
adultery is a violation of God's specific law; and people
in the world are not under any specific law from God.
They are not therefore required to repent of any specific
sins. (*Ibid.*, Aug. 1951, p. 3.)

To summarize this position, it holds that the world is under
civil law exclusively, and will be judged solely by that law. Also,
the world is not under any law from God or Christ on any subject,
and so cannot violate any law or instruction of Christ. Finally,
the salvation of a man in the world does not involve his repenting
of specific sins, and so he does not have to sever "sinful relationships" as viewed by the Law of Christ, while he is (or was) in the
world.

Does the Bible teach that alien sinners are only under civil
law? Paul took a different tack as to why all men are sinners. In
Romans, Paul, whose goal was to show that all men were under
condemnation and needed the gospel, used a clever approach.
Realizing that self-righteous Jews were going to be the hardest

to convince, he showed in chapter 1 that all Gentiles were condemned. Of course, the self-righteous Jews thought this was good preaching! They naturally enjoyed Paul's "pouring it on" the Gentiles. Then in Romans 2, he showed that the Jews had done precisely the same sins, which trapped them as guilty of the same sins. Then in Romans 3, Paul concluded in verse 23, that "all [both Jews and Gentiles—SGD] have sinned and fall short of the glory of God."

We particularly want to notice how Paul showed that all Gentiles were condemned. Was it solely because they were only under civil law? Not at all. Beginning in Rom. 1.18-21, Paul condemned the Gentiles who didn't glorify God because of the evidence in nature of his existence. What nation has a civil law requiring everyone to examine the evidence intellectually and coming to the conclusion that God exists? None! In Rom. 1.21, he condemned them for their ungratefulness to God. What civil law were they violating, do you suppose? In Rom. 1.22-25, he condemned them for their idolatry. What civil law does that violate? In Rom. 1.26-27, he condemned them for their sexual sins, particularly homosexuality. Was that a violation of civil law? Hardly, when many of the Roman Caesars themselves practiced such. In Rom. 1.28-32, Paul affirmed that the Gentiles, who had never even heard of God or the Bible, were guilty of violating a highly sophisticated set of moral precepts:

> ...being filled with all unrighteousness, wickedness, covetousness, maliciousness; full of envy, murder, strife, deceit, malignity; whisperers, backbiters, hateful to God, insolent, haughty, boastful, inventors of evil things, disobedient to parents, without understanding, covenant-breakers, without natural affection, unmerciful: who, knowing the ordinance of God, that they that practise such things are worthy of death, not only do the same, but also consent with them that practise them.

Many times we view godless Gentiles during the Mosaic period as ignorant savages who barely knew how to start fires, but Paul made it clear that God held them to nearly as high a standard as the Jews had under Moses. Rom. 1.28-32 is essentially the Gentiles' version of the ethics of the Sermon on the Mount. These "ignorant savages" were held responsible for knowing that these things were sinful. They were held responsible for knowing that "malignity" (maligning someone's motives) is evil. There are people in most churches who don't know malignity is a serious sin. Know any whisperers? Who doesn't know that's a sin? Covenant-breakers? These people were hardly ignorant savages. They were living and being judged by a law substantially higher than civil law. What civil law makes malignity, whispering, and boastfulness a crime?

Surely the Jews were judged by their behavior under the Mosaic code, but Gentiles were judged by a law essentially as morally refined. Because of this, when Paul addressed the Gentiles in his letters, he referred to their sinful backgrounds in much higher terms than civil law. In Eph. 2.1-4, he said to the predominantly Gentile Ephesian Christians:

> And you did he make alive, when ye were dead through your trespasses and sins, wherein ye once walked according to the course of this world, according to the prince of the powers of the air, of the spirit that now worketh in the sons of disobedience; among whom we also all once lived in the lust of our flesh, doing the desires of the flesh and of the mind, and were by nature children of wrath, even as the rest...

Paul evidently didn't share Fuqua's concept that alien sinners were only under civil law, did he? Likewise, in Col. 3.5-7, Paul wrote the predominantly Gentile Colossian Christians:

> Put to death therefore your members which are upon the earth: fornication, uncleanness, passion, evil desire, and covetousness, which is idolatry; for which things' sake cometh the wrath of God upon the sons of disobedience: wherein ye also once walked, when ye lived in these things...

We know that these sexual sins are wrong, but what about covetousness, wanting another man's possessions, or his wife?

Lusting after another man's wife was something these Gentiles were guilty of. Where in the world does civil law prohibit such?

Incidentally, recall that in one of the previous quotations Fuqua said, "They were not 'living in adultery' in the world, because adultery is a violation of God's specific law; and people in the world are not under any specific law from God." Paul said in these verses that the Gentiles were "living" in fornication. Which will you believe?

When we understand that all men, whether they've heard of God or not, are judged by a very sophisticated moral law, then we're prepared to understand Paul's statement in Ac. 20.21, characterizing his preaching as:

> ...testifying both to Jews and to Greeks repentance to-
> ward God, and faith toward our Lord Jesus Christ.

Paul knew that both Jews and Greeks needed to repent toward God, the Jews for violating the Law of Moses, and the Greeks, not just for violating civil law, but also for violating the highly sophisticated law of their conscience.

Lloyd Moyer Position—
First Act of Fornication Breaks One Marriage
Bond, Second Act Creates Another One

Lloyd Moyer was an extremely well-known gospel preacher who in the 1960s set forth a highly controversial answer to the unscriptural divorce and remarriage problem. Moyer had two brothers who were also gospel preachers. This writer has visited with both of them extensively; they both disagreed with the Lloyd Moyer position, for exactly the same reasons the writer does. A representative statement of the Lloyd Moyer position is given by Lloyd Moyer himself:

> That first marriage has been destroyed by the sin of
> fornication (illicit or unlawful sexual inter-
> course)...Though adultery was committed when they

first joined themselves together in intercourse because they were still the husband or wife of someone else, subsequent sexual intercourse between them is not adultery. They are no longer the husband or wife of someone else...And by this sin of adultery they cause their previous marriage to be dissolved...When a marriage is thus dissolved, the innocent is no longer married to the guilty, nor is the guilty any longer married to the innocent. No marriage exists. Where no marriage exists, the parties may marry someone else...We have shown that by the very act of adultery the first marriage was defiled, adulterated and therefore dissolved. Subsequent sexual intercourse would not be adultery. It would be simply a man and his wife cohabiting in the confines of marriage. (Lloyd Moyer, *Gospel Guardian*, Aug. 22 and 29, 1963, pp. 253, 257.)

Thus, Moyer attempted to work "the problem" of unscriptural divorce and remarriage by affirming that the first act of fornication broke the previous marriage bonds, while the second act of fornication made the new marriage bond. From our study of what constitutes a marriage, and violations of marriage, we know that cohabitation never broke a marriage bond (*putting away* for fornication did), and it never made a marriage (it was a *right* of marriage).

J. T. Smith Positions—(1) One Unjustly Put Away Cannot Put Away a Fornicating Spouse and (2) The Put-Away Fornicator Cannot Remarry

We now come to the two most prevalent positions purporting to answer the unscriptural divorce and remarriage situation in the last quarter of the twentieth century, those of a gospel preacher by the name of J. T. Smith. Though Smith is not the originator, nor is he alone in upholding his doctrines, his work is probably the most influential, due to the extensive public debating he's done. Smith participated in four debates (each six months apart over two years, 1976-1978) with Glen Lovelady, Lyle McCollum, Bob Melear, and Jack Gibbert.

As we've already seen in Figure 23, in order for the couple involved in an unscriptural divorce and remarriage to not have their union result in adultery, two things would have to happen: (1) their previous marriage bonds would have to be scripturally broken, since they were not broken by a not-for-fornication divorce, and (2) their marriage bonds would have to be scripturally made. Each of the positions we've discussed thus far have attempted to answer those two questions. As we come to Smith's two positions, they likewise deal with these same two problems.

One Unjustly Put-Away Cannot Put Away a Fornicating Spouse

First, Smith holds that an innocent party put away not for fornication by one who then commits fornication cannot put that fornicator away for fornication, and therefore he cannot remarry. Most of us probably would agree with Smith that if a woman was not put away for fornication and then remarried, she would commit adultery. However, Smith says that if her husband commits fornication before she remarries, she has lost her right to put him away for his fornication. Smith claims that the fact that this ungodly man lives under an ungodly government, which permits him to treacherously divorce her, negates the right Jesus gave her to put away a fornicating spouse.

The Position Documented

Smith affirmed this position in his debate with Bob Melear. The proposition was:

> The Scriptures teach that when a man puts away his wife for any cause other than fornication and he subsequently marries another, his first wife must either remain celibate or be reconciled to her husband.

We note here that Smith misuses the word "celibate," meaning "not to have a spouse," yet Smith believes this woman has a spouse, and refers to her "husband." On the second night of his debate with Glen Lovelady, Smith replied to a direct question thusly:

> 1. If an innocent woman is put away by her husband for no cause, not for fornication, and then that man marries another, and thereby commits adultery, can the innocent, put-away one, now put away her adulterous mate, or must she remain bound to that adulterer? She is not free. She is not free." (*The Smith-Lovelady Debate on Marriage, Divorce, and Remarriage* [Brooks, KY: Searching the Scriptures, 1976], p. 101.)

Another representative teacher who takes this same position is Roy Deaver. He wrote:

> It should be stressed that according to Mt. 5.32 and 19.9 the innocent party unjustly put away is not allowed to remarry. We are not discussing the innocent party who did the putting away—who put away the companion guilty of fornication. Rather, reference is here made to the innocent person put away by her companion, and without cause. Even this innocent person put away without cause is not given the right of remarriage. If Joe marries Jane, and if Joe later divorces Jane—but not upon the grounds of adultery upon the part of Jane—then Jane has no scriptural right of remarriage and the man who marries Jane 'keeps on committing adultery.' (Roy Deaver, *Spiritual Sword,* VI, #2, January 1975.)

Finally, in documenting this position, we have three questions answered by Smith in the Melear debate, which reflect his position:

> 3. If a man puts away his wife for a cause other than fornication and then he and his wife are reconciled, but following this reconciliation he commits fornication,

what may she now do according to God's law? Put him away for fornication if she desires, as per Mt. 19.9.

4. Suppose a man decides to obtain a civil divorce, but before he does, he commits fornication. What may his wife do according to God's law? In Mt. 5.32, Jesus said, "Whosoever shall put away his wife, saving for the cause of fornication, causeth her to commit adultery, and whosoever shall marry her that is divorced commits adultery." So in this case, both would be guilty according to God's law.

5. May the man in Rom. 7.2, 3 who lives, put his wife away for fornication and marry another according to God's law? No.

We will examine in detail Smith's position set forth here in the next chapter, "The Rights of the Unjustly Put-away."

A Put-Away Fornicator Cannot Remarry

Second, Smith holds that a put-away fornicator may not remarry until his former spouse dies, but must remain celibate, not having a mate.

The Position Documented

Smith affirmed the following proposition in his debate with Lyle McCollum:

The Scriptures teach that the put-away adulterer must remain unmarried or be reconciled to his first wife or husband.

Again, Roy Deaver, a champion of this same position, in reviewing Lewis Hale's book, *Except for Fornication*, said:

Likewise, I agree completely that the marriage bond is broken completely for both parties. The fornication does not automatically destroy the marriage, but the right of continuing or putting away belongs to the innocent party. He concludes that if the marriage bond is broken for both parties then the guilty party (as well as the innocent party) may form another marriage. I insist that this conclusion does not follow. It does not follow because of the law of God on the subject at hand. The guilty party, though free from the innocent party, is still subject to and is amenable to the law of God, and *the law of God states it plainly that God does not give the guilty party the right to remarry.* The innocent party is free to form another marriage not just because the marriage bond has been broken, but also because the law of God gives the innocent party this right. (Roy Deaver,*Spiritual Sword, VI,* #2, p. 15.)

Finally, in documenting his position, Smith offered this syllogism in the Melear debate:

a. Major premise: Everyone put away who remarries commits adultery, Mt. 19.9b. Jesus says if you marry one who has been put away, you commit adultery.

b. Minor premise: Some of those put-away persons are put away for fornication.

c. Conclusion: Fornicators who remarry commit adultery.

This position will be examined in detail in Chapter 11, "The Celibacy Position Examined." For now, we just want to be aware of Smith's two very popular positions.

Conclusion

This concludes our examination of the most influential answers proposed over the decades to the unscriptural divorce and remarriage problem. As we have seen, all these positions have some difficulties as they try to answer the controversial aspects of this subject. Although there are other positions that are held, this selection of positions has had and still has significant influence in the religious world.

In the next chapter, we begin to discuss in detail what we believe the answers to be. First, we will discuss the rights of those unjustly put away by those who then commit adultery. This will be our answer to the first critical and controversial question, i.e., can the first marriage bond be scripturally broken after someone tried to break it without scriptural authority. The chapter following that will deal with the remarriage of a put-away fornicator, which relates to whether the second bond can be scripturally made after someone tried to make it without scriptural authority, resulting in adultery.

Chapter 9

Rights of Those Unjustly Put Away

Highlights

- *There is no "guilty party" in Mt. 5.32 or Mt. 19.9.*
- *Jesus never said one could be put away for fornication.*
- *We can pay too much attention to civil law on this subject.*
- *Some add another exception clause to Mt. 5.32, Mt. 19.9.*
- *May one guilty party put away another?*
- *How an unjustly put away person puts away a fornicating spouse.*

As we come in our study to the rights of those unjustly put away, we have already seen that Jesus' teaching authorizes one to put away a fornicating spouse. Actually, we saw this in the previous chapter in introducing the fact that exception clauses are not meaningless (in dealing with the Roman Catholic position). We also noted that every exception clause in the Bible contains an inescapable conclusion. In Jn. 3.5, Jesus said:

> Except one be born of water and the Spirit, he cannot enter into the kingdom of God.

Jesus never made the direct statement that if one is born of water and the Spirit, he can enter into the kingdom of God. That statement exists nowhere in the Bible. However, through the use of the exception clause, Jesus necessarily implied that, didn't he? We all believe this truth, although we know Jesus didn't say it. We believe it because the exception clause inescapably implied it.

The same principle is true in Mt. 19.9, where Jesus said:

Whosoever shall put away his wife, except for fornication, and shall marry another, committeth adultery.

Jesus never made a direct statement about putting away a mate
for fornication. As a matter of fact, *he never made any statement
about a divorce for fornication.* Only the verses dealing with
divorce and remarriage that also have the exception clause teach
anything at all about a for-fornication divorce, because of the
necessary implications contained in the exception clauses.

This is easily seen when people speak of "the guilty party" in
Mt. 19.9. There is no guilty party in Mt. 19.9 or Mt. 5.32, as
they're written, is there?

Many times when a preacher visits with a congregation with
the prospect of moving to work with that congregation, the
congregation will ask him a question or two about his stand on
divorce and remarriage. If they disagree with his stand, they
probably won't try to "teach him the way of the Lord more
perfectly;" rather they'll send him on his way. In all likelihood,
they don't want to study the question with him or anyone else,
and this procedure assures that they will probably never have to.

The writer recalls one such experience when he was considering working with a small congregation, and in a congregational
meeting, various members were asking his views on these passages, saying something about what "Jesus said about the guilty
party in Mt. 19.9." I pointed out that Jesus excluded for-fornication divorces in Mt. 19.9, so that there were no parties guilty of
fornication in the entire passage. When everyone looked back at
me with the deer-in-the-headlights look, I asked, "If I put away
my wife not for fornication, but for burning the toast, which one
of us is the guilty party?" Some of the audience said, "You are."
Others said, "She is." A few, just to be on the safe side, said,
"Both of you are!"

Of course, when we speak of the guilty party, we mean the
person guilty of fornication, not guilty of speeding, writing hot
checks, etc. Sure, in that example, I'm guilty of something, but
not fornication, and she's guilty of burning the toast, but not
fornication. No one in the passage has committed fornication
before the divorce. There is no guilty party, that is, guilty of
fornication. Until a person sees that for himself, he's not slowing

down enough to read the passage for himself yet. He's going to be restricted to parroting the phrase, "This passage gives the innocent party the right to remarry but not the guilty," and not being able to say much more on the subject.

Once we realize that there is no guilty party in the passage, then we must realize that the only way we can get information about for-fornication divorces out of it, is by noting the necessary implication contained in the exception clause. Just like in Jn. 3.5 above, when you take the exception, the result of the passage changes. Thus, Jesus *said:*

Whosoever shall put away his wife, except for fornication, and shall marry another, committeth adultery.

But Jesus *necessarily implied:*

Whosoever shall put away his wife for fornication, and shall marry another, doth not commit adultery.

Notice that Jesus never *said* a man could put away his wife for fornication, he *necessarily implied* it when he used the exception clause. This is why we say that a person has authority from Christ to put away a fornicating spouse, although Jesus never said any such thing.

Having established that one may put away a spouse for fornication, we recall from Chapter 2 that fornication is "any unlawful sexual intercourse or activity." Thus, one may put away a spouse who engages in illicit heterosexual or homosexual activity, bestiality, or incest. Since we saw in our word study that sexual penetration is not required for fornication, fondling of sexual parts or oral sex would also constitute fornication, and would be scriptural grounds for divorce.

We'll have much more to say about exception clauses, both in this and the following chapters, but for now we notice that myself, J. T. Smith, Roy Lanier, Roy Deaver, and other well-known preachers who agree with Smith on the rights of those unjustly put away all agree that there is authority for a person to put away a fornicating spouse. To put away a fornicating spouse is a right given to us by God, and it cannot be infringed by any preacher, elder, or anyone else. Yet some, including Smith, Lanier, Deaver, and H. E. Philips prohibit Jesus' teaching from applying in certain situations. They say that an unjustly put-away person cannot exercise the right to put away a fornicating spouse. J. T. Smith affirmed the following proposition in his debate with Bob Melear:

> The Scriptures teach that when a man puts away his wife for any cause other than fornication and he subsequently marries another, his first wife must either remain celibate or be reconciled to her husband. (Proposition in Smith-Melear Debate, 1977.)

Likewise, Roy Deaver wrote:

> It should be stressed that according to Mt. 5.32 and 19.9 the innocent party unjustly put away is not allowed to remarry. Even this innocent person put away without cause is not given the right of remarriage. (*Spiritual Sword*, VI, #2, January 1975.)

Recall that we used the illustration of sprinkling salt on a marriage license thinking that it would dissolve the marriage bond just like it dissolves slugs, and how useless that would be. It seems that if Jesus gave a person the right to put away a fornicating spouse, the fact that an ungodly man living under an ungodly government that permitted him to treacherously divorce and subsequently commit fornication wouldn't have any more effect on her right to put him away, than his sprinkling salt on their marriage license would have had. Yet that is entirely the case presented by these preachers in this matter. Why would something no more powerful than a salt shaker take away the right of an unjustly put-away spouse, when it won't break a marriage bond? If a man committed fornication, and his wife got ready to put him away, suppose he got the salt shaker, shook it, and pronounced, "You can't do that! I sprinkled salt on our marriage license!" Surely, we wouldn't fall for that, yet these men all believe that although Jesus gave the innocent party the right to put away a fornicating spouse, the actions of an ungodly man under an ungodly government takes away that right.

Of course, this is a serious matter. These brethren think they're taking a conservative position, but it's never conservative to bind where God did not—it's the rankest form of liberal handling of the scriptures.

Civil Law Argument

The whole point of the divorce and remarriage controversy is, and these brethren would agree, that the laws of man don't nullify the laws of God on the subject. All of us are familiar with passages like Mk. 7.8-9, where Jesus said:

> Ye leave the commandment of God, and hold fast the tradition of men, And he said unto them, Full well do ye reject the commandment of God, that ye may keep your tradition.

In Ac. 4.19-20, when the chief priests told Peter and John not to preach any more in the name of Christ, their reaction was:

> But Peter and John answered and said unto them, Whether it is right in the sight of God to hearken unto you rather than unto God, judge ye: for we cannot but speak the things which we saw and heard.

In Ac. 5:29, after Peter and John had ignored the previous charge and were arrested, they didn't stop preaching:

> But Peter and the apostles answered and said, We must obey God rather than men.

These are passages that we usually read with pride. We understand that man's laws don't overrule God's, and when they do, it's a tradition of men.

In Figure 24 we see how inconsistent it is for Smith and other brethren to take this position. As the chart illustrates, if civil law

Civil Law Argument

If Civil Law Says We Can, Does that Affect Our Teaching or Practice?

Civil Law Says we Can:	Y	N
Refrain from preaching the gospel		☑
Use buttermilk in Lord's Supper		☑
Use instrumental music		☑
Have women bishops		☑
Sprinkle babies to give a name		☑
Pray to Mary		☑
Bind 7th day of rest on Christians		☑
Have Elders over two congregations		☑
Put away not for fornication	☑	

When Man's Law Sets Aside God's Law, Tradition!
Mk. 7.8, 9, Ac. 4.19, 5.29

Figure 24

says one thing and God says another, that doesn't affect our teaching or practice one whit. For instance, if the civil law says not to preach the gospel, it wouldn't affect our actions. If civil law says we should use buttermilk for the Lord's Supper, we wouldn't even think about obeying it. If the civil authorities commanded instrumental music in our worship, we wouldn't do it. If they said we should have women bishops or sprinkle babies

"Bound to Fornicator" Position

Govt. Allows Divorce Only for Fornication	Govt. Allows Divorce for Any Cause
I. Innocent Party cannot be put away	I. Innocent party can be put away not for fornication, according to the law of the land.
II. If innocent party's mate commits fornication, innocent party may put away adulterous mate and remarry.	II. If innocent party's mate then commits fornication, innocent party may not put away and remarry without adultery.

What's the Only Difference?

The Whims of Civil Government!

Figure 25

to christen them, we wouldn't listen. If they demanded we pray to Mary, keep the seventh day of the week as a sabbath, or have one elder over several congregations, that would have no effect on our teaching or practice whatsoever.

But when civil government says couples can divorce not for fornication, all of a sudden civil government has an effect on these brethren's teaching, debating and practice. Although Jesus gave a person the right to put away a fornicating spouse, according to their teaching, an ungodly man living under an ungodly government, which allows him to put away his spouse not for fornication, *takes away his spouse's right to put him away for the very reason Jesus gave!*

Figure 25 illustrates this point even further. It shows two situations, both of which Smith *et al* agree with. While they're under a government that allows divorce only for fornication, an innocent spouse cannot be put away; if the spouse commits

"Bound to Fornicator" Position

Govt. Allows Divorce Only for Fornication	Govt. Allows Divorce for Any Cause
1. PREACH innocent party may put away guilty.	1. MUST PREACH CANNOT in such cases.
2. DEBATE innocent party may put away guilty.	2. DEBATE CANNOT in such cases.
3. IN FELLOWSHIP with innocent parties who have put away guilty.	3. NOT IN FELLOWSHIP with such cases.
4. INNOCENT NOT BOUND TO GUILTY here.	4. INNOCENT BOUND TO GUILTY here.

What's the Only Difference?

The Whims of Civil Government!

Figure 26

fornication, the innocent spouse has a right to put him away. However, if they're under an ungodly government that allows divorce for reasons other than fornication, the innocent party can be put away not for fornication according to the law of the land. If the treacherous partner then commits fornication, these brethren teach that the innocent party cannot exercise the right Jesus gave him. What's the only difference? The whims of civil government!

Figure 26 illustrates the same point yet another way. Again, brethren who hold to this "bound to fornicator" position agree with both sides of this chart. Under a civil government that allows divorce only for fornication, they *preach* that innocent parties may put away guilty parties; they *debate* that innocent parties may put away guilty parties; they're *in fellowship* with innocent

Syllogism on Civil Law

- **Civil law doesn't affect the truth**

  Ac. 4.19, 5.29

- **Civil law affects the "bound to fornicator" position**

  (previous two charts)

- **Therefore, the "bound to fornicator" position is not the truth!**

Since when does the action of an ungodly citizen under an ungodly government affect the rights of the godly?

Figure 27

parties who put away guilty parties; and *innocent parties are not bound to guilty parties*.

On the other hand, under a civil government that allows divorce for other than fornication, they *preach* that innocent parties may not put away guilty parties; they *debate* that innocent parties may not put away guilty parties; they're *not in fellowship* with innocent parties who put away guilty parties; and *innocent parties are bound to guilty parties*. Again, the only difference between the two positions is the whims of civil government!

Figure 27 concludes this point with a syllogism on civil law. The major premise is:

> Civil law doesn't affect the truth, Mk. 7.8-9, Ac. 4.19, 5.29.

The minor premise is:

> Civil law affects the "bound to fornicator" position.

Therefore, the inescapable conclusion is:

> Therefore, the "bound to fornicator" position is not the truth.

We know that the Mormons believe that civil law negated their doctrine on polygamy. Do we believe civil law negates Jesus' teaching on divorce and remarriage?

Smith's "Wrong Order" Argument

The author well remembers the first time he saw J. T. Smith use the chart shown in Figure 28 in the Smith-Lovelady Debate, because it seemed unanswerable. Smith used this very effective chart to oppose the proposition that an unjustly put-away person can put away a fornicating spouse.

As the chart shows, Smith argued that we're getting things out of the Biblical order, which he said reads in Mt. 19.9: marry, put away, commit adultery. He said our order is wrong in that we're teaching: marry, commit adultery, put away. Thus, our order is wrong because it isn't God's order.

To compound our offense, Smith then said that God's order on baptism is believe, be baptized, be saved. When Baptists argue that you believe, then you're saved, then you're baptized, we oppose their order because it's not God's order on baptism. Thus, our argument is no better than Baptist doctrine.

J. T. Smith's "Wrong Order" Chart

"But I say unto you, whosoever shall put away his wife, except it be for fornication, and shall marry another, committeth adultery: and whoso marrieth her which is put away doth commit adultery." Mt. 19.9.

I. GOD'S ORDER

Put Away	Marry	Adultery

II. OPPONENT'S ORDER

Marry	Adultery	Put Away

III. GOD'S ORDER

Believe	Baptized	Saved

IV. BAPTISTS' ORDER

Believe	Saved	Baptized

(Smith-Lovelady Debate, p. 103.)

Figure 28

Smith's "Wrong Order" Chart

I. GOD'S ORDER				
Marry	Put Away	Marry	Adultery	Put Away

Figure 29

Sounds pretty effective, doesn't it? This writer sure thought so! But as you begin to think about it more closely, what Smith was calling God's order is *God's order if you want to result in adultery*! It's the putting away not for fornication and remarriage that results in adultery in Mt. 19.9. If we don't want to end up in adultery, we might suspect that our order needs to be different.

To see what's wrong with Smith's argument, we need to analyze the first line in his chart a little closer in Figure 29. You will see that we have added a marriage at the first of Line 1, which is the original marriage, that is, before the unscriptural putting away. We also added another putting away at the end of Line 1, which is the putting away for fornication. Here we are merely adding a beginning action and an ending action to the actual sequence of events.

In Figure 30, we labeled each of the events in Line 1. The first marriage is a valid one, recognized by God while the first divorce is not for fornication, authorized and recognized only by civil government. The second marriage in Line 1 is authorized and recognized only by civil government, which Jesus said results in adultery. With all these points so far, Smith agrees. The last divorce in Line 1 is the one Jesus authorized for fornication, but

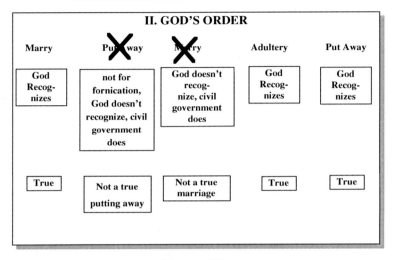

Figure 30

which Smith denies because of the actions of the ungodly man under the ungodly government.

In Figure 31, we cross out civil government's unscriptural actions. The first divorce was not for fornication, and didn't affect the marriage bond. The second marriage was unauthorized and resulted in adultery. We cross them out because we all agree that God doesn't recognize them as valid. This leaves the original scriptural marriage, the adultery, and the scriptural putting away for adultery. This is our order, the same order that Smith calls "The Opponent's Order."

In summary on Smith's "Wrong Order" chart, he is merely listing different items in the same sequence of events, and is paying too much attention to the unscriptural actions of an ungodly man under an ungodly government. His order results in adultery, ours does not.

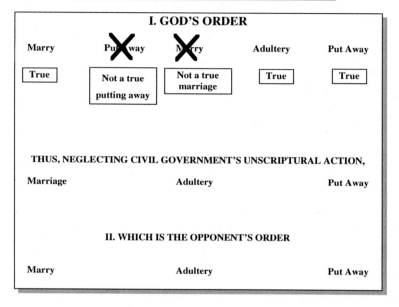

Figure 31

Authority for One Unjustly Put Away to Put Away a Fornicating Spouse

In Figure 32 we establish scriptural authority for one who is unjustly put away to then put away a fornicating spouse, using the necessary implication contained in the exception clause of Mt. 19.9. As we've noticed before, in Mt. 19.9, Jesus said:

> Whosoever shall put away his wife, *except for fornication*, and shall marry another, *committeth adultery.*

Because of the exception clause, Jesus necessarily implied:

Whosoever shall put away his wife *for fornication*, and shall marry another, *doth not commit adultery.*

This is the right of the other spouse to put away a fornicating spouse. Jesus never directly stated it, but it's necessarily implied in the exception clause. The "whosoever" here would include those who have been unjustly put away. Mt. 19.9 necessarily implies authority for those unjustly put away to put away a spouse who commits fornication through the courts.

Smith's prohibition essentially adds another exception clause. His version is:

Those Unjustly Put Away Can Put Away a Fornicating Spouse

MT. 19.9 SAYS:

"WHOSOEVER shall put away his wife, except for fornication, and shall marry another, commits adultery."

MT. 19.9 NECESSARILY IMPLIES:

WHOSOEVER shall put away his wife FOR FORNICATION, and shall marry another, commits no adultery.

YET SOME TEACH:

WHOSOEVER [EXCEPT THOSE UNJUSTLY PUT AWAY] shall put away his wife FOR FORNICATION, and shall marry another, commits no adultery.

Figure 32

Whosoever (*except one unjustly put away*) puts away his wife for fornication, and shall marry another, doth not commit adultery.

So we conclude that if we don't pay too much attention to civil law, as do Smith, Lanier, Deaver, and others, Jesus implicitly authorizes one unjustly put away to put away a fornicating spouse.

May One Guilty Party Put Away Another?

Traditionally, we've read the put-away fornicator into Mt. 19.9, even though the Jews didn't ask Jesus about the fornication case, and Jesus specifically excluded the case from his answer. We then said, "This passage gives the innocent party the right to remarry, but not the guilty." When we faced the highly realistic case of two fornicators in one marriage, we were forced to say that since there was no innocent party, "They are just hung," as one preacher said, and neither party can put away the other and remarry. As we've just seen, Smith must add another exception clause to Mt. 19.9 to prevent an unjustly put-away person from putting away a fornicating spouse. This observation raises the question of whether one guilty party may put away another guilty party. This is easily answered by noticing what Jesus implied:

Whosoever puts away his wife for fornication, and shall marry another, doth not commit adultery.

The "whosoever" here would include a fornicating spouse, unless we wish to imitate Smith and add another exception clause to Jesus' statement as well, producing:

Whosoever (*except one guilty of fornication himself*) puts away his wife for fornication, and shall marry another, doth not commit adultery.

NOTE: This is general authority for one guilty party to put away another and remarry without committing adultery in the new marriage.

How Would an Unjustly Put Away Person Put Away a Fornicating Spouse?

A very practical question arises: How would one who had been unjustly put away in the eyes of God then put away a fornicating spouse? As always, the key is not to allow the civil government to take away a right given by Christ. One option would be for the unjustly put-away one to go to the county courthouse and say, "Hello, you may not remember me, but my husband and I were here last month when he divorced me against my will for a trivial reason, certainly not for fornication. He didn't have the right to do that, but he has now remarried, thereby committing adultery, so I want to put him away for the reason Jesus said." With this approach, the conversation would go no further, because all the clerks would fall down laughing behind the counter.

So the unjustly put-away one must recognize the civil government's interest in divorce. The civil government isn't interested in how a person's spouse treats him, how he treats his spouse, the teaching of Christ, or why the divorce took place. The civil government is interested in only one thing: property, for taxation purposes. When the civil government granted the unscriptural divorce, it took care of its sole interest at that time: it divided up the property of each spouse in its computer database. If the unjustly put-away spouse now privately puts away the fornicating spouse, as Joseph was going to do with Mary, and as was authorized by Moses originally, civil government's interest is already satisfied. So a trip to the courthouse is not even necessary, any more than it was in Deuteronomy 24 or in Matthew 1.

Since the word "put away" literally means "to bid to go away," the unjustly put-away one could go to the now adulterous spouse, or if that's not practical, write him a letter, which says something like this: "When you treacherously put me away, you didn't have a scriptural basis for doing so, and had we not been living under a civil government that allowed it, you wouldn't have been able to do it. However, your ungodly actions under an ungodly government alter not one whit the authority Jesus implicitly gives me to put you away for your fornication, which I hereby now do." In this way, an unjustly put-away one could follow the teaching of Jesus in Mt. 19.9 and scripturally put away a fornicating spouse, which would give that spouse the right to remarry.

Conclusion

We have now dealt with one of the critical and controversial questions and seen that one cannot deny the right of an unjustly put-away person to then put away a fornicating spouse. We next deal with the second critical and controversial question, whether one who is scripturally put away may remarry.

Chapter 10

Remarriage of the Put-Away Fornicator

Highlights

- *A put away fornicator may remarry and still displease God.*
- *Whether a put away fornicator may remarry is hardly the issue.*

We've now covered the first critical and controversial question dealing with "the problem" of unscriptural divorce and remarriage situations. This first question concerns whether an unjustly put-away spouse may put away a fornicating mate. Now we're ready to deal with the second critical and controversial question: Can the put-away fornicator remarry?

A Simple Question That Should Be Answerable

We begin in Figure 33, not with an argument, but with a simple question that should be answerable. The purpose of this chart isn't so much to teach anything, as it is to get people to slow down and make sure they've read Mt. 19.9 and Mt. 5.32. The writer knows he preached about these verses for a long time before he slowed down and actually read these passages for himself. Over the years, he's handed hundreds of people copies of this chart to see if he could get them to stop making creedal statements ("this passage gives the innocent party the right to remarry, but not the guilty") about these verses and preaching about them long enough to actually read the passages, maybe for

A Simple Question
That Should Be Answerable

In Mt. 19.9, Jesus said:

"Whosoever shall put away his wife, except for fornication, and shall marry another, committeth adultery: and he that marrieth her when she is put away committeth adultery."

A typical statement of the commonly accepted view of Mt. 19.9 is as follows:

"There He taught that if the companion be guilty of fornication that the innocent party has a right to put the guilty party away and exercise personal license to remarry. Liberty is not expressed or implied to the guilty party to either disengage his marriage because of his personal guilt, or to benefit thereby the contract of another marriage." (H. L. Bruce, *Truth, XX*, #3, p. 9, January 15, 1976.)

QUESTIONS:

1. Do you agree with this commonly accepted view of Mt. 19.9 concerning the right of remarriage of the guilty party. YES_____ NO_____

2. If yes, do you agree that since Jesus does not either by direct statement or approved example deal with the case of a putting away for fornication in Mt. 19.9, that such conclusions must be reached by necessary implication? YES_____ NO_____

3. If yes, please list the logical sequence whereby you reached the inescapable conclusion from Mt. 19.9 that the put away fornicator commits adultery when he remarries:

Signature_____

Figure 33

the first time in their lives. Perhaps the reader has already done that, but many people have not.

The writer's experience has been that when he held that position, after reading these passages he couldn't talk about the guilty party question for very long, or write about it for very many words. He also noticed that other preachers and writers did the same thing. They would quote the passage, speak quite a bit about the unscriptural divorce situation, but then treat the for-fornication aspect pretty lightly, making; of course, the required statement to show one wasn't a false teacher on the subject. The chart is reprinted here to encourage the student to copy it and use it with those with whom he studies and discusses this subject. The exercise goes like this.

In Mt. 19.9, Jesus said:

Whosoever shall put away his wife, except for fornication, and shall marry another, committeth adultery: and he that marrieth her when she is put away committeth adultery.

A typical statement of the commonly accepted view of Mt. 19.9 is as follows:

"There he taught that if the companion be guilty of fornication that the innocent party has a right to put the guilty party away and exercise personal license to remarry. Liberty is not expressed or implied to the guilty party to either disengage his marriage, because of his personal guilt, or to benefit thereby by the contract of another marriage." (H. L. Bruce, *Truth, XX*, #3, p. 9, January 15, 1976.)

QUESTIONS:

1. Do you agree with this commonly accepted view of Mt. 19.9 concerning the right of remarriage of the guilty party? YES___ NO___

This is not a trick question, nor seeking a commitment to anything the writer has set forth in this volume. It's just a person's declaration to himself of what he presently believes about the passage. Of course, the vast majority of preachers, at least, will answer YES to the question.

2. If yes, do you agree that since Jesus does not either by
direct statement or approved example deal with the case
of a putting away for fornication in Mt. 19.9, that such
conclusions must be reached by necessary implication?
YES___ NO___

The purpose of this question is to help someone realize that
Jesus didn't say anything about a for-fornication divorce or
remarriage in Mt. 19.9. As we've noted earlier, the Jews didn't
care about a for-fornication divorce when they asked the question
as they knew what they could do in such cases. Not only did they
not have any controversy about a for-fornication divorce, but
Jesus *explicitly excluded* the fornication case in his answer! Yet
many come to this passage and say, "This passage gives the
innocent party the right to remarry, but not the guilty." As this
passage is given, there is no guilty party (guilty of fornication,
that is) in the entire passage before the divorce takes place. A
person filling out this chart needs to slow down enough in his
reading of the passage to notice that? If he hasn't, he'd better try
it again. Once he sees it, he is ready to go to the next question.

3. If yes, please list the logical sequence by which you
reached the inescapable conclusion from Mt. 19.9 that
the put-away fornicator commits adultery when he remarries.

When printed, the form from Figure 33 should leave a gener-
ous amount of blank space for the person answering it to present
his logical argument. A signature line is provided for the person
to sign his name if he's sufficiently confident that he can prove
what he believes about the passage. Over the twenty years that
the writer has used hundreds of copies of this form, only a handful
have chosen to fill out the blank space at the bottom, even among
some of the preachers who have preached and debated this
subject the most. One of the most personally powerful debaters
entered only "that's the sense of it." That's hardly a logical
sequence of argument, is it?

These are not trick questions, and they're not presented to
show how the writer powerfully put someone on the spot. It's a

reasonable approach to see if someone can back up his mantra on the subject, and as said before, to aid students of the subject to slow down until they've actually read the passage for themselves and to be responsible with themselves for dealing with it. It's not enough to just assume that the passage teaches what we've always assumed about it.

Thus far in our study, whether or not you agree with the writer's conclusions on this topic, we've already seen that a lot of our assumptions on this subject turned out not to be true at all. First, many of us thought the "unseemliness" or "indecency" in Dt. 24.1-4 couldn't be fornication because all the fornicators were stoned. That assumption was wrong. It led the writer astray for about seventeen years while he studied the subject. Second, many of us assumed therefore that God permitted loose divorce in the Old Testament, tacitly thinking that he shouldn't have, and we certainly wouldn't permit our preacher to do so. It turns out that that assumption wasn't right, either, and we actually think a lot more of God's law and treatment of women in the Old Testament, as a result. Third, we assumed that Mt. 5.32 and Mt. 19.9 were addressed to Christians, where the context shows that there wasn't a Christian in either passage, and Christians weren't talked about. That's another false assumption we're relieved from. Fourth, we assumed that Paul wasn't teaching something different than Jesus in I Cor. 7.12-16, but we found out that after Paul said he was going to teach something Jesus didn't teach, he actually taught something Jesus didn't teach.

Critical Question #2

May one put away for fornication remarry?

If cannot, all argue from one of two reasons:

Adultery will result, Mt. 19.9

No authority for him to do so

Figure 34

Hasn't enough time long past for us to stop making and believing assumptions on this subject? It behooves us not to just assume that Mt. 5.32 and 19.9 teach what we think they do. We need to give careful attention to determine what these passages actually do teach.

Overview of the Issues

We are now ready to slow down and stop and really examine these passages as we deal with the second critical and controversial question: Can the put-away fornicator remarry? To start with, Figure 34 helps us break the issue down a little more. It illustrates the fact that those who teach that the put-away fornicator may not remarry argue that (1) he will commit adultery if he does (Mt. 5.32, 19.9, etc.), or (2) there's no scriptural authority for him to do so. We will deal with both lines of argument.

On controversial issues, it is always helpful to clarify the issue by stating what the issue is not. Figure 35 illustrates what the issue is not. First, *the issue is not whether adultery is a grievous sin, or whether it's ever right*. It is always a grievous sin, and it's never right. A person can never continue in it and be pleasing to God.

The issue is not whether a put-away fornicator has a spouse. Everyone agrees that he does not. Most people understand that he couldn't have a spouse or the person who put him away for fornication couldn't remarry without committing adultery herself.

The issue is not whether the right to marry means that one is pleasing to God. It doesn't. This is important to realize because many times people assume that since one teaches that a put-away fornicator may remarry, that means that person thinks the put-away fornicator is pleasing to God. Not at all! There are hundreds of millions of people who have the right to marry, yet they are not pleasing to God. Never-married fornicators may marry. In fact, we hope many of them settle down and marry, and yet they're not pleasing to God, are they? A murderer may get out of prison (way too many of them do) and, if they don't have a spouse, they have the right to marry. Drunkards who don't have a spouse

What The Issue Is Not:

Whether adultery is a grievous sin

Whether a put-away fornicator has a spouse

Whether the right to marry means one is pleasing to God

Never-married fornicators may marry, yet not pleasing to God. Just not adultery when he marries.

Murderers may remarry without committing adultery, yet not pleasing to God.

Drunkard may marry, but not pleasing to God. Just not guilty of adultery when he marries.

Whether a put-away fornicator may remarry

Nearly all will allow put away fornicator to remarry:

when first spouse dies

if first spouse wants to remarry him/her

Figure 35

have a right to one, yet they are not pleasing to God. Thus, we shouldn't confuse the right to marry with being pleasing to God. They are not the same things.

The issue is not whether a put-away fornicator may remarry. Yes, that sentence is correct! The issue is not whether a put-away fornicator may remarry. Unless the writer is honestly mistaken, everyone that we'll quote in this study who disagrees with, and preaches and debates against our conclusions believes that a put-away fornicator may remarry when his first spouse dies, or if the first spouse wants to remarry him! This being true, the issue

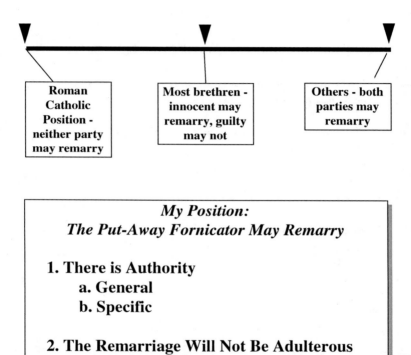

Figure 36

is not whether the put-away fornicator may remarry, but *when* he may remarry.

Last, *the issue is not whether all second marriages can be legitimate*, for the writer doesn't believe they can, either. If one is put away not for fornication and the spouse doesn't commit fornication, no second marriage that the put-away party enters will be legitimate until the first spouse dies, or is put away for his own fornication.

General Authority with No Specific Prohibition

Lending
  Mt. 5.42 - general authority to lend to all
  II Thes. 3.10 - a specific prohibition

Foods
  Mk. 7.19 - general authority for all foods
  I Tim. 4.3-4 - warnings against restrictions
  Ac. 15.29 - a specific prohibition

Bible Classes
  Ac. 20.28 - general authority to feed sheep
  I Pet. 5.1-2 - general authority to feed sheep
  _____ - where is a specific prohibition?
  NOTE: Not parallel to instrumental music argument:
      No general authority for instrumental music!

Remarriage of Put-Away Fornicator
  Gen. 2.18, 24 - general authority for all to have a spouse
  I Cor. 7.2, 9 - general authority for all to have a spouse
  I Tim. 4.3 - warning against prohibition

  _____ - where is a specific prohibition?

If there is no specific prohibition for the put-away fornicator to remarry, there is general authority!

Figure 37

Figure 36 illustrates the spectrum of beliefs on the remarriage of the guilty party. On the left end of the spectrum we have the Roman Catholic position of divorce only for fornication, but no remarriage for either party. Next to them, we have most of our brethren, who believe that divorce is only for fornication, but only the innocent party may remarry. On the right, we will be setting forth the same position Moses taught, that divorce is only for fornication, but that both parties may remarry. We will affirm that there is both general and specific authority for the put-away fornicator to remarry, and also that the remarriage will not be adulterous.

General Authority with No Specific Prohibition

Our demonstration of general authority for the put-away fornicator to remarry is given in Figure 37. We first establish that when there is general authority for a practice, with no specific prohibition for certain people or actions within that practice, then there is general authority for those certain people or actions to engage in the practice.

For example, on the subject of lending, in Mt. 5.42, Jesus said, "Give to him that asketh thee, and from him that would borrow of thee turn not thou away." Here is general authority for one to lend to anyone: a mailman, a farmer, a quadriplegic, anyone at all. However, Paul gave a specific prohibition in II Thes. 3.10, "If any will not work, neither let him eat." Thus, we don't have general authority to lend to anyone at all who will not work.

On the subject of foods, in Mk. 7.19, Jesus gave general authority to eat all foods, as Mark said, "This he said, making all meats clean." So beef, lamb, and pork, all of it were cleansed by Jesus. To make the case even stronger, Paul in I Tim. 4.3, warned of false teachers, who would be "forbidding to marry, and commanding to abstain from meats, which God created to be received with thanksgiving by them that believe and know the truth." However, in Ac. 15.29, we find a specific prohibition against certain kinds of meats: "that ye abstain from things sacrificed to idols, and from blood, and from things strangled, and from fornication; from which if ye keep yourselves, it shall be well with you."

Sometimes brethren question whether there is authority for dividing a congregation up into Bible classes, as there is no example of them in the Bible. I Peter 5.1-2 and Ac. 20.28 give general authority to the shepherds of a local church to tend and feed the flock of God which is among them. If physical shepherds tending physical sheep had orders from their master to feed their flock, and that was all that was said, they would understand that they had authority to divide up the sheep into rams, ewes, lambs, etc., for feeding, although no specific demands were made with respect to them. If there's no specific prohibition to the shepherds against dividing up the sheep, the spiritual shepherds have the same authority.

Someone might ask, "Isn't that the same as saying that if the Bible doesn't say not to, it's authorized?" No, if there is general authority for a practice, and "the Bible doesn't say not to" do a specific part of the practice for which there is general authority, then it's authorized. The general authority must come first.

As we come to the subject of marriage, there is general authority for all adults to have a spouse. In Gen. 2.18, God said, "It is not good for man to be alone." In verse 24 he said, "Let a man leave his father and mother and cleave unto his wife." In I Cor. 7.2, Paul said, "To avoid fornications, let each man have his own wife, and let each woman have her own husband." Likewise, in verse 9, he said of those who can't contain their sexual desires without marriage, "But if they have not continency, let them marry: for it is better to marry than to burn." The case is made even stronger in I Tim. 4.3, where Paul warned that false teachers would be "forbidding to marry, and commanding to abstain from meats, which God created to be received with thanksgiving by them that believe and know the truth."

Thus, *there is general authority for everyone to have a spouse, including a put-away fornicator, unless there is a specific prohibition for a put-away fornicator to have a spouse.* Of course, many will say, Mt. 5.32 and 19.9 contain such a specific prohibition. However, we're going to examine those passages carefully. We've already noticed that they say nothing directly about a for-fornication divorce. If after our examination we find that there is no specific prohibition, we note that there is general authority for a put-away fornicator to have a spouse.

Marriage, Divorce, & Remarriage

Exception Clause
Implies Specific Authority

Mt. 18.3 says:

"Except ye turn and become as little children, ye shall in no wise enter into the kingdom of heaven"

the exception necessarily implies:

those who turn and become as little children shall enter into the kingdom of heaven

Mt. 5.20 says:

"Except your righteousness shall exceed the righteousness of the scribes and Pharisees, ye shall in no wise enter into the kingdom of heaven"

the exception necessarily implies:

when your righteousness shall exceed the righteousness of the scribes and the Pharisees, you shall enter into the kingdom of heaven

Mt. 12.29 says:

"One cannot enter into the house of the strong man, and spoil his goods, except he first bind the strong man"

the exception necessarily implies:

when one first binds the strong man, he can enter into the house of the strong man, and spoil his goods.

Mt. 19.9 says:

"Whosoever shall put away his wife, except for fornication, and shall marry another, committeth adultery"

the exception necessarily implies:

Whosoever shall put away his wife for fornication, and shall marry another, doth not commit adultery.

This is why the "innocent party" can remarry:
by necessary implication!

Figure 38

Specific Authority from the Exception Clauses

Even though Jesus didn't say anything directly about a for-fornication divorce, the fact that he used exception clauses means that he necessarily implied certain truths about such divorce that are just as binding as if Jesus had uttered them in direct statements. In Figure 38, we see that in every case where an exception clause occurs in the New Testament, a necessary implication exists. For instance, in Mt. 18.3, Jesus said, "*Except* ye turn and become as little children, ye shall in no wise enter into the kingdom of heaven." Although Jesus never said it, he necessarily implied that "Those who turn and become as little children shall enter into the kingdom of heaven." We all believe what he necessarily implied.

In Mt. 5.20, Jesus said, "*Except* your righteousness shall exceed the righteousness of the scribes and Pharisees, ye shall in no wise enter into the kingdom of heaven." Although Jesus never said it, he necessarily implied, and we all believe, that "When your righteousness shall exceed the righteousness of the scribes and Pharisees, ye shall enter into the kingdom of heaven."

In Mt. 12.29, Jesus said, "How can one enter into the house of the strong man, and spoil his goods, *except* he first bind the strong man?" Although Jesus never said it, he necessarily implied, and we all believe, that "When one first binds the strong man, he can enter into the house of the strong man, and spoil his goods."

In Mt. 19.9, Jesus said, "Whosoever shall put away his wife, *except* for fornication, and shall marry another, committeth adultery." Although Jesus never said it, he necessarily implied, and nearly all believe, that "Whosoever shall put away his wife for fornication, and shall marry another, doth not commit adultery."

NOTE: This is why the one who puts away a fornicating spouse can remarry, by necessary implication. As we've already seen, the Roman Catholic position denies this necessary implication, because to them, the exception clause has no meaning at all.

In Figure 39, we continue. In Mt. 5.32, Jesus said, "Everyone that putteth away his wife, *saving* for [except for—SGD] the cause of fornication, maketh her an adulteress [when she remar-

**Exception Clause
Implies Specific Authority (Cont'd)**

Mt. 5.32 says:

"Everyone that putteth away his wife, saving for the cause of
fornication, maketh her an adulteress" [when she remarries]

the exception necessarily implies:

everyone that putteth away his wife for the cause of fornication,
doth not make her an adulteress [when she remarries]

---

*This is why the "guilty party" can remarry:
by necessary implication!*

***If the right of remarriage of the put-away fornicator
is not necessarily implied in Mt. 5.32, why is the
right of the innocent party to remarry necessarily
implied in Mt. 19.9?***

***If the right of remarriage of the put-away fornicator
is not necessarily implied in Mt. 5.32, then one
cannot enter into the kingdom of God when he is
born of the water and the Spirit!***

Figure 39

ries—SGD]." Although Jesus never said it, he necessarily implied, and we all should believe, that "Everyone that putteth away
his wife for the cause of fornication, doth not make her an
adulteress [when she remarries—SGD]." Suppose he did make

her an adulteress; it would be quite an indictment of the innocent party, wouldn't it?

NOTE: *This is specific authority for the put-away fornicator to remarry without committing adultery.* If someone objects that he doesn't make her an adulteress because she was already one before the divorce, let's don't change the subject. We, and Jesus, were talking about committing adultery when remarrying.

If the right of remarriage of the put-away fornicator is not necessarily implied in Mt. 5.32, why is the right of the innocent party to remarry necessarily implied in Mt. 19.9? The same process that proves one proves the other, i. e., that every exception clause contains a necessary implication.

We might parallel this to baptism. In Jn. 3.5, Jesus said, "*Except* one be born of water and the Spirit, he cannot enter into the kingdom of God." Although he never said it, Jesus necessarily implied, and we all believe, that "When one is born of water and the Spirit, he can enter into the kingdom of God." If the above implication that the put-away fornicator can remarry without committing adultery is not necessarily valid, then we have no assurance that one can enter the kingdom of God when he is born of water and the spirit.

Having seen how the exception clause in Mt. 5.32 necessarily implies that a put-away fornicator may remarry without committing adultery, we have also learned that this passage contains no specific prohibition to the remarriage of the guilty party. Thus, since we have already seen that there is general authority for everyone to have a spouse, *we also have general authority for a put-away fornicator to have a spouse with no specific prohibition.*

We see the same result in Mt. 19.9b, the remarriage clause, where Jesus said, "Whosoever puts away his wife, except for fornication, and shall marry another, committeth adultery; and he that marrieth her committeth adultery."

Substituting the phrase "the wife put away except for fornication" for the pronoun "her," which is entirely legitimate since pronouns are "for nouns," we get: "Whosoever puts away his wife, except for fornication, and shall marry another, committeth adultery; and he that marrieth *the wife put away except for fornication* committeth adultery." This is true, as we have seen before, and we believe it.

We then reverse the exception clause as we have before, since every exception clause in the Bible contains a necessary implication, an inescapable conclusion. We get the following necessary implication: "Whosoever puts away his wife *for fornication*, and shall marry another, *doth not commit adultery*; and he that marrieth the wife put away *for fornication doth not commit adultery*." Here again is specific authority for a put-away fornicator to remarry, from Mt. 19.9b. Also notice, that far from prohibiting a put-away fornicator from remarrying, the verse necessarily implies that he will not commit adultery if he does remarry. The use of pronouns in these verses (both Mt. 19.9b and Mt. 5.32) prohibits us from confusing what woman we're considering. While we're not reading the exception clause into the remarriage clause, the pronouns do serve to keep us talking about the same woman in the first and last parts of the verse.

Substituting for the pronouns "her" and "she" in Mt. 5.32 gives a similar result. Jesus said, "Everyone that putteth away his wife, saving for the cause of fornication, maketh her an adulteress: and whosoever shall marry her when she is put away committeth adultery." Replacing the pronouns with the person for whom they stand, the wife put away except for fornication, we get: "Everyone that putteth away his wife, saving for the cause of fornication, maketh *the wife put away saving for fornication* an adulteress; and whosoever shall marry *the wife put away saving for fornication* when *the wife put away saving for fornication* is put away committeth adultery."

Reversing the exception clause gives us the following necessary implication: "Everyone that putteth away his wife *for fornication, doth not make the wife put away for fornication* an adulteress; and whosoever shall marry *the wife put away for fornication* when *the wife put away for fornication* is put away *doth not commit adultery*."

As we've seen, this is specific authority for a put-away fornicator to remarry.

NOTE: Some of our readers will be aware that there is a textual question concerning Mt. 19.9b. It may be reflected in a footnote in Mt. 19.9 in your translation. Many textual scholars contend that this remarriage clause does not belong in the text, arguing that it is an interpolation from Mt. 5.32b. While the present author is not a textual scholar, he does observe that even if Mt. 19.9b doesn't belong in the text, the same inescapable conclusion is reached from Mt. 5.32, where there is no question of textual integrity.

A Put-Away Fornicator Has No Spouse

We now want to remind ourselves that a put-away fornicator has no spouse. No one who takes any position on marriage, divorce, and remarriage, whether they agree with the positions set forth in this book or not, disagrees with this statement. If someone were even slightly tempted to say he did have a spouse, the spouse would have to be the mate who put him away. We can't say the previous mate is the spouse or the innocent party couldn't remarry without committing adultery. *Thus, since the put-away fornicator has no spouse, he cannot commit adultery when he remarries, as long as he marries someone who has no spouse.* By definition, two spouseless people cannot commit adultery.

Recall that the definition of adultery is "illicit sexual intercourse involving a spouse." Let's read Mt. 5.32 as Jesus stated it, and then substitute the definition of the word adultery for the word itself. Substituting a definition for the word it defines is always a useful check to see if one is using a word correctly. Thus, in Mt. 5.32 Jesus said:

>...every one that putteth away his wife, saving for the cause of fornication, maketh her an adulteress: and whosoever shall marry her when she is put away committeth adultery.

Substituting the definition of adultery for the word adultery itself, we have:

>...every one that putteth away his wife, saving for the cause of fornication, maketh her to commit illicit sexual

Syllogism on Mt. 5.32

- Since the "her" of Mt. 5.32 commits adultery, she must be a spouse, Mk. 10.11-12, Ro. 7.2, 3

- But, a put-away fornicator has no spouse

- Therefore, the "her" of Mt. 5.32 cannot be a put-away fornicator

There is no prohibition for a put-away fornicator to remarry in Mt. 5.32

- By definition, adultery is limited to intercourse involving the spouse of another

- A put-away fornicator is not the spouse of anyone

- Therefore, a put-away fornicator cannot commit adultery when he remarries one who is not a spouse

There is no prohibition for a put-away fornicator to remarry in Mt. 5.32

Figure 40

intercourse involving a spouse: and whosoever shall marry her when she is put away committeth illicit sexual intercourse involving a spouse.

Now, since a put-away fornicator doesn't have a spouse, it's absolutely impossible by definition for him to commit adultery, the sin Jesus spoke of in Mt. 5.32 and Mt. 19.9, by remarrying someone who doesn't have a spouse.

We can see this illustrated in logical form in Figure 40, which by the definition of adultery, establishes that Mt. 5.32 does not prohibit the remarriage of the put-away fornicator. In the first

syllogism (a major premise, a minor premise, and a valid conclusion—SGD), we have:
Major premise:

> Since the put-away woman of Mt. 5.32 is committing adultery when she remarries, she must be a spouse of another. This is true since Jesus in Mk. 10.11-12 said adultery is against your spouse, and God's definition of adultery in Rom. 7.2-3 requires the involvement of a spouse to commit adultery.

Minor premise:

> A put-away fornicator has no spouse.

Conclusion:

> Therefore, the put-away woman of Mt. 5.32 cannot be a put-away fornicator.

In the second syllogism in Figure 40, we have:
Major premise:

> By definition, adultery is limited to illicit intercourse involving the spouse of another, Rom.7.2-3.

Minor premise:

> A put-away fornicator is not the spouse of anyone.

Conclusion:

> Therefore, a put-away fornicator cannot commit adultery with one who is not a spouse.

This is not complicated. These are simple, powerful arguments based solely on the definition of adultery.

In Figure 41, we offer a summary chart on Mt. 5.32 and Mt. 19.9. In the *not-for-fornication* case, we consider each of the three

Summary on Mt. 5.32, 19.9

Except for Fornication

The man putting away the woman commits adultery

    REASON: THE WOMAN IS STILL A SPOUSE

The put-away woman who remarries commits adultery

    REASON: THE WOMAN IS STILL A SPOUSE

The man who marries her commits adultery

    REASON: THE WOMAN IS STILL A SPOUSE

For Fornication

The man putting away the woman and remarrying commits no adultery

    REASON: THE WOMAN IS NOT STILL A SPOUSE

The put-away woman who remarries commits _____.

    REASON: THE WOMAN IS NOT STILL A SPOUSE

The man who marries her commits _____.

    REASON: THE WOMAN IS NOT STILL A SPOUSE

Figure 41

persons involved in the marriage-divorce-remarriage situation. (1) The man putting away the woman and remarrying commits adultery *because the woman is still his spouse.* (2) The woman put away who remarries commits adultery *because the woman is still a spouse of another.* (3) The man who marries the put-away woman commits adultery *because the woman is still a spouse of another.*

In the divorce *for fornication*, we consider the same three people. (1) the man putting away the woman and remarrying commits no adultery *because the woman is not still a spouse.* (2) The woman put away who remarries commits _____, *because the woman is not still a spouse.* (3) The man who marries the put-away woman commits _____ *because the woman is not still a spouse.* Historically, we have said the put-away fornicator commits adultery upon remarriage, but since we know he's not a spouse, what do we put in the blank? Surely, consistency will prevent us from putting the word "adultery" in it.

One Loosed from a Spouse May Have One

We have already noticed in I Cor. 7.2 that there is general authority for every person to have a spouse. In I Cor. 7.27-28, a passage we've not discussed before, Paul gave specific authority for one loosed from a spouse to have one. Paul said:

> Art thou bound unto a wife? Seek not to be loosed. Art thou loosed from a wife? Seek not a wife. But shouldest thou marry, thou hast not sinned; and if a virgin marry, she hath not sinned. Yet such shall have tribulation in the flesh: and I would spare you.

These instructions were given in the context of the Corinthian Christians facing an imminent distress, where in their case it was better not to marry. To the Corinthians Paul told the married to not seek to be loosed, a reference to divorce, unless one thinks he was telling them not to kill their wives. If they were loosed, they would be better off not seeking a wife, but if those loosed from wives did marry, they wouldn't commit sin.

Who are those loosed from a wife? Those divorced not for fornication would not be loosed because, still having a wife, they would commit adultery when they remarried. Widowers would be loosed from a wife. Would never-married bachelors be loosed from wives? Hardly, for they never had wives to be loosed from.

Those divorced for fornication would be loosed from wives, wouldn't they? Paul said, if they marry, they have not sinned.

A Syllogism on the Put-Away Fornicator

- **One loosed from a spouse may have one**

  I Cor. 7.27-28

- **A put-away fornicator has no spouse**

  Why his "innocent" ex-spouse may remarry

- **Therefore, a put-away fornicator may have a spouse**

NOTE:

This is specific authority for a put-away fornicator to have a spouse!

Figure 42

Here is specific authority for those loosed from a spouse to marry without sin.

This is shown in logical form in Figure 42.

Major premise:

One loosed from a spouse may have one, I Cor. 7.2, 27-28.

Minor premise:

A put-away fornicator has no spouse.

Conclusion:

Therefore, a put-away fornicator may have a spouse.

Summary on the Remarriage of the Put-Away Fornicator

In this chapter, we have shown that while the unscripturally divorced person may not remarry because he already has a spouse, the scripturally divorced person may remarry, because he does not have a spouse. The put-away fornicator also may remarry because there is general authority for everyone to have a spouse, but no one may have anyone else's spouse. He may remarry because Jesus necessarily implied that put-away fornicators might remarry without committing adultery. He may remarry because since he doesn't have a spouse, he cannot, by definition, commit the sin of adultery mentioned in Mt. 5.32 and Mt. 19.9. Finally, he may remarry because Paul gave specific authority for those loosed from wives to remarry without sin.

This position is not new, for it's the same principle Moses taught in Dt. 24.1-4. Nor is it new because Jesus necessarily implied the same truth in Mt. 5.32 and Mt. 19.9. However, it's not even as new as the present century. The legendary J. W. McGarvey, historic preacher in the restoration movement in America in the nineteenth century, wrote:

HER THAT IS PUT AWAY—That is, put away for some other cause than fornication. Whether it would be adultery to marry a woman who had been put away on account of fornication, is neither affirmed nor denied. No doubt such a woman is at liberty to marry again if she can, seeing that the bond which bound her to her husband is broken. (J. W. McGarvey, *Commentary on Matthew and Mark* [Delight, AR: Gospel Light, 1875], p. 165.)

We would agree with McGarvey that "Whether it would be adultery to marry a woman who had been put away on account of fornication, is neither affirmed nor denied." We would say that it is necessarily implied that it would not be adultery to marry a woman who had been put away for fornication.

Three Things The Negative Must Do

To successfully negate the position we've set forth herein, it appears there are three things which must be done:

1. One must insert the put-away fornicator into the remarriage clauses of Mt. 5.32 and Mt. 19.9 as written, although the Jews didn't ask Jesus about a putting away for fornication, and Jesus specifically excluded the case from his answer. This is historically what has happened to these passages, although it is very hard to get anyone taking this position to fill out the chart we started this chapter with. Basically, when students slow down enough to really read these verses, they realize that there is no guilty party anywhere in the text. We have just been conditioned to read in the guilty party.

2. One must change the definition of adultery. Within recent years, several brethren have done this, setting forth definitions different from God's definition in the Bible (Rom. 7.2-3) and all the standard lexicons of the original languages. These are new definitions that no one on earth ever heard of until the last quarter of the twentieth century. This raises the specter of men urging people to break up marriages and remain celibate when they didn't even know what the word adultery meant.

A few of those having already taken a stand in support of the standard definition of adultery include Bryan Vinson, Jay Bowman, Gene Frost, Roy Lanier, Maurice Barnett, J. D. Thomas, and J. T. Smith. New definitions have come from J. T. Smith, David Bonner, and Olan Hicks. We've already examined Hicks' definition. Smith's and Bonner's will be reviewed in the next chapter, "The Celibacy Position Examined."

3. One must deny the general authority Paul gives in I Cor. 7.2 for everyone to have a spouse, as well as the specific authority he gives for the loosed person to have one, I Cor. 7.27-28.

We close this chapter with Figure 43, which shows our plan of study completed.

Plan of Study

Old Testament

Not for fornication

No, Mt. 5.32, 19.9

Neither party can remarry
   without committing
   adultery

For fornication

Yes, Dt. 24.1-4

Both parties could remarry

Mixed Marriages Not Considered: Ex. 34.14-16, Dt. 7.3, Josh. 23.12-13, Neh. 10.29-30, 13.23-30

New Testament

Not for fornication

No, I Cor. 7.10-11

Mt. 5.32, 19.9
Mk. 10.11
Lk. 16.18
Neither party can remarry
without committing adultery.

For fornication

Yes, Mt. 5.32

Both parties may remarry

Mixed Marriages: I Cor. 7.12-16

Figure 43

Chapter 11

The Celibacy Position Examined

Highlights

- *Conservative positions aren't always safe.*
- *We don't disagree whether put-away fornicators may remarry, merely when.*
- *Yes, bread burners may be guilty, and fornicators innocent.*

In the previous chapter, we set forth our understanding of the right of the put-away fornicator to remarry. Since this is not a prevalent position among many Christians, in this chapter we wish to consider arguments that have been advanced against it.

The Seriousness of the Question

Regardless of the position one takes on the question of whether or not a put-away fornicator can remarry, it is, indeed, a serious question. If God does not allow the put-away fornicator to remarry, and it is in fact adultery or scripturally unauthorized for him to do so, we are guilty of encouraging his adultery or otherwise unscriptural actions. On the other hand, Figure 44 shows the seriousness of opposing our position should it be the truth.

First of all, if we forbid a put-away fornicator from having a spouse when God actually permits it, then I Tim. 4.3, where Paul warned of false teachers who would "forbid to marry" applies to us. Although Paul's teaching probably applied to Gnostics (who taught celibacy, not to have a spouse, for higher spirituality) in the eyes of his first century audience, many of us have heard these verses applied with relish to Roman Catholic celibacy. In any event, none of us would enjoy hearing the warning applied to ourselves.

Additionally, if we get a put-away fornicator who has remar-

The Celibacy Position Examined

The Seriousness of the Question:

If we forbid one to have a spouse when God permits it, I Tim. 4.3 applies to us.

If we get someone out of a valid second marriage, Mt. 19.6 applies to us.

⇨ **It's not always safe to take a more conservative position.**

It's never safe to bind where God didn't!

Figure 44

ried out of a second marriage that God permits, then Jesus' statement in Mt. 19.6 ("whatsoever God hath joined together, let not man put asunder") applies to us as well. As we've said before, it's not always safe to take the more conservative position, especially if we're attempting to bind it on others. If I want to take the more conservative position for myself, that's fine. But it's never safe to bind on others what God has not, and it's not conservative at all to make a law where God has not.

The Celibacy Position Stated

We present several quotations from prominent brotherhood scholars and preachers, and others, to let the reader see the celibacy position for himself. First, J. W. McGarvey, an authentic scholar of the restoration movement in America in the latter 1800s and early 1900s stated his opposition to the put-away fornicator remarrying this way:

> It is implied that divorce for unchastity breaks the marriage bond, and it is therefore held almost universally, both by commentators and moralists, that the innocent party to such a divorce can marry again. Of course the guilty party could not, for no one is allowed by law to reap the benefits of his own wrong. (J. W. McGarvey and Phillip Y. Pendleton, *The Fourfold Gospel* [Cincinnati, OH: Standard Publishing Foundation, 1914], p. 252.)

While we're not attempting a detailed refutation of McGarvey's position here, we do wish the reader to notice several facts about this statement for his own study. Since this statement was made from his commentary on the gospels, it undoubtedly reflected his views on Mt. 5.32 and 19.9. Of course, McGarvey is reading the guilty party (guilty of fornication, that is) into a passage where the Jews weren't interested in the for-fornication case, and Jesus explicitly excluded it from his answer. Notice also his use of the word "lawful" here. When the Jews asked "is it lawful," they were asking from the point of view of the Mosaic Law; McGarvey undoubtedly was not. Finally, notice the statement that "no one is allowed by law to reap the benefits of his own wrong." Although McGarvey gave no scriptural foundation for this statement, it figures mightily in the writing and thinking of legions of people on this subject.

Interestingly, McGarvey earlier had written quite a different thought on the subject:

> ...her that is put away. That is, put away for some other cause than fornication. Whether it would be adultery to

marry a woman who had been put away on account of fornication, is neither affirmed nor denied. No doubt such a woman is at liberty to marry again if she can, seeing that the bond which bound her to her husband is broken." (J. W. McGarvey, *Commentary on Matthew. and Mark* [Delight, AR: Gospel Light, 1875], p. 165.)

H. Leo Boles, another legendary preacher in the restoration movement, wrote:

Unlawful intercourse with any other person permits the innocent party to break the marriage tie; the guilty party has deserted forever the marriage partner; and has become unfit for further association; the guilty party can never again enter a pure and lawful marriage covenant. (H. Leo Boles, *Commentary on Matthew* [Nashville, TN: Gospel Advocate Company, 1936, 1964 Reprint], p. 389.)

If the reader thinks this is good preaching, he needs to ask himself, what passage would he appeal to in the Bible to sustain the statements "The guilty party has become unfit for further association," and "The guilty party can never again enter a pure and lawful marriage covenant"? Surely the put-away fornicator is a grievous sinner, and until he repents in obedience to the gospel, he cannot be in fellowship with God. However, our desire to see him get his just desserts doesn't relieve us of our obligation to have divine authority for such a regulation. Boles offered none to help us. From past experience, the writer knows he has the courage to preach this way; he'd just like to have a passage of scripture to base the sermon on.

W. M. Foley, an encyclopaedist, wrote:

Hence it is maintained that the passage in Matthew may be taken as a fuller expression of the Lord's mind than the briefer passages in the other Gospels, that we have His *express sanction for divorce in case of adultery* [emphasis mine—SGD], with the consequent permission to marry again in the case of the innocent partner. It is not, of course denied that, if the bond is broken, it is broken alike for both partners, but, as the guilty partner is, or has been, living in notorious sin, and can give no evidence of repentance except by abstaining altogether from marriage, such guilty partner must necessarily be refused the Church's benediction in the case of remarriage. The latter principle has been invariably and universally accepted." (James Hastings, editor and W. M. Foley, *Encyclopaedia of Religion and Ethics,* VIII, [New York, NY: Charles Scribner's Sons, 1958], p. 438.)

There are several notable things about this quotation. First, Foley said Jesus gave an "express sanction for divorce in the case of adultery." This is simply not true, whether the author's positions are true or not. As we have seen, whatever Jesus taught about divorce for fornication, he taught not expressly, but by necessarily implying it. He expressly taught about not-for-fornication divorce, and expressly taught *nothing* about for-fornication divorce. Anybody who would make such a statement probably didn't even know how to demonstrate the right of an innocent party to put away a fornicating spouse.

It is interesting to note that Foley thought that the marriage bond was broken alike for both partners. However, what is the basis that the put-away fornicator "can give no evidence of repentance except by abstaining altogether from marriage"? Surely, if Foley had known of a passage telling the put-away fornicator to abstain from marriage, wouldn't he have stated it? Then he wouldn't have had to resort to such a statement as this. This statement has no more scriptural basis than Roman Catholic arguments for priestly celibacy.

Finally, notice "such guilty partner must necessarily be refused the Church's benediction in the case of remarriage." The interjection of the Church (whether he means universal, local, or in a denominational sense, he doesn't say) is something new. Marriage and divorce in the Bible was private. Isaac took Rebekah into his tent and knew her. As we've noted before, there was no preacher, no marriage license, no county record, no church, no wedding, and now, no benediction of the Church.

Joseph was minded to privily divorce Mary, again with no county record or benediction of the Church.

One final quotation to establish the celibacy position is from J. D. Thomas, scholarly professor at Abilene Christian University:

> The original marriage called for a union until death, which each spouse was obligated to uphold. The only thing that can ever break the marriage bond while both parties are alive is fornication; and that only for the innocent party! "Except for fornication" is the one justifying ground for remarriage to another, but the guilty party does not have this justifying ground. It is possible only for the innocent spouse. The guilty one is therefore still under all obligations toward the first marriage that he ever was, in the sense of being "bound to it" by God's law. Nothing has happened to give him freedom! He is still "handcuffed to God's law," though not to his former wife...Therefore he would commit adultery if he remarried. (Matthew 19:9) (J. D. Thomas, *Divorce & Remarriage* [Abilene, TX: Biblical Research Press, 1977], p. 57.)

There are several things in this quotation the reader should note. First, fornication never broke a marriage bond, only a putting away for fornication and death did that. Second, Thomas doesn't prove any of his conclusions about a for-fornication divorce. He just sprinkles down a proof text, in which Jesus excluded for-fornication divorces! Third, Thomas' treatment of the exception clause is completely vaporous. Fourth, Thomas claimed that the put-away fornicator is still "bound to the marriage" after the divorce. However, we can read where the wife is bound to the husband in marriage (Rom. 7.2-3), and the husband is bound to the wife (I Cor. 7.39), but nowhere does the Bible say anything about anyone ever being bound to a marriage. Fifth, Thomas treats us to the "handcuffed to God's law" mantra, with nary a Bible passage to base it on.

With these cursory observations about these statements of the celibacy position, we now review arguments advanced for the celibacy position. As we have pointed out, the issue of the put-away fornicator is not really about whether he may remarry, but when. This is true since the vast, vast majority of those who contend he cannot remarry admit he can if (1) his first spouse dies, or (2) his first spouse takes him back. This negates every argument we're about to see in these two cases. It may become tiresome to see this negation pointed out, but it needs to be done. These teachers make some awfully powerful sounding arguments, yet everyone of them self-destruct when (1) the first spouse dies, or (2) the first spouse takes him back. If the proponents of these arguments don't believe them when the first spouse dies or takes the partner back, why should anyone else believe them under any circumstance? It's like we tell our Mormon friends. If they don't believe Joseph Smith enough to obey him and publicly defend his claims to be a prophet of God when he commands them to "confute your enemies publicly and privately; and inasmuch as ye are faithful, their shame shall be made manifest" (*Doctrine & Covenants* 71.7), why should we believe him? In like manner, if the teachers of the celibacy position won't defend their arguments in all situations, why should we accept their interpretation of limited, specialized situations?

"Remarriage of Guilty Party Encourages Deliberate Sin"

This is probably the most popular argument made against the right of remarriage of the guilty party. Many believe, "It just cannot be the case that the put-away fornicator can remarry, for men would deliberately commit fornication in hope that their wife would divorce them so they could remarry." This is extremely powerful logic in the minds of some, but let's notice the following fallacies of this argument:

1. This argument is nullified if those who make it believe that the put-away fornicator may remarry after the first spouse dies. It doesn't make any difference how deliberate the sin was; if the first spouse just dies, the argument goes away.

2. This argument is nullified if those who make it believe that the put-away fornicator may remarry the first spouse. It doesn't

make any difference how deliberate the sin was; if the first spouse just takes him back, the argument goes away.

3. We all teach that an alien sinner may kill, steal, get drunk, and repent and be baptized to be forgiven. Does that mean that we encourage killing, stealing, or drunkenness? Even if it does, the Bible still teaches it (Ac. 2.38)!

4. We teach repentance, confession, and prayer for remission of sins for Christians. Does that encourage sin? Even if it does, the Bible still teaches it (Ac. 8.22, I Jn. 1.6-10)!

5. When we teach that the put-away fornicator may remarry, someone may ask, "If that's true, what's to stop a married man from seeing another woman, deciding he would like to be rid of his wife, let her put him away for fornication, and remarry the newer model?" Here's the answer: Absolutely nothing! What's to keep the man from murdering his wife? Absolutely nothing! This is where the Pharisees wanted to step in and close loopholes in God's law. As someone wisely said, "Pharisees are like law-yers, and you know how lawyers are: they build high fences around the laws they want to have obeyed, and leave loopholes around the ones they don't want to obey." It's not our job to close loopholes God left in his own law. God didn't even do that. God gave us our free will, and doesn't force us to do right. So let's not help God out by closing the loopholes we don't like.

In I Tim. 1.8, Paul said, "We know that the law is good, if a man use it lawfully." If someone wants to use the law unlawfully, it can be done, but that doesn't change the law, does it? The law is still good.

The celibacy position is not immune from such abuse, either. The Roman Catholic argument that even the innocent party cannot remarry is based upon a similar argument: "All he has to do is provoke his spouse to commit adultery, then he can put her away and remarry." That's true, but that still doesn't change God's law, even if a man uses it unlawfully.

6. Such high-handed sinners are not likely to care about the scripturalness of their marriage. If they do, they're overlooking much more serious spiritual problems.

7. The conduct of high-handed sinners doesn't determine the truth on any subject. For example, wife murderers may remarry

without committing adultery. Do the actions of high-handed murderers mean all murderers must remain celibate?

"No One Is Allowed to Enjoy the Fruit of His Own Sin"

This argument is an extremely influential one. Why should the scoundrel that is unfaithful to his wife be allowed to enjoy a new marriage?

1. This argument is nullified if those who make it believe that the put-away fornicator may remarry after the first spouse dies. Why should the scoundrel that is unfaithful to his wife be allowed to enjoy a new marriage?

2. This argument is nullified if those who make it believe that the put-away fornicator may remarry his first wife. Why should the scoundrel that is unfaithful to his wife be allowed to enjoy an old marriage?

3. This is the argument we've already seen from J. W. McGarvey, who said, "Of course, the guilty party could not, for no one is allowed by law to reap the benefits of his own wrong." Question: Where is the passage in the law that teaches that? This is a legitimate question. Don't we need some Bible teaching as a basis before we forbid to marry, command celibacy, and put asunder marriages that God may in reality permit? The writer thinks as much of McGarvey as anyone, but he still needs a passage of scripture, doesn't he?

4. If the guilty party cannot enjoy the fruits of his own sin, is it proper for the innocent party to enjoy the fruits of it, if she finally got rid of a scoundrel for a husband?

5. In II Sam. 12.27, David kept Bathsheba, which was a case of adultery followed by murder! He got to keep children from that marriage. Evidently, folks couldn't find a passage for McGarvey's position in the Old Testament, either.

6. In Ac. 2.37-38, Peter preached the first gospel sermon to the very people who had killed the Messiah, and were proud of it. When Peter convinced them that they had killed the very one they were looking for, here was their reaction:

Now when they heard this, they were pricked in their
heart, and said unto Peter and the rest of the apostles,
Brethren, what shall we do? And Peter said unto them,
Repent ye, and be baptized every one of you in the name
of Jesus Christ unto the remission of your sins; and ye
shall receive the gift of the Holy Spirit.

Could these men benefit from their deliberate shedding of the
blood of Christ? If not, Peter preached false doctrine in his first
sermon!

7. How far do we take this? Do we use this principle to take
away babies from unwed mothers so they can't enjoy them?
Suppose a man ran a stop sign and killed his rich aunt; could he
receive the estate she left him in her will? Would we say, "No,
you can't have it. J. W. McGarvey said, 'No one is allowed by
law to benefit from his own wrong.' "? If a woman nagged her
drunkard husband till he committed fornication (or shot himself),
could she put him away for fornication (or bury him) and remarry
a tea-totaller?

8. Again, using a law unlawfully doesn't change the law.

J. T. Smith's Absurdity Chart

In his debate with Bob Melear, J. T. Smith, who has debated
this subject many times, produced the tremendously effective
chart shown in Figure 45. Smith said:

If one is put away for some cause other than fornication,
when that person remarries, he commits adultery. My
opponent agrees, I agree. BUT if one is put away for
fornication, when that person remarries, he does not
commit adultery. My opponent agrees, I disagree. ONE
REASON FOR DISAGREEING: God said he would
judge adulterers (Heb. 13.4). But according to my opponent's position, God judges the "bread burner" guilty and
the fornicator innocent. Thus God's consequences are
much greater for the "bread burner" than for the fornicator. THIS IS ABSURD!

Objection #3: J. T. Smith's Absurdity Chart

Opponent's Position Reduced to An Absurdity
(Smith-Melear Debate)

"If one is put away for some cause other than fornication, when that person remarries, he commits adultery. My opponent agrees, I agree. BUT if one is put away for fornication, when that person remarries he does not commit adultery. My opponent agrees, I disagree. ONE REASON FOR DISAGREEING: God said he would judge adulterers (Heb. 13.4). But according to my opponent's position, God judges the 'bread burner' guilty and the fornicator innocent. Thus God's consequences are much greater for the 'bread burner' than for the fornicator. THIS IS ABSURD!"

This argument is nullified if those who make it believe the put-away fornicator may remarry after the first spouse dies.

This argument is nullified if those who make it believe the put-away fornicator may remarry the first spouse.

Agree "God will judge adulterers" - but where is celibacy part of that judgment?

"God judges bread burner guilty" - yes, but of adultery, not for burning bread!

"God judges fornicator innocent" - not of fornication! But he's not guilty of adultery because he remarries after having been put away - he has no spouse!

Figure 45

The first time the writer saw this chart, it bowled him over, so no one should feel bad if it does the same thing to him the first time he sees it. It's an ingenious, but incorrect argument, for the following reasons:

1. This argument is nullified if the one who makes it believes the put-away fornicator can remarry after the first spouse dies. It just doesn't make any difference how absurd an argument is!

2. This argument is nullified if the one who makes it believes the put-away fornicator can remarry the first spouse. If she'll just take him back, absurdity is acceptable, apparently.

3. We agree that "God will judge adulterers," but where does the Bible say celibacy is part of that judgment?

4. When Smith said, "God judges the bread burner guilty," stop and think. What is the bread burner guilty of? Bread burning? What is the Biblical penalty for burning the bread? No, he's guilty of committing adultery because it is a sin to take another spouse when you already have one, and the bread burner already had a spouse. When the bread burner remarries, she is guilty of the same sin as the fornicator.

5. When Smith said, "God judges the fornicator innocent," we reply that God doesn't judge him innocent of fornication. He is a fornicator, and will be eternally condemned if he doesn't repudiate it. However, he's not guilty of adultery when he remarries after having been put away for fornication, as he no longer has a spouse. A more correct description would be that "God judges the bread burner bound to a husband and unable to have another, and judges the fornicator loosed and able to have another."

When God Put Israel Away, Israel Couldn't Remarry Other Gods

Since we've noticed several parallels between God's treatment of Israel on divorce and remarriage, this argument attempts to build another parallel. Since Israel couldn't remarry other gods, then, the argument goes, neither should the put-away fornicator be allowed to remarry.

1. This argument is nullified if the one who makes it believes the put-away fornicator can remarry after the first spouse dies. It doesn't matter what Israel could or could not do.

2. This argument is nullified if the one who makes it believes the put-away fornicator can remarry the first spouse. Apparently, if she will take him back, we can just forget the Israel argument!

3. However, the argument is not parallel to the divorce and remarriage situation because idolatry is never right. Idolatry wasn't right before Moses, during Moses, nor now. Marriage has been right since the creation, so the parallel is not true. To be a valid parallel, the argument would forbid a put-away fornicator from marrying one of the same sex. Homosexuality, like idolatry, has never been right.

Ezra 10.1-3

Some argue from Ez. 10.1-3 that "God commanded people to put way their wives and children, so men should be expected to do so today."

1. This argument is nullified if the one who makes it believes the put-away fornicator can remarry after the first spouse dies. It no longer matters what God commanded the Israelites.

2. This argument is nullified if the one who makes it believes the put-away fornicator can remarry the first spouse. Again, it no longer matters what God commanded the Israelites.

3. The writer agrees that men should be expected to put away their wives and children today, if it's a marriage disallowed by God in the first place, which is exactly what these marriages were. This was a remedy for their disobeying God, Ez. 9.2, "For they have taken some of their [Gentile—SGD] daughters as wives for themselves and for their sons, so that the holy race has intermingled with the peoples of the lands; indeed, the hands of the princes and the rulers have been foremost in this unfaithfulness." The Jews had intermarried with the idolatrous and ungodly people of the lands, which God had prohibited in Dt. 7.1-3. They were guilty of *forbidden international marriage*, not adultery.

4. God commanded this putting away; therefore, God doesn't hate all putting away.

God Hates Putting Away

We've noticed this passage in Mal. 2.10-16, where the children of Israel were putting away the Jewish wives of their youth to marry foreign women. God told them, "I hate divorce."

1. This argument is nullified if the one who makes it believes the put-away fornicator can remarry after the first spouse dies, no matter what God told Israel.

2. This argument is nullified if the one who makes it believes the put-away fornicator can remarry the first spouse, no matter what God told Israel.

3. Joseph was not condemned for determining to divorce Mary, whom he thought was an impenitent adulteress. Instead, he was pronounced "a righteous man."

4. God commanded the putting away in Ez. 10, and put away Israel himself in Jer. 3.8. These acts of putting away weren't wrong; they were scriptural.

5. Those who make this argument don't believe it's wrong for the innocent party to put away the guilty party.

6. Verse 11 teaches that these marriages were contracted with foreigners, violating Dt. 7.1-3. However, they were also violating Moses' teaching in Dt. 24.1-4 by divorcing their Jewish wives not for fornication and remarrying. We would have told them the same thing. These verses do not conflict with our positions.

It Wasn't Lawful for Herod to Have Philip's Wife

In Mk. 6.17-18, we read:

> For Herod himself had sent forth and laid hold upon John, and bound him in prison for the sake of Herodias, his brother Philip's wife; for he had married her. For John said unto Herod, It is not lawful for thee to have thy brother's wife.

People argue from this passage, "We need more preachers like John the Baptist, who condemned unscriptural remarriage, not these quislings who permit put-away fornicators to remarry."

1. This argument is nullified if the one who makes it believes the put-away fornicator can remarry after the first spouse dies. It doesn't matter how many quisling preachers we have.

2. This argument is nullified if the one who makes it believes the put-away fornicator can remarry the first spouse. It doesn't matter if quisling preachers have taken over the church.

3. We agree that we need more preachers like John the Baptist.

4. We disagree that Moses was a quisling because he permitted put-away fornicators to remarry, Dt. 24.1-4.

5. We disagree that Jesus was a quisling because he taught the same thing Moses did, Mt. 5.19-20.

6. We disagree that Paul was a quisling because he taught the same thing Jesus did, I Cor. 7.10-11.

7. A good quotation that typifies this position is from Jim Waldron in the Waldron-Hicks Debate concerning the remarriage of Herod:

> Beloved, that is what we are saying. When a woman is divorced unscripturally, she is bound to the husband of her youth. She will go on being bound to him until he dies, if it is unscriptural divorce. (*Waldron-Hicks Debate* [Ft. Worth, TX: Star Bible & Tract Supply, 1977].)

8. If this was an unscriptural divorce, we agree, but if this verse is being applied to scriptural divorce, it has no bearing on our subject.

9. The marriage of Herod to Herodias was unscriptural, and the writer would have told Herod the same thing John the Baptist did.

10. From Josephus, *Antiquities*, Book 18, chap. 5.1, 5.4, we find that Herod made a pretense at least of living under Jewish law. His family was intermarried with Simon the High Priest's family, and Herod went to Jerusalem for feasts to offer sacrifices to God. Everybody in this story was at least claiming to live under the Mosaic Law. The Mosaic Law was why it wasn't lawful for Herod to have Herodias, although the Mosaic Law would have

permitted her to remarry had she been scripturally divorced. However, Josephus said that Herodias hadn't been scripturally divorced, and she was his brother's wife, violating Lev. 20.10. Notice what John said: "It is not lawful for thee to have thy brother's wife."

11. There is no evidence of fornication before the divorce, so this case has no bearing on the present question.

Handcuffs in Marriage

Roy Deaver explains the handcuffs argument:

> In the marriage situation there are THREE sets of hand-cuffs—not one set. The husband is handcuffed to God (to the law of God); the wife is handcuffed to God (the law of God); and the husband and the wife are hand-cuffed to each other. The marriage law is God's law, and all men are amenable to that law. When the wife is guilty of fornication the husband has the right to put away the wife—to take off the handcuffs by which he is bound to the wife. But he is still handcuffed to the law of God, and the wife (the guilty party) is still handcuffed to the law of God. The law of God allows the husband (the innocent party) to form another marriage union. But, the law of God does not allow the wife—the guilty party—to form another marriage union. The guilty party is still hand-cuffed to the law of God—not to the husband she sinned against. (Quoted by J. D. Thomas, *Divorce & Remarriage* [Abilene, TX: Biblical Research Press, 1977], p. 55.)

1. This argument is nullified if the one who makes it believes the put-away fornicator can remarry after the first spouse dies, handcuffs notwithstanding.

2. This argument is nullified if the one who makes it believes the put-away fornicator can remarry the first spouse, handcuffs notwithstanding.

3. Find even one set of handcuffs in the Bible, write the passage where you found them right here _____, and send it to the author as well.

4. This argument still assumes that the law of God doesn't permit the remarriage of the put-away fornicator. What passage did Deaver give? If he was thinking Mt. 19.9, did he show the necessary implications concerning putting away for fornication?

Bound to God and New Definition of Adultery

David Bonner, another preacher and debater who affirms the put-away fornicator cannot remarry, makes a "handcuffs" argument of his own, which results in a new definition of adultery, which no one ever heard of until the mid-1970s. He argues from Rom. 7.1-3, which says:

> Or are ye ignorant, brethren (for I speak to men who know the law), that the law hath dominion over a man for so long time as he liveth? For the woman that hath a husband is bound by law to the husband while he liveth; but if the husband die, she is discharged from the law of the husband. So then if, while the husband liveth, she be joined to another man, she shall be called an adulteress: but if the husband die, she is free from the law, so that she is no adulteress, though she be joined to another man.

From this passage, where Paul used the language "bound by law to the husband," Bonner argues that "bound" means not "tied," but "restrained." "To" doesn't mean "to," but "in reference to." Bonner knows the put-away fornicator isn't a spouse, so he argues that "husband" means "husband of previous reference." Thus, Paul's "bound to a husband" becomes Bonner's "restrained in reference to a husband of previous reference." No, this is serious. This is not made up. Other than that, he sounds just like Paul, word for word!

1. This argument is nullified if the one who makes it believes the put-away fornicator can remarry after the first spouse dies, regardless of how words are redefined.

2. This argument is nullified if the one who makes it believes the put-away fornicator can remarry the first spouse, regardless of how words are redefined.

3. The subject of Romans 7 is not divorce and remarriage, but the Christian's relationship to the Mosaic Law and the gospel.

4. Romans 7 doesn't teach anything the Mosaic Law didn't teach about marriage and divorce, yet Bonner does. Though putting way in Dt. 24.1-4 allowed remarriage of the put-away fornicator, and therefore Jesus, as a faithful rabbi, did as well, Bonner doesn't. Also, Bonner has a new, different definition of adultery (for illicit sexual intercourse involving a spouse of another, Bonner has *marrying one restrained in reference to a spouse of previous reference*), yet this very passage gives God's definition of the term. God's definition agrees with all the lexicons and with Jesus in Mk. 10.11 (adultery is against the spouse).

5. If "bound" here meant "restrained in reference to a husband," these verses are still speaking of one who "hath a husband," and he's mentioned five times in the passage. Thus, to apply these verses to a put-away fornicator who has no spouse is clearly wrong.

6. God said that one bound to a spouse who joins to another is an adulteress. Bonner says that one without a spouse who joins to another is bound to God ("restrained in reference to a husband of previous reference"), and is an adulterer.

Conclusion

This concludes our examination of the celibacy position. As we saw in the introduction, to impose celibacy on someone God has not is indeed serious because someone is making law where God did not, as did the false teachers of the first century. With this chapter, we conclude our development of the subject of marriage, divorce, and remarriage. In the next chapter we will attempt to apply what we have learned to practical real-life problems that we have collected over the years.

Chapter 12

Practical Examples

Highlights

- *Four questions, which if answered, may lead to solution of every marriage, divorce, and remarriage situation.*
- *Is divorce and remarriage private or church business?*
- *Church limitations in dealing with divorce.*

The writer offers you his compliments and gratitude if you're still participating in this study. In addition to whatever previous serious study you've done before taking up his material, it's taken a significant amount of reading, thinking, rethinking, rereading, and examination for you to get to this point. He hopes your investment of time has been worth it, whether you agree with his major conclusions or not. Surely most of us can see how ridiculous it is to expect to read a couple of proof texts to some novice Bible student and expect him to understand and obey the truth on many of these matters. Some might conceive their duty to God to be breaking up his marriage and telling him to remain celibate the rest of his life, when he probably can't even say the books of the Bible in order.

Four Questions Which Must Be Answered

In Figure 46, we present an approach for breaking down and analyzing practical divorce and remarriage situations. We present these examples in order of increasing complexity, hoping to develop our skills at helping ourselves and others sort out their

Practical Applications:

Four Questions Which Must Be Answered

> Regardless of positions on two critical and
>   controversial questions
>
> If know the facts, which local churches often do not,
>   then such situations can be dealt with
>
> NOTE: No consideration of number of children, time,
>   nor civil government, or whether Christian or
>   aliens

---

1. Identify scriptural marriages

2. Identify any unscriptural unions and urge to quit

   adultery is never right

3. Identify any scriptural bonds that can now be scripturally
   broken for impenitent fornication, and let those breaks
   take place

4. Identify any unbound people who can remarry and let
   those bonds be scripturally made

Figure 46

own situation and determine what God would have them to do.
We think that these four questions will be useful to the reader
regardless of his position on the two critical and controversial
questions of (1) whether one unjustly put away can then put away
a fornicating spouse, and (2) whether the put-away fornicator
may remarry.

Question 1: Identify scriptural marriages.

Question 2: Identify any unscriptural unions and tell them to stop; adultery is never right.

Question 3: Identify any bonds that can now be scripturally broken for fornication, and let those breaks take place, if necessary.

Question 4: Identify any unbound people who can scripturally remarry, and let those bonds be scripturally made.

The Right to Divorce: Should One Exercise It?

Note on Question 3: Just because one has the right to divorce doesn't mean he should. God had the right to divorce Israel for decades before he did, yet he worked patiently, trying to get his wife to repent. When she wouldn't, God exercised his right. While it would be good if everyone in this position could be as mature as God, such often isn't the case, and impenitent fornication isn't spoken of in Jesus' teaching. After encouraging people to exercise patience and to try to heal the marriage, the ultimate decision is the spouse's as Moses taught in Dt. 24.1-4 and Jesus taught in Mt. 19.8. Review Chapters 5 and 8 for a discussion of "hardness of heart." Thus, it's even conceivable that a sinful spouse could truly repent, and the offended spouse could forgive the fornicator, yet still not reconcile. Such reconciliation or maturity is not a requirement of Jesus' teaching regarding scriptural divorce.

If the innocent spouse studies how God reconciles adulterers, homosexuals, fornicators, and effeminate men to himself, and then follows that example, he or she will be on safe ground in dealing with an adulterous mate. In I Cor. 6.9-11, God gives a three-part formula for reconciling sexual sinners to himself:

I Cor. 6.9-11: "Do not be deceived: neither fornicators, nor idolaters, nor adulterers, nor effeminate, nor abusers of themselves with men [homosexuals—SGD], nor thieves, nor covetous, nor drunkards, nor revilers, nor extortioners, shall inherit the kingdom of God. And such were some of you: but ye were washed, but ye were

sanctified, but ye were justified in the name of the Lord
Jesus Christ, and in the Spirit of our God."

After listing a group of sexually immoral people who had
some of the worst problems imaginable with knowing how to
love, Paul added that none of these sinners would inherit the
kingdom of God. Then Paul reminded the Corinthian Christians,
"And such were some of you." What a comforting statement full
of great hope! The Gospel possesses the power to change the most
hideous sexual sinners into loving sincere people who reflect
God's own love for mankind.

Fortunately, Paul told us how this transformation took place.
The Corinthians followed three steps that reconciled them to
God: (1) they were washed, (2) they were sanctified, and (3) after
these two steps, they were finally justified before God.

The first step, "they were washed," is the most obvious—
washing away the sins of adultery and fornication through the
blood of Jesus. The non-Christian finds forgiveness through
baptism (Ac. 22.16) while the Christian seeks forgiveness
through repentance and prayer (Ac. 8.22). Thus, the Christian
must begin by asking for forgiveness from the wronged mate and
God. Unfortunately, the reconciliation often stops at this beginning step, and the process is never completed and justification
with either God or the mate is not realized.

The second step, "they were sanctified," must be completed
for true healing to take place in the marriage and for the sinner
to become justified before God. Basically, "sanctification"
means to take something and set it apart for special use. Paul
admonished Christians in I Thes. 4.4 to sanctify their sexual lives.
He told them that it wasn't enough for them to avoid sexual
immorality, but that God commands his people to "possess their
own vessels unto sanctification and honor." In other words, a
Christian can't be pleasing to God and just say, "I've repented of
my adultery and I've stopped it." While that is what a Christian
must do, that is only going half the way towards being justified.
The Christian must go all the way and say, "I've repented of my
adultery and I've stopped it and I now use the sexual relationship
with my mate to God's glory." Thus, the sexual sinner not only
repudiates his past sins, but he moves forward to replace the sin

in his life with a healthy and loving sexual relationship with the mate.

True sanctification is a learning process that requires diligent mental effort as reflected in Rom. 12.2 which says that Christians are not to be conformed to this world, but are to be "transformed by the renewing of their minds." "Transformed" is an interesting word that means "to change into another form, to transfigure, transform." The modern word "metamorphosis" comes from the same Greek word. In the English language the word refers to the process whereby the insect larva spins a cocoon around itself and undergoes drastic change and maturation. After a certain period of time, the ugly caterpillar emerges as a beautiful butterfly—a completely transformed insect. Not only does the insect's outer appearance change, but also its function changes. The butterfly has left behind the caterpillar's compulsion to eat plants and destroy foliage. Instead, the butterfly pollinates flowers and makes the world more lovely.

A similar "metamorphosis" happens to the adulterer. He seeks forgiveness as a repulsive sinner. While pure and clean, he is not yet mature and adorned with all the beauty of Christ. As the adulterer deliberately studies the word of God and renews or changes his mind, he is set apart from the conduct of the world and is gradually transformed into a beautiful loving person who glorifies God in his daily life. Even homosexuals, adulterers, fornicators, prostitutes, revilers, drunkards, etc. can be transformed into pure and holy individuals through forgiveness and the power of God's word in their lives.

Many times after a mate's promiscuity comes to light, the mate promises, "It will never happen again." The mate may even go forward in a public assembly to confess sin and ask for prayers. No doubt, the mate is genuinely sorry and determined to never commit the sin again. Unfortunately, often the healing stops at this first step of the "washing" by accessing the blood of Jesus for forgiveness. While forgiveness is essential for one's relationship with God, one's self, and the mate, forgiveness is only the first step. Stopping with forgiveness dooms the person to repeat the sin again. Indeed, this cycle of sinning, repenting and determining never to do it again, only to backslide even deeper into the same sin happens over and over. Yet the person involved in the sin is probably deeply committed to stopping the behavior when he repents.

The problem is not the person's sincerity. Nor is it a problem with the power of Jesus' blood to cover sins. The problem comes from completing only the first step for changing behavior—the washing. Without the next step of true sanctification, or thorough mental housecleaning that changes and reorganizes the thinking, the sinner stays locked in his former pattern of behavior. The metamorphosis takes place by the "renewing of their minds," "the renewing by the Holy Spirit." Sanctification doesn't require just any renewing of the mind, but it requires "renewing by the Holy Spirit through God's words that are preserved in the Bible."

For greater understanding of this sanctifying process, the author highly recommends his wife Patsy Rae Dawson's booklet "Adultery & Sexual Addiction: A Plan for Healing the Soul and the Marriage," which gives a step-by-step process for sanctifying the mind after sexual sin. The reader will also benefit from studying her book *Marriage: A Taste of Heaven, Vol. II: God's People Make the Best Lovers,* which not only contains help for solving sexual problems, but also goes on to prove that God's people really do make the best lovers when they sanctify their love lives.

Only after the adulterer has (1) asked for forgiveness and (2) then gone on to sanctify the mind, can the sinner (3) become justified before God. So without these first two steps, a sexual sinner cannot be fully reconciled to God. Likewise, without these first two steps being completed, the marriage is going to continue in a state of decay and the problem will not really be solved. Two real-life examples show the harm of not following God's three-part formula for overcoming sexual sin:

One husband had engaged in a long-term affair that resulted in a child. The wife learned about the affair after it had gone on for over ten years. The husband, who claimed to be a Christian, went forward and confessed sin. After learning of the affair, the wife realized why their marriage had not grown emotionally although she had worked hard to make it a success. Since her husband was mentally attached to another woman, it was impossible for the wife to create a true emotional bond with him. She told him now they needed to repair the emotional void between them and make their marriage be what it should be. Her husband said he had done everything he needed to do by asking for forgiveness and if problems still existed—they were her problems—not his. He concluded, "You just need to learn how to forgive better."

To the contrary, repentance is much more than asking for forgiveness. *It is both repudiating the past conduct and then moving forward to embrace righteous behavior.* Because that husband was unwilling to repair the damage done to his marriage, that marriage continued to deteriorate. Because the wife fought feelings that came from sin in the home that had not been properly covered by the blood of Jesus, while having all the blame unjustly cast onto her, she wrestled with thoughts of suicide.

God gives the mate the right to insist on full repentance taking place after sexual sin because that sinner is not pleasing to God until he can truthfully say, "I don't commit adultery anymore and I use the sexual relationship to God's glory" (I Thes. 4.3–4). Anything less does not please God and leaves the marriage in a state of decay. In fact, Paul concluded this discussion about the sanctification of the sexual relationship with, "Consequently, he who rejects this *is not rejecting man* but the God who gives his Holy Spirit to you" (I Thes. 4.8). Thus, a person who is not willing to both (1) repudiate the sin and (2) embrace righteous living is not rejecting the mate (man) when he refuses to treat the mate right, but *a person is rejecting both God and the words God has preserved in the Bible through the Holy Spirit.* That person is not sanctified and is not overcoming his or her sin as the Corinthians overcame theirs.

Another husband who committed adultery with several young women repented of his adultery and promised never to do it again. But when his wife told him, "Now I want us to work on our marriage to make our relationship right so you won't be tempted again," he refused. This husband had the Victorian Madonna-prostitute view of a woman and had a problem feeling sexual desires for his wife. Because he was not satisfying his legitimate desires at home, he was very susceptible to affairs. In addition, his wife fought continual sexual frustration because he neglected to satisfy her God-given desires. Since he was unwilling to go all the way in making his adultery right by correcting the problem with his wife that led to his sin in the first place, his wife eventually divorced him for "impenitent" adultery. Although he claimed he had repented, his actions proved otherwise. Repentance involves not only turning one's back on the sinful behavior, but also going forward to embrace righteous behavior. To please God, it's not enough to say, "I don't commit adultery anymore." A person must be able to also say, "And I find my sexual fulfillment with my mate" (I Thes. 4.3–4).

We hope that this brief discussion of how adulterers are reconciled to God will aid the reader in answering question 3: Identify any bonds that can now be scripturally broken for fornication, and let those breaks take place, if necessary.

Approval of Churches: Is It Required?

We ask the reader explicitly to notice that we are not suggesting these questions for churches to use in order to pass approval on everyone's divorces and remarriage in their midst. Throughout our study, we've seen that marriage and divorce were private matters in both the Old and New Testaments. Centuries after the New Testament was finished, Roman Catholicism made marriage a sacrament of the church. In their eyes, this gives them the right to legislate and regulate concerning marriage, divorce, and remarriage.

Most denominations followed Roman Catholics down that road, and many Christians who are trying their best to be nondenominational have, as well. We follow their practice of having the preacher perform the ceremony, giving the appearance of reading the ceremony from the Bible. Thanks to Roman Catholicism, civil governments license preachers to do it. As we've mentioned before, civil governments' only interest in marriage and divorce is property, for taxation purposes.

Our recommendation is that those who have serious practical questions concerning aspects of divorce and remarriage exercise great care in revealing those problems and questions to churches. In most churches, most individual members, and sadly, even the preachers and other church leaders haven't studied the subject seriously. An ignorant but well-meaning zealot can easily make a private matter a church problem in the blink of an eye. Perhaps a well-studied person can be found that can help you study the problem for yourself and still the keep the matter private.

Not only have most congregations not studied the scriptures sufficiently on the subject to be of real help, but they are not scripturally equipped to deal with them justly. Years ago, the writer learned that even well-taught, well-meaning churches are severely limited in their ability to gather facts and deal justly with such situations. We don't mean that God left the church ill equipped in this regard. We do mean that churches are probably engaging in activity that God never intended for them to be involved in. When people move in from far off and tell a local church one side of a divorce situation, that's all we know: one side. The wise man in Proverbs 18.13 wrote, "He that giveth answer before he heareth, It is folly and shame unto him." It's entirely possible and commonplace for people to hear just one side of a story and make shameful and foolish decisions regarding serious matters. Elders in local churches don't have subpoena power to subpoena witnesses from churches in other states, and compel their testimony. Many times, they attempt to make decisions they're ill equipped to make. If God had expected them to make such decisions, he would surely have equipped them to do it.

Of course, if someone begins working with a congregation and advertises that he's an impenitent adulterer and rather likes it that way, that church should move to exclude him from their fellowship. Likewise, if a member begins actively committing adultery and refuses to repent, the church should take action. However, in most cases, local churches shouldn't get into the business of passing on everyone's divorce and remarriage and recognize that those individuals will have to answer to God for the choices they've made.

Christians or Non-Christians: Does It Matter?

Note that these four questions contain no considerations of how long someone has been involved in a marriage, how many children they have, the stance of civil government on these matters, nor even whether the people involved are Christians or non-Christians (with the exception of Christians in mixed marriages). What constitutes a marriage is the same whether those involved in it are Christians or not. Fornication and adultery are the same whether those involved are Christians or not. We noted in an earlier discussion that in Mt. 5.27-32, Jesus spoke of three ways adultery is committed: (1) with the feet, overtly, (2) with the mind, mentally, and (3) with the courts, legally. In all three cases, exactly the same activity is involved. This is true whether the one committing adultery is an alien or a Christian.

The change in behavior that God wants is the same in all cases, whether the one committing adultery is an alien or a Christian. God wants him to stop the adultery whether he's doing it with his feet, his eyes, or with the courts. However, when one won't stop such activity, punitive divorce is in order, again whether the adulterer is an alien or a Christian. Punitive divorce is what God himself did with Israel after patiently trying to get her to repent (Jer. 3.8). Aliens, strangers from covenant relationship with God such as Abimelech, knew overt adultery was wrong.

Likewise, non-Jews like Job knew adultery with the eyes was wrong. In Job 31.1, Job said, "I made a covenant with mine eyes; How then should I look upon a virgin?" Later, Job said that if he had done such a thing, he deserved the misery he was in. Aliens and Christians know that God wants them to stop such behavior. In cases where adulterers use the civil courts which permit treacherous divorce, whether aliens or Christians, God wants them to stop it.

When such adulterous activity isn't stopped, where do efforts at reconciliation cease? In Dt. 24.1-4, one could divorce a fornicating spouse, and yet be reconciled until the put-away fornicator had married someone else. Then, he could never have her back. In Mt. 5.31-32, by necessary implication, we've seen that if one unjustly put away a spouse, then committed adultery by remarrying, reconciliation no longer was the order, but putting away the fornicating spouse for his adultery is permitted. Likewise, in I Cor. 7.12-16, when an unbeliever deserted the Christian, the Christian was no longer under the bondage the Christian married to a Christian was, to (1) remain unmarried to anyone else, or (2) be reconciled.

We now proceed through our examples, applying the four questions we gave above:

Analyzing Examples with Four Questions

Example 1

When divorce has been granted on an unscriptural ground and one of the parties is considering remarrying, what should that party be advised to do?
Question 1: Identify scriptural marriages.

Both parties are still scripturally bound to each other.

Question 2: Identify any unscriptural unions and tell them to stop; adultery is never right.

There are no unscriptural unions.

Question 3: Identify any bonds that can now be scripturally broken for fornication, and let those breaks take place, if necessary.

There are no bonds to scripturally break.

Question 4: Identify any unbound people who can scripturally remarry, and let those bonds be scripturally made.

None may be scripturally bound to another. I Cor. 7.10-11 applies here. They should remain unmarried to anyone else, or be reconciled to each other.

Example 2

When divorce has been granted on an unscriptural ground and neither party remarries or indulges in illicit sexual relations, what should they be advised to do?
Question 1: Identify scriptural marriages.

They are still scripturally bound to each other.

Question 2: Identify any unscriptural unions and tell them to stop; adultery is never right.

There are no unscriptural unions to break.

Question 3: Identify any bonds that can now be scripturally broken for fornication, and let those breaks take place, if necessary.

There are no scriptural grounds for divorce.

Question 4: Identify any unbound people who can scripturally remarry, and let those bonds be scripturally made.

None may remarry. They should be advised to reconcile. To satisfy civil government, they probably will need to remarry civilly, depending on the jurisdiction.

Example 3

When divorce has been given on a scriptural ground and neither party remarries, is there any reason why the divorced persons may not come together again on the repentance of the guilty party?
Question 1: Identify scriptural marriages.

There are no scriptural bonds.

Question 2: Identify any unscriptural unions and tell them to stop; adultery is never right.

There are no unscriptural unions to break.

Question 3: Identify any bonds that can now be scripturally broken for fornication, and let those breaks take place, if necessary.

There are no scriptural bonds to be broken.

Question 4: Identify any unbound people who can scripturally remarry, and let those bonds be scripturally made.

Both parties are free to remarry, whether or not the guilty party repents. However, the ex-spouse would be foolish to remarry the guilty party without his repentance. Repentance is a condition of reconciliation with the ex-spouse and God, not a condition of the right of remarriage.

Example 4

A divorce has been granted on an unscriptural ground. The husband (A) who sued for divorce remarries and thereby commits adultery. After some time his second wife (C) dies. He repents of his wrong and wishes to return to his first spouse (B), who has in the interval remained unmarried. May he do so, and is remarriage necessary in such an event?

Question 1: Identify scriptural marriages.

A was scripturally tied to B all along.

Question 2: Identify any unscriptural unions and tell them to stop; adultery is never right.

The remarriage of A and C was unscriptural all along.

Question 3: Identify any bonds that can now be scripturally broken for fornication, and let those breaks take place, if necessary.

B could now scripturally divorce A. She should be encouraged to imitate God's behavior with Israel, and accept him back because of his repentance. However, as our study of the meaning of "hardness of heart" indicates, she is under no obligation to accept him back.

Question 4: Identify any unbound people who can scripturally remarry, and let those bonds be scripturally made.

Thus, A and B are still scripturally bound to each other. If A is willing to accept B back rather than scripturally divorce him, to satisfy civil government, they probably will need to remarry civilly, depending on the jurisdiction.

Example 5

A husband (A) has secured a divorce on an unscriptural ground and remarries. After some time he divorces his second wife (C) on an unscriptural ground and wishes to return to his first wife (B). May he legitimately do so?

Question 1: Identify scriptural marriages.

A was scripturally bound to B all along.

Question 2: Identify any unscriptural unions and tell them to stop; adultery is never right.

The marriage of A and C was unscriptural all along.

Question 3: Identify any bonds that can now be scripturally broken for fornication, and let those breaks take place, if necessary.

B could now scripturally divorce A. She should be encouraged to imitate God's behavior with Israel, and reconcile with him based on his repentance. However, as our study of the meaning of "hardness of heart" indicates, she is under no obligation to accept him back.

Question 4: Identify any unbound people who can scripturally remarry, and let those bonds be scripturally made.

A and B are still scripturally bound to each other. If A is willing to accept B back rather than scripturally divorce him, to satisfy civil government, they probably need to remarry civilly, depending on the jurisdiction.

Example 6

A woman (B) has been divorced from her husband (A) for the cause of adultery and she remarries. After a while her second husband (C) dies. She is penitent for her sins and wishes to return to her first husband who has remained unmarried. May she do so?

Question 1: Identify scriptural marriages.

There are none.

Question 2: Identify any unscriptural unions and tell them to stop; adultery is never right.

There are none.

Question 3: Identify any bonds that can now be scripturally broken for fornication, and let those breaks take place, if necessary.

There are none.

Question 4: Identify any unbound people who can scripturally remarry, and let those bonds be scripturally made.

A and B could now be scripturally bound unless the restriction on the man from Dt. 24.1-4 is binding on Christians. If it's not, a civil ceremony would be required to satisfy civil government.

Example 7

Mr. and Mrs. A have been divorced on an unscriptural ground, and Mr. and Mrs. B likewise. Mr. A marries Mrs. B and Mr. B marries Mrs. A. After a while, let us suppose, all four have become truly penitent and deplore their sin. They wish to put everything right. May they all resume their first marital relationships, and thus, return to their original partners?

Question 1: Identify scriptural marriages.

Scripturally, Mr. and Mrs. A and Mr. and Mrs. B are still bound.

Question 2: Identify any unscriptural unions and tell them to stop; adultery is never right.

There are no unscriptural unions left after all four people stop the adultery.

Question 3: Identify any bonds that can now be scripturally broken for fornication, and let those breaks take place, if necessary.

There are scriptural grounds for divorce, but none want to, which is as it should be.

Question 4: Identify any unbound people who can scripturally remarry, and let those bonds be scripturally made.

Yes, they may thus return to their original partners to whom they are still bound. They must correct their marital situation in accord with the laws of the land, i.e., a civil divorce and remarriage. They should also probably find someone else to play bridge with.

Example 8

Mr. C is guilty of adultery and Mrs. C knows this. However, Mr. C will not publicly confess to his sin and Mrs. C cannot secure the necessary evidence to prove it before an ecclesiastical or civil court; and thus, cannot sue for a divorce on this proper ground. But Mr. C is quite willing to be divorced on other grounds. May Mrs. C secure a civil divorce on these improper grounds, knowing, of course, that the real ground is the adultery of which her husband is guilty but which she cannot prove?
Question 1: Identify scriptural marriages.

Mr. and Mrs. C are still scripturally bound.

Question 2: Identify any unscriptural unions and tell them to stop; adultery is never right.

Mr. C's extramarital affair was adulterous.

Question 3: Identify any bonds that can now be scripturally broken for fornication, and let those breaks take place, if necessary.

Mrs. C may put Mr. C away, especially if he's not willing to repent, with no requirement to prove anything to any ecclesiastical or civil court. She couldn't lie, but "no fault" divorce would be permissible, as long as she and Mr. C understood that she was repudiating their marriage for his fornication.

Question 4: Identify any unbound people who can scripturally remarry, and let those bonds be scripturally made.

Both parties would be free to remarry without committing adultery.

Example 9

Mr. D divorces Mrs. D without scriptural cause. Mrs. D remarries and in doing so, of course, commits adultery. May Mr. D now remarry?
Question 1: Identify scriptural marriages.

Mr. D is still scripturally bound to Mrs. D.

Question 2: Identify any unscriptural unions and tell them to stop; adultery is never right.

Mrs. D's remarriage was unscriptural, and she should stop the adultery.

Question 3: Identify any bonds that can now be scripturally broken for fornication, and let those breaks take place, if necessary.

Mr. D can now scripturally put away Mrs. D.

Question 4: Identify any unbound people who can scripturally remarry, and let those bonds be scripturally made.

Both Mr. and Mrs. D may remarry.

Example 10

Mr. E falls in love with another woman. Mrs. E knows that she has lost her husband's matrimonial affection and devotion and that such have been transferred to the other woman. May she sue for a divorce on the ground that this is virtual adultery on the part of her husband, even though she has no reason for thinking that there has been any overt act of adultery?

Question 1: Identify scriptural marriages.

Mr. and Mrs. E are still bound to each other.

Question 2: Identify any unscriptural unions and tell them to stop; adultery is never right.

While the man's mental bonds with the other woman cannot be condoned, there is no evidence of unscriptural unions, even mental sexual ones. If "matrimonial affection transferred to the other woman" means he's committing mental adultery with her, then that would have to stop.

Question 3: Identify any bonds that can now be scripturally broken for fornication, and let those breaks take place, if necessary.

There are none, unless there is evidence of mental adultery.

Question 4: Identify any unbound people who can scripturally remarry, and let those bonds be scripturally made.

There are no unmarried people who can be married to each other, unless Mrs. E divorces Mr. E for mental adultery, in which

case both parties would be free to remarry, since neither one
would have a spouse.

Example 11

Mr. and Mrs. F lived happily together for several years and
had children. After some time Mr. F became enamoured of
another woman and desired to marry her. The state in which he
lives grants divorce only for the cause of adultery. He publicly
avowed having committed adultery with this other woman and
secured witnesses to testify before the court to adultery on his
part. Divorce from Mrs. F was granted. Thereupon Mr. F married
the other woman. After some years, however, his second wife
wished to be separated from him and he was able to secure a
decree of nullity on the ground of her impotence. So the state
decreed Mr. F's second marriage to be null and void. Mr. F is
penitent of his waywardness and wishes to return to his former
wife and perform the duties of husband and father, which he had
renounced. He also alleges that the charge of adultery, which he
himself had instituted and on the basis of which the divorce had
been granted, was false and had simply been an expedient to meet
the requirements of the law. Mr. F's former wife, who had not
remarried in the interval, is willing to have Mr. F as her husband.
May Mr. and Mrs. F be remarried and resume marital relations?
  Question 1: Identify scriptural marriages.

If Mr. F was lying the first time, he is still bound to Mrs. F. If
he is lying the second time, he is bound to his second wife.

  Question 2: Identify any unscriptural unions and tell them to
stop; adultery is never right.

If he was lying the first time, his union with the second wife
was always adulterous.

  Question 3: Identify any bonds that can now be scripturally
broken for fornication, and let those breaks take place, if necessary.

If Mr. F was lying the first time, Mrs. F could now put him away for fornication. If he is lying the second time, he is still married to his second wife as there is no scriptural concept of nullity, and there are apparently no scriptural grounds for divorce here.

Question 4: Identify any unbound people who can scripturally remarry, and let those bonds be scripturally made.

If Mr. F was lying the first time, Mrs. F could remarry. If Mr. F is lying the second time, Mrs. F and Mr. F could be reconciled, but a civil ceremony would probably be necessary to satisfy civil government.

Example 12

This is the average case, illustrated in Figure 47. Mr. and Mrs. A are married, as are Mr. and Mrs. B. Both couples divorce unscripturally, whereupon Mrs. A marries Mr. B. What should they be told to do to please God?
Question 1: Identify scriptural marriages.

Both are still bound to the previous mates.

Question 2: Identify any unscriptural unions and tell them to stop; adultery is never right.

The new union is adulterous, and must stop.

Question 3: Identify any bonds that can now be scripturally broken for fornication, and let those breaks take place, if necessary.

Both previous mates could now put away their partners, but wouldn't have to if they're penitent and willing to reconcile to the original partners.

Question 4: Identify any unbound people who can scripturally remarry, and let those bonds be scripturally made.

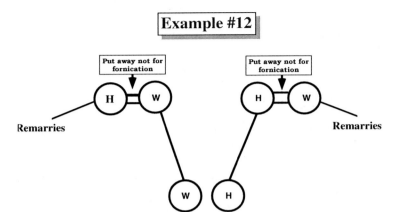

1. Identify scriptural marriages

2. Identify any unscriptural unions and urge to quit; adultery is never right

3. Identify any scriptural bonds that can now be scripturally broken for
   impenitent fornication, and let those breaks take place

4. Identify any unbound people who can remarry and let those bonds be
   scripturally made

---

1. Both are still bound to previous mate

2. New union is adulterous, must stop

3. Both could put away mates scripturally

4. The two innocent parties could now remarry without
   committing adultery, and so could their ex-spouses

Figure 47

If the two fornicators are put away for adultery, they could
now marry each other without committing adultery. Also the two
innocent parties may now remarry.

Example 13

Mrs. H discovers homosexual pornography and confronts Mr. H. Mr. H confesses that he is a practicing homosexual.
Question 1: Identify scriptural marriages.

Mr. and Mrs. H are still bound to each other.

Question 2: Identify any unscriptural unions and tell them to stop; adultery is never right.

Mr. H's homosexual union(s) and use of pornography are adulterous, and must stop.

Question 3: Identify any bonds that can now be scripturally broken for fornication, and let those breaks take place, if necessary.

Depending on Mr. H's repentance and her ability to reconcile with him, Mrs. H may put Mr. H away for his fornication. If Mr. H won't repent, she must divorce him, for one cannot be one body with an impenitent fornicator.

Question 4: Identify any unbound people who can scripturally remarry, and let those bonds be scripturally made.

If Mrs. H puts her husband away, since neither party has a spouse, both parties may remarry without committing adultery. However, Mr. H stands condemned before God until he repents of his use of pornography, his homosexual union(s), his sin against Mrs. H, and against God.

Example 14

Mrs. I catches Mr. I masturbating while looking at pornography. Mr. I confesses that he does this on a regular basis and often goes to strip bars to watch the women and engages in phone sex. While Mrs. I recognizes that Mr. I has a problem with sexual

addiction, Mr. I defends his actions claiming that no one is getting hurt and that his activity is totally harmless.
Question 1: Identify scriptural marriages.

Mr. and Mrs. I are scripturally bound to each other.

Question 2: Identify any unscriptural unions and tell them to stop; adultery is never right.

Mr. I's use of pornography, strip bars, and phone sex constitutes adultery, and is not going to stop, since he claims "no one is getting hurt."

Question 3: Identify any bonds that can now be scripturally broken for fornication, and let those breaks take place, if necessary.

Mrs. I may put Mr. I away for his fornication, and since he's impenitent, she must, to avoid being one body with a fornicator.

Question 4: Identify any unbound people who can scripturally remarry, and let those bonds be scripturally made.

After Mrs. I puts away Mr. I, both are without spouses, and may remarry without committing adultery. However, Mr. I stands condemned before God until he repents of his use of pornography, strip bars, and phone sex, his sin against Mrs. I, and against God.

Example 15

Mrs. J discovers that Mr. J has been involved with a much younger woman. Mr. J denies that he has had sexual relations with the younger woman. He claims that they have only fondled each other and engaged in oral sex. (This is being taught in many public schools as a safe alternative for sexual intercourse so this case will be seen more and more.)
Question 1: Identify scriptural marriages.

Mr. and Mrs. J are scripturally bound to each other.

Question 2: Identify any unscriptural unions and tell them to stop; adultery is never right.

Mr. J's involvement with the younger woman is adulterous, as fondling and oral sex are, scripturally speaking, fornication, and must stop.

Question 3: Identify any bonds that can now be scripturally broken for fornication, and let those breaks take place, if necessary.

Mrs. J may put Mr. J away for fornication.

Question 4: Identify any unbound people who can scripturally remarry, and let those bonds be scripturally made.

After the putting away for fornication, both Mr. and Mrs. J may remarry without committing adultery.

As stated in the beginning of this book, the high rate of divorce in society demands, if we're going to teach members of society, that we teach God's view of divorce and remarriage to those striving to live according to the Gospel so that they may bring their lives into harmony with it. The author hopes these examples illustrate the value of the four questions given at the beginning of this chapter for helping to sort out how God's teaching affects individual marriage and divorce situations.

Chapter 13

Fellowship on Marriage, Divorce, & Remarriage

Highlights
• *Denominational splits occur over these controversial matters among people who have long fought denominationalism.* • *Can a local church study these issues for itself and determine its own conduct on these matters? If not, let's not hear any more about local church autonomy.*

In the late 1840s, a small group of Christian men met in a room in Cincinnati, Ohio and made some decisions that affected every church of Christ in America. The action of those men resulted in the American Christian Missionary Society, which in turn produced two coalitions of churches—those for the society and those against it.

In the latter part of that same century, another group of men met in Ridgeway, Kentucky and made some decisions that again influenced every church of Christ in America. Their decision concerned the use of instrumental music in Christian worship. Their action resulted in another denominational split within churches of Christ, i.e., two camps of churches—those churches for it and those against it.

In the mid-1900s, a small group of men met in a room in Abilene, Texas and made decisions that impacted every church of Christ in America. The elders of the Fifth and Highland Church of Christ determined to be a sponsoring church, i.e., to oversee the work of thousands of churches of Christ across the land. It was a decision that affected every church of Christ in America.

Their action resulted in two parties of churches of Christ—those against the concept and those for it.

Most of us are indignant at the idea that anyone could meet in Cincinnati and make decisions that impacted every local church, and it makes us realize that some unhealthy relationships existed between those churches, for such a division to take place. We are also provoked that men could meet in Ridgeway and make decisions with similar results, and we realize that again, some unhealthy relationships existed between those churches that participated in the division. Likewise, we realize that had churches of Christ been as independent as they claimed, such a division could not have arisen from a meeting in Abilene. The very idea that anyone could meet anywhere, especially Cincinnati, Ridgeway, or Abilene, and make decisions that influenced every local church in America, ought to exasperate us all.

However, in 1988, a small number of men met concerning a small church in Belen, New Mexico and made decisions that again threaten to affect every church of Christ in America. It is a fact that a great controversy confronts churches of Christ, this time, on the subject of marriage, divorce, and remarriage. Although there is not just one issue, but many, the question arises as to what we should tell those we attempt to reconcile to Christ to do, when they have been involved in divorce and remarriage situations. This chapter does not attempt to deal with those important issues, but rather with how a local congregation should conduct itself in the midst of controversy. Its main thrust is *that each local church should study the issues for itself, determine its own conduct on these matters, and not allow any outside preacher, paper, college, or coalition of congregations to determine its action.* This is not to say that a preacher, paper, or college might not aid in the procedure of determining what that local group of Christians conceives to please God, but that they should not interfere with that church's study, deliberation, and determination of its own action.

History of Denominational Divisions Among Churches of Christ

Missionary Society Issue in Mid-1800s

When a doctrinal split occurred over whether local churches could support an external organization to preach the gospel, the history of the "restoration movement" shows that the split occurred before very much study took place on this issue. Brethren chose up sides and an ugly grab for the loyalty of congregations took place. The result was a denominational split among churches of Christ. By denominational, we mean that by and large, two camps, or coalitions of churches resulted. It was denominational in nature, because that's exactly what a denomination is—a coalition of congregations. Such a split could not have taken place without denominational concepts of the body of Christ. Had congregations been more independent, not allowing preachers, papers, or colleges to exercise undue influence on their study and to determine their own congregational action, it could never have occurred. This was evidenced by the fact that Christians on both sides of the issue were not that familiar with the others' arguments. The split took place before much study had been done.

Instrumental Music in Latter 1800s

The split over whether Christians should use instruments of music in their worship also occurred before much study was done by Christians in general. Line-ups of congregations resulted, due to unwarranted influence by preachers, papers, and colleges, which in many cases precluded open study and deliberation on the part of each congregation.

During this controversy, David Lipscomb, a highly regarded preacher of the gospel and editor of the *Gospel Advocate*, constantly upheld the importance of open discussion in local churches:

> The Church that stifles investigation, but [only—SGD] prepares and nourishes the elements of violent explosion

and division within its own bosom. We will freely, gladly hear ourselves and let our readers hear both sides of every question we present. (David Lipscomb, *Gospel Advocate*, 1866, p. 111.)

I would like to see all of us get along pleasantly and harmoniously in obeying the commands of God. But if the *Gospel Advocate* were to adopt this policy of criticizing others and refusing to let them reply, I would cease to read it. (David Lipscomb, *Gospel Advocate*, 1912, pp. 44, 45.)

Congregations, which did not discuss these issues for themselves, and determine their own action, were doomed to participate in another denominational split.

Institutional Controversy of 1950s

Likewise, the split over institutionalism occurred without much study. Many congregations split before brethren really understood the arguments on both sides. Preachers and papers quarantined each other, and applied great pressure to side with this group or that. Lipscomb's own *Gospel Advocate* initiated a quarantine, so that had Lipscomb still been alive, he wouldn't have read it! This split occurred because of undue outside influence which in many cases precluded much deliberation and study. The idea that a meeting of "sponsoring-church elders" in Abilene, Texas could affect congregations across the land is abhorrent to many. A denominational split could not have occurred without a denominational idea of the body of Christ. Had congregations been independent, such a split would have been impossible.

At the time, Reuel Lemmons, editor of the *Firm Foundation* spoke well of the need for independent congregational study:

I don't want any committee of editors deciding for me what the truth is. I will decide that for myself. And every reader of every paper in the brotherhood should feel the same way. Neither an infallible man nor an infallible paper exists. Not man, nor committee of men—even though they be editors—can tell me what to believe. (Reuel Lemmons, *Firm Foundation*, May 28, 1957, cited by Herbert E. Winkler, *Congregational Cooperation of the Churches of Christ* [Herbert E. Winkler Publisher, 1961], p. 10.)

Another Denominational Split Coming

The author prepared this chapter because the same process began happening again. Brethren have differed long about the various issues encompassed within marriage, divorce, and remarriage. But all of a sudden, though, a few preachers and editors felt that congregations must line up, and that open discussion and study in each congregation was dangerous. These few began advocating that lines of fellowship must be drawn. They began bringing undue influence to bear on congregations, which will inevitably result in many congregations being split, and there will be another denominational line-up of congregations.

It's not the author's responsibility to ensure the independence of all congregations. That is the responsibility of each congregation. But the author does have the responsibility to teach how we should behave ourselves in the midst of this controversy. Thus, this chapter doesn't deal with the various doctrinal issues of divorce and remarriage. Rather, it deals with how individual Christians and local churches should conduct themselves to avoid participation in another denominational split.

Although there has been disagreement and discomfort over marriage, divorce and remarriage since the earliest days of the "restoration movement," the present heated controversy began in Belen, New Mexico in March, 1988. At that time, Homer Hailey, a gospel preacher highly regarded for decades, was involved. For forty-five years, he held a different-than-mainstream position on divorce and remarriage, and was asked to come to Belen to explain his position in a private congregational study. Many of the preachers who later attacked Hailey had known of his position for those forty-five years, but since Hailey didn't openly propagate it, they were content to leave him alone. The study in Belen was to be private, as Hailey said:

> The meeting was private, and they insisted we keep it that way. A friend of mine from a different congregation wanted to attend, but they did not want it. The meeting was to be private. We sat around a table, fourteen or sixteen, I believe, and for an hour and a half I went though the Scriptures pointing out the ground of my position; then we spent an hour asking and answering questions. I then left. They had assured me that what they wanted was my view to compare with the differing view, that they might make a decision. I didn't even make any special preparation, just went as one would meet and discuss a matter. (Homer Hailey, Letter to *Christianity Magazine*, November 1988, p. 7.)

The session was videotaped, and the tape was then widely circulated across the United States. Had the study remained private, the resulting controversy would not have ensued. With the widespread distribution of the tape, many became alarmed.

Connie Adams, editor of *Searching the Scriptures* and one who was aware of Hailey's position for nearly forty-five years, wrote one of the first articles citing the "potential for all out war," because Hailey was openly preaching his position. The author's purpose is not to defend Hailey at all, but to ask, was this alarm the result of Hailey teaching his position to less than twenty people sitting around a table in Belen, New Mexico (at their request), or because some didn't leave a private study private?

At that same time, some raised a voice against harsh treatment of a brother of Hailey's stature, among them Ed Harrell, co-editor of *Christianity Magazine*:

> Must we label every person who disagrees with us a false teacher? Then I must surely judge almost every other brother to be a false teacher in some regard. The end of such thinking is rampant factionalism.

A false teacher is surely one whose dishonest motives and/or ignorance distinguish him from the sincere brother who has reached an erroneous conclusion. If that is not the case, then I am surrounded by false teachers.

I judge him to be one of the most godly and learned men I have ever known. I have walked proudly with him through the years, learning, and loving, finding him always willing to probe those questions where his views conflicted with mine. Through sixty years of service Hailey has proven himself to be a tireless student, a profound preacher and a selfless builder of the cause of Christ. He has left behind a trail of praiseworthy achievements. He is a great and a good man, and brethren have sought to use him and to honor him. At this late date, he deserves nothing less. (Ed Harrell, *Christianity Magazine*, November 1988, p. 9.)

The author agrees with these remarks, but they were too limited. We should not have treated Hailey right because of his advanced years; we all need to treat each other right, regardless of our years! Everyone won't, but that shouldn't keep the rest of us from behaving ourselves.

As expected, Harrell's plea to treat Hailey right brought abuse upon him. Ken Leach, in a bulletin circulated across the United States, was quick to charge Harrell with thinking too highly of men:

A perfect example of thinking more highly of man than one ought to think is the Ed Harrell editorial ("Homer Hailey: False Teacher") in *Christianity Magazine*, November, 1988 issue. In spite of admitting that Hailey believes and teaches error on divorce and remarriage, brother Harrell writes:

[Quotation from Harrell is given above and is not repeated here.]

The scriptures teach to expose those who teach such false doctrines as does Hailey (Eph. 5:11) and to rebuke them (Titus 2:15). This is to be done openly (I Tim. 5:20), sharply (Titus 1:3) and towards repentance (Rev. 3:19). Ones providing shelter and safety for those teaching such things as Hailey teaches on divorce and remarriage stand in violation of 2 John 9-11 and share in the evil deeds.

Recommending that congregations disregard Hailey's teaching on divorce and remarriage and continue to use him for gospel meetings is not according to truth.

Leach didn't point out what was wrong with Hailey's teaching, but decided that Harrell's disagreement with parts of it should be good enough for his readers. He, thus, assumed that Hailey taught false doctrine, deserved national rebuke, and admonished congregations not to listen to Hailey.

Did Hailey deserve sharp national rebuke for a private study? No, these admonitions resulted because the church in Belen didn't leave it private. The issue is not what Hailey believed. The issue is whether these men and papers had the right to decide who congregations ought to listen to, and when all out war was necessary.

These Men Are Not Qualified to Incite a Split

After congregations study these questions for themselves, and prayerfully deliberate how the scriptures should be applied to real situations, there may still have to be lines of fellowship drawn *within those congregations*. However, the author simply agrees with David Lipscomb that there should be much study before matters arrive at that dismal result:

When differences exist, the discussion of these differences is the only hope of union. The suppression of discussion is the direct and open road to division. Whoever opposes the free discussion of differences among brethren, in that favors speedy division. Differences existing will manifest themselves. If they are discussed freely, there is hope of reconciliation and harmony. Suppress the discussion, and unless the strong hand of arbitrary and despotic power holds by the terror of physical force, disruption and division must follow. When persons having a community of interest differ, so long as those who differ show a kindly interest in the others, listen to the remonstrances, treat with considerate kindness their feelings, wishes, and reasonings, they remain one. The moment the one party says: "We wish to hear no more your reasonings; we intend no longer to regard your feelings or wishes; we intend to go our own way, regardless of your course or purposes," those people become two distinct people. Division or an unmanly and unchristian submission to what we believe to be wrong is the only alternative. (*Gospel Advocate*, 1906, p. 552.)

In other words, Christians should have the character to treat each other right while they study controversial questions. In addition, *these men who pressed for division, and would draw lines of fellowship within congregations and between congregations that have not seriously studied these issues, are not themselves qualified to incite such a split:*

J. T. Smith, Editor of *Torch Magazine*

For example, one of the preachers who pressed for division, J. T. Smith, participated in four debates (each six months apart over two years, 1976-1978) with Glen Lovelady, Lyle McCollum, Bob Melear, and Jack Gibbert. He contradicted himself on the definition of adultery, a concept basic to the whole topic. In the first two debates, Smith limited adultery to fornication involving a spouse. In the last two, Smith abandoned this position and said that adultery could be committed by two people, neither of whom had a spouse. Notice, in his debate with Lyle McCollum, he responded to a formal question:

Do you agree that the definition of adultery is limited to
sexual intercourse with the spouse of another? Yes.
(Smith-McCollum Debate, Night 1, October 4, 1976,
Question No. 5.)

Five months later, in his debate with Bob Melear, Smith
asserted that adultery was not limited to sexual sins with another's spouse. Commenting on Mt. 5.28, Smith said:

If it does not include one who is single looking on one
who is single, then, according to that, that means, as
we've already pointed out, and as one commentator said,
that it does not involve them, and therefore they're free
to look on them and lust after them as they will. (Smith-
Melear Debate, March 8, 1977.)

That same night, Smith said:

The word adultery in the Old Testament does include
those who are not married as well as those who are
married because this is the only instruction that God
gave: "Thou shalt not commit adultery," and the word
fornication is not used. (Smith-Melear Debate, March 8,
1977.)

The issue in this chapter is not the definition of adultery, and
it's certainly not Smith's integrity, intelligence, or sincerity. The
issue is whether one who doesn't even know the definition of the
word adultery has any business telling people to separate and
instigating drawing lines of fellowship between brethren.

Likewise, Smith gave conflicting answers on another question. He was asked in all four debates how a put-away fornicator
would answer Paul's question in I Cor. 7.27-28, "Art thou loosed
from a wife?" In the first debate, he told Glen Lovelady:

How can the put-away fornicator answer Paul's question
on I Cor. 7.27b, "Art thou loosed from a wife?" No.
(*Smith-Lovelady Debate*, March 26, 1976, question 4
[Brooks, KY: Searching The Scriptures, 1976], p. 265.)

Then he told Lyle McCollum seven months later:

> How would the put-away fornicator answer Paul's question, art thou loosed from a wife, I Cor. 7.27? Yes, but I've been divorced for fornication and would be guilty of adultery if I married. (Smith-McCollum Debate, October 7, 1976, Question 1.)

In response to the same question five months later, he told Bob Melear:

> Do you say that the put-away fornicator is loosed from a mate as per I Cor. 7.27 but nevertheless bound or obligated to the law of her husband? I don't know what loosing Paul is discussing in the passage. He does not say. (Smith-Melear Debate, March 8, 1977, Question 2.)

Finally, thirteen months later, Smith answered Jack Gibbert this way:

> What answer would a put-away fornicator give the apostle Paul? I presume with reference to what was asked in question five. The put-away fornicator would say no to this and we'll see why as the discussion continues. (Smith-Gibbert Debate, April 17, 1978, Question 6.)

The issue is not that some disagree with Smith on I Cor. 7.27-28—even he does that! The issue is that one who answers the same question by "No," "Yes," "I don't know," and "No," needs to get his own answers straight before debating and drawing lines of fellowship. Should he tell people to separate and participate in an all out war?

Smith also gave inconsistent answers to the question of whether one must remain bound to an adulterous mate. In the Lovelady debate, March 22, 1976, he said:

> Must a mate remain bound to an adulterous partner? No, if the adulterous partner does not repent. (*Ibid.*, p. 36.)

The next evening, Smith responded just the opposite:

> If an innocent woman is put away by her husband for no
> cause, not for fornication, and then that man marries
> another, and thereby commits adultery, can the innocent,
> put-away one, now put away her adulterous mate, or
> must she remain bound to that adulterer? She is not free.
> She is not free.

Likewise, in the Melear debate, Smith again answered the
same question two different ways. On the first night, he responded:

> Does God require that one must remain bound to either
> his adulterous partner or to the law of his adulterous
> partner? No. (Smith-Melear Debate, March 10, 1977,
> question 1.)

The next night he said:

> Doesn't the proposition you affirmed last night demand
> that the put-away woman remain bound by the law to her
> adulterous husband? Yes, but her husband was not an
> adulterer when they got a divorce. (Smith-Melear De-
> bate, March 11, 1977, Question 3.)

About a year later, he told Gibbert:

> Must any innocent woman remain bound to an adulterous
> mate? It depends on whether it's before or after the fact.
> (Smith-Gibbert Debate, April 2, 1978, Question 3.)

As stated before, the issue is not what Smith believes or his
sincerity. The issue is whether or not a man who answers the same
question "Yes," "No," and "It depends," has his own thinking
together enough on the subject to qualify him to take such hard
stands on these issues and to insist that others stand with him.

Connie Adams and H. E. Phillips, Editors of *Searching the Scriptures*

Likewise, Connie Adams, editor of *Searching the Scriptures*, is not qualified to determine when "all out war" ought to take place, because of the careless way he bandies about inflammatory terms, particularly the term "Moyer Position." Lloyd Moyer taught in the 1950s that when a man was unfaithful to his wife, the first act of fornication breaks his old marriage, and the second makes a new one. A concise statement of Lloyd Moyer's position follows:

> That first marriage has been destroyed by the sin of fornication (illicit or unlawful sexual intercourse). Though adultery was committed when they first joined themselves together in intercourse because they were still the husband or wife of someone else, subsequent sexual intercourse between them is not adultery. They are no longer the husband or wife of someone else. And by this sin of adultery they cause their previous marriage to be dissolved. When a marriage is thus dissolved, the innocent is no longer married to the guilty, nor is the guilty any longer married to the innocent. No marriage exists. Where no marriage exists, the parties may marry someone else. We have shown that by the very act of adultery the first marriage was defiled, adulterated and therefore dissolved. Subsequent sexual intercourse would not be adultery. It would be simply a man and his wife cohabiting in the confines of marriage. (Lloyd Moyer, *Gospel Guardian*, Aug. 22 and 29, 1963, pp. 253, 257.)

Lloyd was the only Moyer who taught this position. Both his brothers rejected it for the same reason many people do: fornication never made a marriage bond, and it never broke one, that is, without a putting away for fornication.

At the time of the Smith-Lovelady debate, H. E. Phillips, editor of *Searching the Scriptures*, moderated for Smith. In this debate, neither Smith nor Lovelady believed the Moyer position, nor did the only Moyer who attended the debate believe that position. The word "Moyer" was in none of the propositions, and no one spoke the word "Moyer" in the course of the debate. In fact, Gene Frost, another prolific writer on the subject has said:

> I know of no one today who believes the position that brother Moyer took. ("The Divorce Issue," *Gospel Anchor*, July 1978, pp. 2-7.)

But Connie Adams and H. E. Phillips, editors of *Searching the Scriptures,* published the debate, and their advertisements said, "This debate examines the Moyer Position." Even if it did, the debate must not have done a very good job of it, since the word "Moyer" never occurred the whole week! We have no problem with the sincerity or integrity of Connie Adams and H. E. Phillips, but as they bandied that term about, they either didn't know enough about it, or weren't careful enough, to be qualified to decide when "all out war" should take place.

Later, Connie Adams wrote about brother Hailey and the Bales position, and in so doing misrepresented Bales' position. Bales believes that all men are under law to Christ, but not that all men are under *all* the Law of Christ. Bales believes that aliens are under the entrance requirements, so they are not commanded to partake of the Lord's Supper, contribute to preaching the gospel, nor take the gospel to the lost. But Adams said that Bales doesn't believe alien sinners are under law to Christ at all. Bales also believes that alien sinners are condemned because they violate the law of their conscience. Adams asked why we should preach the gospel to aliens if they're not amenable to all the Law of Christ. He wonders how he got to be a sinner in the first place. Bales teaches that it's because he violated his conscience, just like the Gentiles Paul spoke of in Romans 1-2 violated the law of their conscience. One who knows no more than this about the issue, isn't qualified to decide when "all out war" should take place.

Gene Frost, Editor of *Gospel Anchor*

Gene Frost, editor of the *Gospel Anchor,* has also written a tremendous amount on this subject over the years, but the thing we wish to note is his disparagement of study:

> The subject of divorce and remarriage is yet an unresolved study with many. It is one of controversy wherein many positions are advocated. And yet we must conclude that differences are the result of the weakness of man rather than a failure in the revelation of God. (Gene Frost, "Gift of Celibacy," *Gospel Anchor*, October 1976, pp. 20-22.)

If by weakness Frost means imperfect knowledge or limited intelligence, he is surely correct. But Frost didn't leave it at that. About Jack Gibbert, who debated Smith, he said:

> Gibbert stated that the subject of divorce and remarriage is an "unsettled question." What false teacher would not subscribe to such a position? (Gene Frost, "The Divorce Issue," *Gospel Anchor*, July 1978, p. 4.)

Many conclude from this that *unresolved study* means one is *weak*, and is thus a *false teacher*. Many false teachers don't believe their question is unsettled (e.g., denominational preachers, Jehovah's Witnesses, premillennialists, Mormons, charismatics, etc.). Most seriously, this statement chills tremendously the atmosphere for study, and makes many Christians take hardened stands on matters which they haven't studied thoroughly themselves.

However, in his earlier days, Frost took a number of years for quiet study himself on this very subject:

> Through the years following, I have had relatively little to say upon the subject, for the most part speaking on it as requested. My disposition has been to avoid a heated, brotherhood controversy in favor of a period of calm,

deliberate study. ("The Divorce Issue," *Gospel Anchor*,
July 1978, pp. 2-7.)

Don't we all need what Frost needed then? If not on divorce
and remarriage, on some other subject? We do, and the next
generation will, too. Just because Frost studied the issue out for
himself, that doesn't mean that thousands now don't need to do
the same thing. New converts will have to study, for surely we
won't teach them to rely on Frost's conclusions, will we? *The
conclusions of his study aren't "case law" for others.* When a
state supreme court decides a matter, that decision becomes case
law for the courts throughout the state. When the editor of a paper
decides a matter, his decision does not become case law throughout the brotherhood. When prominent Jewish rabbis did this, they
called it the *Talmud!* Why can Frost have years of calm, deliberate study, but others who claim it's an "unsettled question" are
branded as false teachers? It's not fair for someone who has been
able to study for years to write off someone else who hasn't, and
is honestly searching for truth.

Recall Reuel Lemmon's statement concerning the earlier
controversy on institutionalism:

> I don't want any committee of editors deciding for me
> what the truth is. I will decide that for myself. And every
> reader of every paper in the brotherhood should feel the
> same way. Neither an infallible man nor an infallible
> paper exists. Not man, nor committee of men—even
> though they be editors—can tell me what to believe.
> (Reuel Lemmons, *Firm Foundation*, May 28, 1957.)

As with the others, the issue is not Frost's intelligence, sincerity, or love of the Lord at all. As Christians, we have the right
and responsibility to study *any issue* for ourselves. We should be
extremely leery of anyone who stifles study, whether it's the
Catholic Church, or a preacher, paper, or anyone else.

Sensible Words from James W. Adams, Editor of the *Gospel Guardian*

James W. Adams, former editor of the *Gospel Guardian*, wrote many sensible things about fellowship on divorce and remarriage several years before the controversy over Hailey's teaching began. His influence probably held off a denominational split among us in the mid-1970s. His comments don't deal with the truth on the issues as much as they deal with how we ought to treat each other while we're studying. In the *Gospel Guardian* of June 1, 1976, James Adams said:

> The Marriage and Divorce Question, Carnal Warfare and Peace Officers, The Artificial Covering and Long Hair for Women. All of these matters and others which could be named have one thing in common. They have to do with the practice of the individual Christian and not of a congregation as a congregation. In this, they differ radically from questions concerning the support of human organizations and sponsoring churches by the congregations as congregations. The practice of a single individual in these areas does not of necessity involve the conscience or practice of another individual. They do not of necessity, therefore, have to become matters of fellowship on the congregational level. This is not to say that truth does not lie on one side or the other of every one of these matters. It is to say that they are to be dealt with in a manner different from that utilized in dealing with congregational matters.
>
> I am not attempting, in this article, to pose a workable solution to our differences in these areas. I am attempting only to appeal to the good sense of serious, reflecting, dedicated brethren of good will not to press their views in these areas to the inevitable destruction of fellowship and peace. Some profess not to make such "tests of fellowship," yet constantly harp upon these subjects in their preaching and in the church bulletins (many such

bulletins are simply sounding boards for the preachers' idiosyncrasies and not mediums of the congregation at all). (James W. Adams, "False Conclusions from Just Principles," *Gospel Guardian*, pp. 220-221.)

Two years later, Adams wrote:

The divorce and remarriage question is highly complex. Many suppose that their *ipse dixits* in the matter constitute Revelation or Law. Over-simplification of the issue coupled with arbitrary dictums have obscured rather than exposed truth on the question. Too many hesitate not to play god with the lives of other people. I have no disposition whatsoever to adjust God's will to make it compatible with the permissive ethics of our time, nor do I have any disposition to usurp Divine prerogatives in making overly human, arbitrary, and uncertain application of Divine principles to particular situations. I understand the stated principles of Holy Scripture on divorce and remarriage and preach them unequivocally. However, I am not always absolutely certain how they may apply in complex marital difficulties involving divorce and remarriage. In this respect, I do not know as much as some brethren. Where I am uncertain, I move with great caution. In my teaching, I maintain unequivocally that marriage is for life—one man and one woman and that divorce and remarriage are only permissible when there is violation of the marriage vows—fornication. In a class situation, I do not permit open discussion of the solution of either hypothetical or real situations. (James W. Adams, "Speak for Yourself John," *Gospel Guardian*, January 15, 1978, p. 29.)

Adams' sensible attitude on conduct during study has prevented him from making many mistakes. He hasn't contradicted himself on the definition of adultery. We don't find him making contradictory statements about I Cor. 7.27-28. He doesn't contradict himself on the "bound to fornicator" position. He doesn't carelessly bandy about prejudicial terms like "Moyer

Position." Neither has he discouraged others from studying for themselves.

A few months later, Adams wrote:

> Recently, I wrote an editorial entitled: "Johnny-Come-Lately-Sommerites" in which I addressed my remarks to the senseless and potentially ruinous spirit at work, among conservatives which is ready at "the drop of a hat" to divide and disfellowship over every divergent point of view. Since becoming editor of the paper, I have not written anything in it which has evoked more universal approval than this article. Brethren everywhere are becoming increasingly tired of senseless strife and bickering over every difference. Some are slow to learn (among them, my correspondents) and slower still to cease their activities, but their tirades must not be allowed to obstruct reasonable, scriptural, and patient handling of said differences among us. Love, mercy, patience, forbearance, longsuffering, and "the unity of the Spirit" must not be sacrificed on the altar of sectarian bigotry and pride. (James W. Adams, "Every Way of Man is Right In His Own Eyes," *Gospel Guardian, XXX,* No. 10, May 15, 1978, p. 221.)

Note particularly Adams' reference to "sectarian bigotry." If we substitute the position of a coalition of congregations imposed by preachers or papers (a denominational idea) for our own independent congregational study, *we are indeed sectarian!*

About debates on the issue, Adams wrote:

> Formal, oral, public debates that are designed for the benefit of the brotherhood at large, are advertised as such, and are participated in on that basis have a tendency to promote the party spirit among brethren as no other medium of discussion does. There is something so intimately personal about such face to face confrontations when coupled with the inevitable temptation to save face and preserve reputation that causes such confrontations to polarize rather than eradicate divergent views. The

result is party alignment and disruption of fellowship. This does not indict all debates nor does it preclude debates between brethren. There can be a place and need for such debates when they are properly arranged, involve qualified and representative disputants, and the propositions for discussion involve matters that have become an issue of sufficient magnitude to affect the unity and fellowship of the Lord's disciples generally. However, to invoke this means of dealing with moot questions in the realm of personal morals and individual responsibilities to God and thereby project them into "tests of fellowship" falls infinitely below what is ordinarily connoted by the term "folly." (James W. Adams, *Gospel Guardian, XXX,* No. 12, July, 1978, p. 269.)

Concerning fellowship in general, Adams said:

Brethren, we cannot make everything about which we disagree a test of fellowship. Some things in individual practice about which we differ are just going to have to be tolerated. We are just going to have to let the Lord decide about some things. I confess that I do not have all the answers to all problems in these realms. We can live together concerning these matters if we are satisfied not to *press* our divergent views. Let those with permissive views hold them, not press them. Let those with conservative views in these matters not arrogate to themselves prerogatives of judgment that belong only to "Him who judgeth wisely." On the basis of charity, I might conceivably have fellowship with some person in this life whose life in the Lord will in the judgment judge as not having been worthy of such fellowship. I think, however, I had rather risk this than to run the risk of driving away from the Lord, as did Diotrophes, those worthy of my fellowship in the eyes of the Lord and thus become the cause of the loss of their souls and the souls of those whom they influence in the world to come. My plea is for sanity, forbearance, and tolerance in these areas of disagreement in which the matter is individual and not collective in character.

I will take second place to no person in my absolute respect for the institution of marriage as ordained by God. The principle of one man and one woman for life, I unequivocally accept. That there is only one cause for divorce and remarriage acceptable to God, fornication, I believe unreservedly. However, relative to how to solve the problems caused by sinful breaking of marriages by imperfect human beings so as to be infallibly certain of the eternal security of those involved, I must often confess my ignorance and even bewilderment. In this respect, others seem to know a great deal more about the subject than do I. My own lack of knowledge and the acute consciousness of my own fallibility cause me to move with great caution. I do not anticipate a time when it will be different. If others, out of a false sense of devotion to a Divine institution, wish to usurp Divine prerogatives and pronounce infallible judgments, so be it. The risk is theirs, and they are welcome to it. (James W. Adams, *Gospel Guardian, XXX,* No. 13, August 1978, pp. 303-304.)

After the attack on Hailey, Adams wrote, in an article entitled "Splendid Murder" (so named from what an eighteenth century Scottish poet wrote concerning war: "Rash, fruitless war, from wanton glory waged, is only splendid murder"):

I admit with embarrassment and shame that such "murder" is committed by professed New Testament Christians in our time. Whenever otherwise faithful brethren are openly and publicly attacked because of difference of understanding some point of Bible teaching when the point of view has been merely voiced as a personal conviction and no effort has been made to press the view upon others, such warfare is both "rash and fruitless." This being true, for what purpose could it be waged but for "wanton glory?" We presume not to judge, but maintain the right to ask the question.

Spiritual warfare is right, but let us always be sure that the cause justifies the response. A doctor does not remove a leg because of a lesion when an antibiotic will effect a cure. Your automobile may not be legally searched on the highway by an officer of the Law unless he can show "probable cause." In the church of the Lord, one does not seek to manufacture issues. There are plenty of real ones without unnecessarily creating others. Too often, strife and division, intrachurch or interchurch, which claim a doctrinal basis and profess to be for "love of the truth," at their root emanate from "lusts that war in our members" or "wanton glory." There is not even "probable cause," much less "adequate cause." It is possible to hide this embarrassing fact from ourselves by convincing ourselves that we are nobly motivated by devotion to a "thus saith the Lord." This article pleads only for the principle of fighting only when we have to! (James W. Adams, "Splendid Murder," *The Apostolic Messenger*, July 1989, p. 3.)

Guardian of Truth Magazine Pressed for Break in Fellowship

The irony of this is that when James Adams wrote the above article, he also wrote articles published in the *Guardian of Truth* which said that such views as his on fellowship were worse than false doctrine on marriage, divorce, and remarriage itself! For example, Mike Willis, editor of *Guardian of Truth* (whose roots go back to the *Gospel Guardian* and *Truth Magazine*), wrote of the Hailey conflict in this way:

As this issue was discussed among us, another group of brethren began teaching that the divorce and remarriage issue should not be made a test of fellowship. In many respects this looser view of fellowship is a more dangerous doctrine than is the loose view of divorce and remarriage. (Mike Willis, "Fellowship and the Divorce and Remarriage Issue," *Guardian of Truth, XXXVI,* No. 1, January 2, 1992, p. 1.)

In the same issue, Tom Roberts wrote:

Truthfully, these arguments to encourage fellowship on the marriage-divorce-remarriage issue are more dangerous, if possible, than the marriage-divorce-remarriage issue itself. (Tom Roberts, *Ibid.,* p. 17.)

On the next page, Mike Willis, in an article entitled, "Just Like the War Question," wrote:

Some have argued, "The differences over divorce and remarriage are just like our differences over the war question." (*Ibid.,* p. 18.)

Willis was correct, some had argued so. But did these men actually believe that James W. Adams, who wrote the following words earlier in the *Gospel Guardian,* was more dangerous than the ones who held false doctrine on divorce and remarriage? Adams wrote:

The Marriage and Divorce Question, Carnal Warfare and Peace Officers, The Artificial Covering and Long Hair for Women. All of these matters and others which could be named have one thing in common. They have to do with the practice of the individual Christian and not of a congregation as a congregation. (James W. Adams, "False Conclusions from Just Principles," *Gospel Guardian,* June 1, 1976, p. 220.)

If, as Willis said, one who holds such views was more dangerous than the false teacher on divorce and remarriage, could Willis still use James W. Adams' material in the *Guardian of Truth*? Was this the "unity in diversity" he so readily decried in his paper regarding others? Could it have been that his own concept of fellowship was loose, or perhaps he just didn't realize what Adams' views were? Willis would have done well to have dwelt on these words of Adams:

> My own lack of knowledge and the acute consciousness of my own fallibility cause me to move with great caution. I do not anticipate a time when it will be different. If others, out of a false sense of devotion to a Divine institution, wish to usurp Divine prerogatives and pronounce infallible judgments, so be it. The risk is theirs, and they are welcome to it. (James W. Adams, *Gospel Guardian, XXX*, No. 13, August, 1978, pp. 303-304.)

We shouldn't leave the view that Willis' special issue on Fellowship on Marriage, Divorce and Remarriage was completely unfruitful as far as wise counsel on this subject. Not surprisingly, Bill Cavender gave several recommendations to promote unity, peace, and good will among brethren:

> We can cease using papers published by brethren and churches for dissections of opinions and foolish questions which engender strife. No one's opinion on matters of personal faith or "conscience" are necessary to salvation, and are not to be bound upon anyone in their service and worship to God. We have so many divisive opinions among us nowadays, so many written and unwritten party "shibboleths," that we are rapidly appearing as a sect, a part of divided people, who have no certain foundations, doctrines and directions to offer the world of saints and sinners alike, and are not sure anymore of anything we say and teach. We are "shooting ourselves in the feet," decimating ourselves in numbers, diminishing our resources by divisions, beginning churches which are not needed, and discouraging brethren who do want to do God's will. There is hardly a growing "conservative" church of Christ anymore, i.e., growing by baptisms, restorations, and internal spiritual development. (*Ibid.*, p. 5.)

Likewise, Colly Caldwell wrote:

> ...all decisions on unity must be decided personally or congregationally, not nationally or by some individual Christian or association of Christians for all other Christians. (*Ibid.*, p. 6.)

Again, the issue is not Willis' intelligence, sincerity, or love for Christ. The issue is that he might have been more unified with diversity than he realized, and didn't need to be inciting breaks in fellowship, as the following section suggests.

Always Have Been Differences, and Still Are

Always Been Differences

There have been significant differences on these issues since the beginning of the restoration of the New Testament way of Christ in America. For example, Alexander Campbell in the *Millennial Harbinger* of 1834, pp. 70-72, took the same position as James Bales. Campbell took the position that I Cor. 7.12-15 had not been legislated on by the Lord when he gave the legislation of Mt. 19.9, and that when the unbeliever deserted, the believer was free from the marriage bond and could scripturally remarry. He also said that one should accept aliens who had been divorced and remarried while in the world. At the conclusion of the article, he said that Walter Scott also approved of that position. Alexander Campbell had tremendous influence among millions for calling people back to the proper standard for Christians, the Bible. Walter Scott won renown for formulating the "invitation" at the conclusion of services as we know it today. R. L. Whiteside, the author of many books we use today, took the same position on I Cor. 7.10-15. (*Reflections of Robertson L. Whiteside* [Denton, TX: Inys Whiteside, 1965], pp. 102, 107.) David Lipscomb, in the *Gospel Advocate*, advised the young preacher G. C. Brewer, who later became a tremendously influential gospel preacher, regarding this matter. (James D. Bales, *Shall We Splinter?* [Searcy, AR: J. D. Bales Publisher, n.d.], p. 4.) Brewer had baptized someone who had been divorced and remarried. Some members of the congregation objected because the person did not leave his wife. Lipscomb counseled him to let such cases alone instead of separating them.

J. W. McGarvey, a truly great scholar, who wrote several commentaries still popular today, took the position that the put-away fornicator could remarry. The renowned gospel preacher John T. Lewis said he would not tell aliens to separate. W. W. Otey, who we esteem for his opposition to the missionary society in the early 1900s and the sponsoring church concept in the 1950s, didn't tell divorced aliens to separate when they obeyed the gospel. F. B. Srygley, another giant of earlier times, believed a put-away fornicator could remarry, and quoted McGarvey in his argumentation. The esteemed N. B. Hardeman believed I Cor. 7.15 gave a deserted believer the right to remarry. R. L. Whiteside, as query editor of the *Gospel Advocate* in the 1930s, took the same position. Foy Wallace, Jr. said it was a presumptuous procedure to break up families in *The Sermon on the Mount and the Civil State.* (Nashville, TN: Foy E. Wallace, Jr. Publications, 1967, p. 41.)

One might wonder if the author believes all those positions. Of course not, no one could! The point is that we regard these men as giants, and rightly so. We use their commentaries, often quote from them, and are thankful for their service. Why all of a sudden must we now press each other to draw lines of fellowship when men of similar stature have such differences? Why must we now split because of a private study of less than twenty people in Belen, New Mexico, of all places? The last denominational split among us began in Abilene, a small, windblown town in West Texas. If this one starts in Belen, one wonders where the next one will start. Could it be Cut Bank, Montana?

Differences Exist Among Those Inciting a Denominational Split on Significant Aspects of Divorce and Remarriage

Those who continue to press these issues to the division of fellowship are not immune from such a spectrum of differences either. They might give some people the impression that they hold to a monolithic position, but not so! Among them exist significant disagreements about what makes a marriage. They disagree about what divorce actually is. They disagree on their definition of adultery, some espousing definitions no one heard of until the last decade.

They even disagree on one of the major debate propositions: J. T. Smith debated that one unjustly put away cannot put away a fornicating spouse, and said that he draws lines of fellowship with those who disagree with his teaching in those debates. Concerning this proposition, James W. Adams wrote: "I do not believe it to be true! It is a human inference (opinion) from the teaching of Jesus that is purely gratuitous." (James W. Adams, "Identical Abominations," *Gospel Guardian, XXX,* No. XIII, August 1978, p. 302.) Yet Willis continues to publish articles by both Smith and James W. Adams. Ron Halbrook and Marshall Patton also disagree with Smith on this proposition, but they're not drawing big, black, bold lines of fellowship on each other. Does Smith draw lines of fellowship on Halbrook and Patton? Does he draw them on any of the legendary restoration preachers? Does Mike Willis? If they don't, is this more "unity in diversity" that should be condemned? Why isn't it "unity in diversity" for Willis to continue to publish articles by both J. T. Smith and James W. Adams who differ on this very proposition? Someone has well said that *Pharisees are like lawyers, and you know how lawyers are: they build big fences around the laws that are important to them, but find loopholes around the ones that are not so important.*

What Is a False Teacher?

All of this makes us wonder, just what is a false teacher, anyway? This term is bandied about quite casually, and many use it of just about anybody who is doctrinally off on nearly anything. For example, J. T. Smith said about Ed Harrell's plea for humane treatment of Hailey:

> Brother Harrell thinks brother Hailey has been abused because he has been referred to as a false teacher, even though Ed says he "does not believe brother Hailey is correct." If he is not correct, then that means he is incorrect. (J. T. Smith, *Torch*, *XXIV*, No. 2, February 1989, p. 5.)

Note again that Harrell never pointed out where he disagreed with Hailey, or why. He didn't even prove Hailey was incorrect, yet Smith accepted that conclusion without question. Have we reached the point where if someone *says* someone is wrong, that *makes him* wrong? Smith argued from Harrell's disagreement with Hailey that therefore Hailey was not correct. Then Smith argued that if Hailey was not correct, 'he was incorrect, and thus he was a false teacher!

In contrast to the way some toss around the term "false teacher" so casually, the New Testament used the term only once, in II Pet. 2.1, "as also among you shall arise false teachers." Peter listed *twenty-nine characteristics* of these false teachers in verses 1-22. In verse 1, Peter mentioned their privily (sneakily) working, their heresies (divisive opinions) that will destroy their followers, and the fact that they deny Jesus! In verse 2, he described their lascivious doings, and that non-Christians would speak evil of the way because of them. In verse 3, he showed that they were covetous and used counterfeit words designed to make merchandise of Christians. This is a good description of some of the "televangelists" of our day, but were these the characteristics of Homer Hailey, or just anyone else who is incorrect? In verse 10, Peter affirmed that these walked after the flesh, they operated from the lusts of defilement, and they despised dominion, and were daring, self-willed, and trembled not to rail at dignities. In verse 11, he said they railed in matters of which they were ignorant. In verse 13, Peter said they enjoyed the hire of wrongdoing, and counted it pleasure to revel in the daytime. He said they were spots and blemishes, reveling in the deceivings while they feasted with Christians. In verse 14, Peter explained that they had eyes full of adultery, could not cease from sin, and enticed unstedfast souls with hearts exercised in covetousness, and were thus children of cursing (destruction). In verse 15, Peter said they forsook the right way because they loved the hire of wrongdoing. In verse 18, he described how they uttered great swelling words of vanity while they enticed in the lusts of the flesh. In verse 19, he called them bondservants of corruption, and concluded in verse 21 by saying it were better for them to have never known the way of righteousness.

When some so casually describe Hailey and others as false teachers, are they using the term scripturally? Is it proper to use the term to describe anyone who is not correct, therefore incorrect, therefore a false teacher? If it's right to so use the term, who would that make a false teacher?

For example, J. T. Smith, who was incorrect in his definition of adultery at one time or the other, labels himself a false teacher by his own definition. Likewise, he has been incorrect in his interpretation of I Cor. 7.27-28, as evidenced by his inconsistent answers to questions on those verses. In addition, his inconsistencies about whether one must remain bound to an adulterous mate demonstrate that, *according to his own terminology,* he is a false teacher. Does Smith brand Ron Halbrook and Marshall Patton as false teachers when they disagree with him on one of his major debate propositions? Do they brand Alexander Campbell, Walter Scott, and David Lipscomb as false teachers because they were incorrect? How about McGarvey, Otey, Srygley, Hardeman, Whiteside, and Wallace? According to Willis, Smith, Connie Adams, and Frost, none of these men could hold meetings in most churches today, nor could they write for most of the papers.

A Local Church Shouldn't Let Outsiders
Determine Its Course of Action

As Lipscomb wrote:

When differences exist, the discussion of these differences is the only hope of union. The suppression of discussion is the direct and open road to division. Whoever opposes the free discussion of differences among brethren, in that favors speedy division. Differences existing will manifest themselves. If they are discussed freely, there is hope of reconciliation and harmony. Suppress the discussion, and unless the strong hand of arbitrary and despotic power holds by the terror of physical force, disruption and division must follow. When persons having a community of interest differ, so long as those who differ show a kindly interest in the others, listen to the remonstrances, treat with considerate kindness their feelings, wishes, and reasonings, they remain one. The moment the one party says: "We wish to hear no more your reasonings; we intend no longer to regard your feelings or wishes; we intend to go our own way, regardless of your course or purposes," those people become two distinct people. Division or an unmanly and unchristian submission to what we believe to be wrong is the only alternative. (*Gospel Advocate*, 1906, p. 552.)

A more modern expression of these sentiments is found in the words of Robert F. Turner, a gospel preacher universally respected for his calm, nondenominational views. Turner wrote:

If divided brethren are serious about wanting unity, they *must* keep open channels of communication with reference to God's word. The universal laboratory test to determine the spirit of man with reference to redemption and unity is his reaction to examination of his faith and practice in the light of the written sword of God's Spirit. When the door to further study of God's word is closed, we have closed the door to further *seeking* and *striving* in its light. We have closed the door to unity, and to heaven. It is here, and here only, that men learn and accept the power of God by which they are changed from darkness to light, and *become one*. May God help us to open our hearts to Him, and to one another. (Robert F. Turner, "The Biblical Concept of Unity," *1982 Florida College Lectures, Their Works Do Follow Them* [Temple Terrace, FL: Florida College Bookstore], p. 15.)

Earlier in the same article, Turner spoke of sectarian or denominational attitudes which prevent continued, deliberative study:

Self-serving pride will prevent fellowship with God and with brethren. The sectarian spirit that separates us from God will splinter us as a people. To the extent we act like the Devil, we will be his children (Jn. 8:41-47) and will forfeit our place in the family of God and in a unified brotherhood. Brethren, we must quit kidding ourselves. God's kind of unity is as difficult, and no more so, as coming to God and being faithful to Him. It requires the same selfless dedication, commitment, and complete dependence upon God. "Narrow is the gate and few are they that find it" (Matt. 7:14). (Robert F. Turner, *Ibid.*, p. 10.)

Turner also warned of letting others do our study for us:

In the first place, many (perhaps most) divisions occur because people are stubborn and self-willed. With hurried and inadequate study, someone draws an erroneous conclusion—and would "split a hame" before he would admit he is wrong. Sides are drawn, and away we go. We compromise points to fit our background or to justify some human weakness, as a solution for what we consider some "greater" wrong, and so, on and on. Peer pressures cause many divisions, for we are often too lazy or feel ourselves incompetent to study for ourselves; so we "go along" with big-name preachers, papers, or other centers of influence. Pride is a great underlying factor. Serving self is more important to us than serving God. (Robert F. Turner, *Ibid.*, p. 13.)

On another occasion, Turner discussed a brotherhood debacle which illustrated his major proposition for an article:

ANY PROJECT OR INSTITUTION OPERATED BY OR FOR THE BENEFIT OF THE CHURCH AT LARGE, "THE BROTHERHOOD," TENDS TO DE-NOMINATIONALIZE THAT BROTHERHOOD. The institution itself may not be so much to blame as the "brotherhood" conceptions that produce and maintain the institution. Party ties are made and strengthened, opinions accepted by the majority become traditions, are crystallized into party tenets; and accepted in the second or third generation as proof of orthodoxy. When the "brotherhood" functions, there must be the acceptance of common direction and guidance; the "brotherhood voice" must be heard. And "brotherhood schools" have paved the way for denominational organizations among members of the Lord's church. No amount of denying can change this obvious historical and current fact. (Robert F. Turner, "The Schools, and Denominational-ism," *The Preceptor, XI*, No. 8 [Beaumont, TX: The Preceptor Company, June 1962], p. 124.)

If we cannot properly conduct ourselves with each other in a local church, are we really the caliber of people who are qualified to tell others what to do in these matters? If we cannot study with each other, when we know we accept a common standard and are trying to live by God's word, how can we study with outsiders who don't share that common standard? *Thus, many in churches of Christ throughout the country have not only lost the ability to study with one another, they have lost the ability to study with those outside of Christ as well.* Lipscomb assailed the same problem in his day:

The Church that stifles investigation, but [only—SGD] prepares and nourishes the elements of violent explosion and division within its own bosom. We will freely, gladly hear ourselves and let our readers hear both sides of every question we present. (David Lipscomb, *Gospel Advocate*, 1866, p. 111.)

Rather than disparaging the need for study, we need to disparage the attitude that stifles it. Truth has nothing to fear in open investigation. Truth only gets brighter as it's polished in the search for truth. *When a congregation fails to do its own studying, but depends on papers, preachers, and other outsiders to do its studying, deliberation, and determination of its action, it participates in the inevitable denominational split.* History shows this procedure has always led to a denominational split before much study was done by a lot of good people on both sides of the issue. This is evidenced by the missionary society, instrumental music, and institutional splits. Churches of Christ are doomed to undergo a series of splits until they learn how to study, give others the right to study, and behave themselves while they do it.

What Should a Local Church Do?

The purpose of this chapter is to enhance study of these matters, and to elevate our behavior while we do it. It is not the author's purpose to suggest that the issues on divorce and remarriage are so complex that we cannot understand them. He doesn't believe it. But just because some have settled these issues for themselves doesn't mean that *all of us* have settled them, *for all time*.

If we want to avoid participating in the next denominational split, we must make sure that our congregation conforms to those churches pleasing to Christ in the New Testament. New Testament congregations were independent teams of disciples. "Disciples" means they were students, they were willing to study for themselves, and they did study. God intended for each congregation to be a working group, not two distinct people as Lipscomb described above. The congregations were independent in that each congregation determined its understanding of God's will for itself.

The congregation that will not or cannot study for itself, and behave itself while it does so, will have to depend on outside preachers and papers. It won't be an independent team of disciples. Regardless of which side of the issue it's on, *it will play a definite role in another denominational split,* this time on the subject of divorce and remarriage.

This chapter is not about the truth of various divorce and remarriage questions. We can and must study these issues for ourselves. This chapter is about how Christians in local churches can avoid letting outside forces propel them into another denominational split. As James W. Adams said:

> Brethren of influence and ability can stop our progress
> toward oblivion on the road of "partyism" if they have
> the courage to speak out against it boldly and plainly. No
> one person, church, or paper can do it.

Note: You can help prevent a denominational split. This chapter is available in booklet form for your use. If you are a preacher and are agreed that local churches should be able to study these matters and determine local church action without outside interference, won't you help get copies of the booklet into the hands of the local elders, and other influential members? Think of others who would benefit from being warned of the danger that confronts us all.

If you are an elder in a local church, you of all people should object to outside stifling of study within your local congregation. Copies of the booklet could help alert your members to the denominationalizing tendencies of previous divisions in churches of Christ, so they will not be willing to inadvertently participate in another one.

If you are a Christian who is a Bible student, copies of the booklet will serve to admonish those you influence to study for themselves.

Bibliography

Adams, Connie and Phillips, H. E., editors. *Searching the Scriptures.*

Adams, James W. "Every Way of Man Is Right in His Own Eyes." *Gospel Guardian,* May 15, 1978.

Adams, James W. "False Conclusions from Just Principles." *Gospel Guardian,* June 1976.

Adams, James W. *Gospel Guardian,* July 1978.

Adams, James W. "Identical Abominations." *Gospel Guardian,* August, 1978.

Adams, James W. "Speak for Yourself John." *Gospel Guardian,* January 15, 1978.

Adams, James W. "Splendid Murder." *The Apostolic Messenger,* July 1989.

Adams, Jay E. *Marriage, Divorce & Remarriage in the Bible.* Phillipsburg, NJ: Presbyterian and Reformed Publishing Company, 1980.

American Standard Bible. Nashville, TN: Thomas Nelson & Sons, 1929.

Baird, James O. *And I Say unto You.* Oklahoma City, OK: B & B Bookhouse, 1982.

Bales, James D. *Shall We Splinter?* Searcy, AR: J. D. Bales Publisher, n.d.

Barnett, Maurice. *Alien Sinners and the Law of Christ.* Phoenix, AZ: Westside Church of Christ, n.d.

Bassett, Jerry F. *Rethinking Marriage, Divorce & Remarriage.* Eugene, OR: Western Printers, 1991.

Boles, H. Leo. *Commentary on Matthew.* Nashville, TN: Gospel Advocate Company, 1936, 1964 Reprint.

Bowman, Jay. *Tract on Marriage.* No publisher, n.d.

Brewer, G. C. *Contending for the Faith.* Reprinted from the *Gospel Advocate*, August 3, 1933.

Britnell, Eugene. *The Sower,* January 1978.

Bruce, H. L. *Truth Magazine,* January 15, 1976.

Bullinger, E. W. *Figures of Speech Used in the Bible.* Grand Rapids, MI: Baker Book House, 1898.

Caldwell, Colly. *Guardian of Truth,* January 2, 1992.

Campbell, Alexander. *The Millennial Harbinger,* 1834. Reprinted Rosemead, CA: The Old Paths Book Club, 1950.

Cavender, Bill. *Guardian of Truth,* January 2, 1992.

Chappalear, Floyd, editor. *Sentry Magazine.*

Dabney, J. Luther and Frost, Gene. *Dabney-Frost Debate.* Fort Worth, TX: The Manney Co., 1959.

Dawson, Patsy Rae. "Adultery and Sexual Addiction: A Plan for Healing the Soul and the Marriage." Puyallup, WA: Gospel Themes Press, 1998.

Dawson, Patsy Rae. *Marriage: A Taste of Heaven, Vol. II: God's People Make the Best Lovers.* Puyallup, WA: Gospel Themes Press, 1996.

Dawson, Samuel G. *Fellowship: With God and His People, The Way of Christ without Denominationalism.* Santa Maria, CA: Gospel Themes Press, 1988.

Deaver, Roy. Quoted by Thomas, J. D. *Divorce and Remarriage.* Abilene, TX: Biblical Research Press, 1977.

Deaver, Roy. *Spiritual Sword,* January 1975.

DeHoff, George W. *Sermons on First Corinthians.* Murfreesboro, TN: The Christian Press, 1947.

Estes, Maurice W. *Marriage, Divorce, and Remarriage, God's Answer to Man's Problem.* Cayucos, CA: The Meco Foundation Inc., 1979.

Frost, Gene and Moyer, Lloyd. *Frost-Moyer Exchange on Marriage, Divorce, and Remarriage.* Cullman, AL: Printing Service, n.d.

Frost, Gene. "Gift of Celibacy." *Gospel Anchor,* October 1976.

Frost, Gene. "The Divorce Issue." *Gospel Anchor,* July 1978.

Fuqua, E. C. *The Vindicator,* May 1950, August 1951, October 1951, December 1951, and February 1952.

Hailey, Homer. *Christianity Magazine,* November 1988.

Hailey, Homer. *The Divorced and Remarried Who Would Come to God.* Las Vegas, NV: Nevada Publications, 1991.

Halbrook, Ron. *Searching the Scriptures,* September 1991.

Hale, Lewis G. *Except for Fornication.* Oklahoma City, OK: Hale Publications, 1974.

Harrell, Ed. "Homer Hailey: False Teacher." *Christianity Magazine,* November 1988.

Harrell, Pat E. *Divorce and Remarriage in the Early Church.* Austin, TX: R. B. Sweet Co. Inc., 1967.

Hastings, James, editor and Foley, W. M. *Encyclopaedia of Religion and Ethics,* VIII. New York, NY: Charles Scribner's Sons, 1958.

Heth, William A. and Wenham, Gordon J. *Jesus and Divorce.* Nashville, TN: Thomas Nelson Inc., 1985.

Hicks, Olan and Holt, Jack. *Divorce and Remarriage.* Searcy, AR: Gospel Enterprises, 1990.

Hicks, Olan. *Divorce and Remarriage, The Issues Made Clear.* Searcy, AR: Gospel Enterprises, 1990.

Hicks, Olan. *What the Bible Says about Marriage, Divorce & Remarriage.* Joplin, MO: College Press Publishing Co., 1987.

International Standard Bible Encyclopedia. Grand Rapids, MI: Wm. B. Eerdmans Publishing Co., 1939.

Josephus, Flavius. *Complete Works.* Translated by Whiston, William. Grand Rapids, MI: Kregel Publications, 1960.

King James Authorized Version Bible. New York, NY: Collins' Clear-Type Press, n.d.

Lanier, Roy H., Sr. *Marriage, Divorce and Remarriage.* Shreveport, LA: Lambert Book House, n.d.

Lemmons, Reuel. *Firm Foundation,* May 28, 1957. Cited by Winkler, Herbert E. *Congregational Cooperation of the Churches of Christ.* Second Edition. Herbert E. Winkler Publisher, 1961.

Lipscomb, David. *Gospel Advocate.* Nashville, TN: Gospel Advocate Publishing Co., 1866, 1906, and 1912.

MacDonald, George. Cited by Tolle, James. *The Beatitudes.* Fullerton, CA: Tolle Publications, 1966.

McGarvey, J. W. and Pendleton, Philip Y. *The Fourfold Gospel.* Cincinnati, OH: Standard Publishing Foundation, 1914.

McGarvey, J. W. *Commentary on Matthew and Mark.* Delight, AR: Gospel Light, 1875.

Melear, Bob and Williams, Ralph. *Melear-Williams Debate.* Huntington Beach, CA: Bob Melear, 1976.

Menninger, Dr. Karl. Cited by Landers, Ann. Chicago, IL: News America Syndicate.

Moffitt, Jerry. *Bales' Position Explained and Denied.* Austin, TX: Jerry Moffitt, 1982.

Moyer, Lloyd. *Gospel Guardian,* Aug. 22 and 29, 1963.

Murray, John. *Divorce.* Philadelphia, PA: The Presbyterian and Reformed Publishing Co., 1961.

"Nation." *TIME Magazine,* August 17, 1998.

New American Standard Bible. LaHabra, CA: Lockman Foundation, 1977.

Packer, J. I. *"Fundamentalism" and the Word of God.* Grand Rapids, MI: William B. Eerdmans Publishing Co., 1958.

Peters, Edward N. *100 Answers to Your Questions on Annulments.* Necedah, WI: Basilica Press, 1997.

Roberts, Tom. *Guardian of Truth,* January 2, 1992.

Semmelmeyer, Madeline and Bolander, Donald O. *Instant English Handbook.* Mundelein, IL: Career Institute, 1968.

Septuagint Version of the Old Testament. Grand Rapids, MI: Zondervan Publishing House, 1970.

Smith, J. T. and Gibbert, Jack. Smith-Gibbert Debate tapes, April 17, 1978.

Smith, J. T. and Lovelady, Glen. *The Smith-Lovelady Debate on Marriage, Divorce, and Remarriage.* Brooks, KY: *Searching the Scriptures.*

Smith, J. T. and McCollum, Lyle. Smith-McCollum Debate tapes, October 4, 1976.

Smith, J. T. and Melear, Bob. Smith-Melear Debate tapes, March 8, 1977.

Smith, J. T. *Torch,* February 1989.

Smith, Joseph. *Doctrine & Covenants.* Salt Lake City, UT: The Church of Jesus Christ of Latter-day Saints, 1921.

Thayer, Joseph Henry, D.D. *Thayer's Greek-English Lexicon of the New Testament.* Grand Rapids, MI: Associated Publishers and Authors Inc., n.d.

Thomas, J. D. *Divorce and Remarriage.* Abilene, TX: Biblical Research Press, 1977.

TIME Magazine, February 11, 1966.

Tolle, James. *The Beatitudes.* Fullerton, CA: Tolle Publications, 1966.

Turner, Robert F. "The Biblical Concept of Unity." *1982 Florida College Lectures, Their Works Do Follow Them.* Temple Terrace, FL: Florida College Bookstore, 1982.

Turner, Robert F. "The Schools and Denominationalism." *The Preceptor,* June 1962.

Vine, W. E. *Expository Dictionary of New Testament Words.* Westwood, NJ: Fleming H. Revell Company, 1950.

Vinson, Bryan. *Preceptor,* April 15, 1965.

Waldron, Jim E. *Waldron-Hicks Debate.*

Wallace, Foy E., Jr. *Sermon on the Mount and the Civil State.* Nashville, TN: Foy E. Wallace, Jr. Publications, 1967.

Whiteside, R. L. *Reflections of Robertson L. Whiteside.* Denton, TX: Inys Whiteside, 1965.

Willis, Mike. "Fellowship and the Divorce and Remarriage Issue." *Guardian of Truth,* January 2, 1992.

Willis, Mike. "Just Like the War Question." *Guardian of Truth,* January 2, 1992.

Wykoff, George S. and Shaw, Harry. *The Harper Handbook,* Third Edition. New York, NY: Harper & Row, 1962.

Scripture Index

Topical Index

A

Abimelech on adultery 39
Abraham, taking a wife for Issac 11
Adams, Connie
  Belen, NM meeting 296
  misrepresents Bales position 304
  pressing for division 303
Adams, James W.
  article "Spendid Murder" 311
  on value of public debates 307
  sensible words on fellowship
    from 307
  vs. J. T. Smith 317
Adams, Jay, on unbeliever abandoning believer 160
adulterers
  most not stoned to death 49
  reconcilation with mate and
    God 267
adultery
  Abimelech on 39
  Bryan Vinson on definition
    of 36, 245
  David Bonner on definition of
    246, 265
  death penalty for 43
  defined 30
  defined in Rom. 7.2-3 31, 169
  figurative 181
  Gene Frost on definition
    of 36, 245
  God's definition of 31, 169
  how enduring 175
  importance of definition 24
  includes sexual intercourse 182
  J. D. Thomas on definition
    of 37, 246
  J. T. Smith inconsistent on defini-
    tion of 299
  J. T. Smith on definition
    of 37, 246
  Jay Bowman on definition
    of 36, 246
  living in 175, 198

Maurice Barnett on definition
    of 37, 246
  new definitions of 37
  New Testament prohibitions 40
  Olan Hicks on definition
    of 180, 246
  Old Testament examples of 38
  pornography, strip bars, and phone
    sex 288
  recent changes in definition of 246
  requires a spouse 31, 36
  Roy Lanier, Sr. on definition
    of 36, 246
  suspected 44
  testing for 44
  three ways committed in Mt. 5.27-
    32 165
  verified 43
  vs. bill of divorcement 109, 124
  vs. fornication 29, 32
  vs. lust 107
  with feet, with eyes, with
    courts 165
affirmations, vs. oaths 109
Albert Sweitzer, on Sermon on the
    Mount 65
aliens
  amenable to God's law 194
  how condemned 196
  under sophisticated moral law 196
aliens or Christians, does it
    matter? 275
annulment
  Roman Catholic concept 16, 191
  statistics 16
  vs. divorce 16

B

Bales position
  Alexander Campbell took 315
  Connie Adams misrepresents 304
  R. L. Whiteside took 315
  Walter Scott took 315

How to Study the Bible:

A Practical Guide to Independent Bible Study

Samuel G. Dawson

446 pages with comprehensive indexes

A tradition-challenging publication without denominational bias!

If you've listened to this popular cassette album, you know how valuable this material is. However, the book contains significant new material not on the cassettes. It begins with a new chapter on "Jesus' Call for Disciples" that demonstrates what it means to be a true disciple or student of God's word, rather than just a spectator sitting in a pew. Another chapter explores "The Importance of the Old Testament to New Testament Christians," while it exposes many of our unfounded prejudices against the Old Covenant. A great help is a list of "Old Testament Passages Quoted in the New Testament," which points us to the inspired commentary on those prophetic verses.

Also, the 42-page "Outline of the Bible" provides a valuable tool for grasping the overall view and context of the Bible and is a fascinating read in itself. Other items of importance are a strategy for both individuals and churches to use in teaching and studying all of the books and topics of the Bible in a timely fashion and an analysis of how all of us have two reservoirs of Bible knowledge: topical and book-by-book.

You can read a detailed table of contents at www.gospelthemes.com/htsbk.htm. You can also read what others say about the material. When one Christian used the material to teach a class, the elders asked him to repeat the class the next year.

Although written by a serious non-denominational Bible student, preacher, and teacher of nearly 40 years, this book is not for the professional Bible scholar or theologian. It is for the independent Bible student who would like to know more of the Bible's teaching without a denominational slant or dependence on a professional. In recent years, the availability of helpful reference works has exploded, as have resources on the Internet. As modern Bibles and the religious world are becoming more premillennialistic and Calvinistic, the emphasis on online easy-to-use Bible aids helps today's student remain true to God's word-for-word inspired text. You can take advantage of these new opportunities for yourself.

This book brings the Bible to life and makes it relevant for today. Lessons progress from examining basic attitudes toward the Bible to choosing a dependable translation to rules for interpretation to dealing with difficulties in the Bible. Not only will you learn how to study the Bible, but you'll also come away with good, basic Bible knowledge from all the examples given in the book.

Christians, Churches, & Controversy:
Navigating Doctrinal & Personal Clashes

Samuel G. Dawson

216 pages with comprehensive indexes

An eighteenth century Scottish poet wrote concerning war: "Rash, fruitless war, from wanton glory waged, is only splendid murder."

An older preacher used this quotation when he wrote concerning a particularly brutal doctrinal attack on another elderly preacher by a group of younger, treacherous preachers. While many controversies among Christians and churches aren't this vicious, many Christians and congregations simply don't know how to navigate personal and doctrinal clashes; and thus, do more harm than good. Such situations expose some noble and naïve souls to some pretty treacherous Christians. Yet, many Christians consent to much worse than Saul did at Stephen's stoning while "consenting to his death" by just holding the coats of the stone-throwers.

Most members, whose jobs aren't even on the line, refuse to ratchet up their courage to be bothered by congregational problems and decisions. They may just want difficulties handled by the congregational leaders so they can avoid being involved. Consequently, many Christians go blithely on, consenting through ignorance to mistreatment of others that goes on behind the scenes.

This book is not for you if:
- You're not a serious student of the Bible
- Your concept of Bible study is listening to your teacher go through a quarterly class book
- Your concept of being a Christian consists mainly of "going to church"
- You depend on the preacher to do your studying for you
- You're in a denomination where all the thinking is done at the top
- You're an elder who is afraid for the congregation to study controversial subjects

Ideal for: Individual Study, Preaching, Elders, Adult Classes, Personal Evangelism, New Converts, Gifts

The Teaching of Jesus
From Sinai to Gehenna: A Faithful Rabbi Urgently Warns Rebellious Israel

446 pages
Samuel G. Dawson

This Book Will Change Your View of Jesus' Teaching and the Entire New Testament as It Exposes Many of Our False Concepts

This work begins with a study of covenant concepts in the Bible, the reign of God prior to the coming of Christ, and the sophisticated expectations God has always had of non-covenant people. After demonstrating that forgiveness of sins existed under the Mosaic Law, the author develops the preaching of John the Baptist and Jesus as an urgent attempt to turn the Jewish nation back to God through faithful obedience to the Mosaic Law in order to avoid imminent national destruction.

The Sermon on the Mount is viewed, not as a contrast between the Mosaic Law and the teaching of Christ, but as Jesus correctly interpreting Moses to the Jews of his day. Thus, every syllable of that sermon is Old Testament teaching. That most of that teaching is also contained in the New Covenant is demonstrated.

The parables of Jesus are then briefly analyzed, showing that each one of them is first related to the attempted reform of the Jews by Jesus. The theme of the relative importance of one's treatment of his fellowman over his formal religious service is traced throughout the Old and New Covenants. The study of *The Teaching of Jesus* concludes as Jesus concluded it, with a study of his pronouncement of imminent national destruction in Matthew 24.

MARRIAGE: A TASTE OF HEAVEN
Patsy Rae Dawson

480 pages each with comprehensive indexes

What People Are Saying!

• *Most exciting books I've read!* • *I couldn't put them down!* • *I'm falling in love all over again!* • *We were ready to divorce—now we have a great marriage!* • *I didn't know the Bible had so much to say about marriage!* • *Must-read books!* • *Ideal for most women's AND MEN'S studies!*

Volume I: God's People Appreciate Marriage

You'll learn the Biblical formula for solving every marriage problem. You'll examine current medical evidence for the physical and mental differences between men and women. At the same time, you'll find your self-esteem growing along with increased respect for the opposite sex. The verse-by-verse study of the Song of Solomon will thrill you as it captures the emotion God put into this wonderful love story. Perhaps best of all, you'll discover that God put a blessing instead of a curse in subjection as you examine both the husband's and the wife's parts and learn where God tells wives to draw the line. "I'm falling in love all over again!" is the most common statement readers make.

Volume II: God's People Make the Best Lovers

This exciting volume deals with a popular subject, sexual love, from a fresh perspective—the Bible. You'll learn the key for sexual satisfaction for both the husband and the wife that science discovered only recently, but it has always been present in the Bible. The Bible provides proper sex education for each stage of development from puberty through the temptation for middle-aged affairs. You'll find the discussion of Victorian morals so fascinating you won't want to put the book down. Deals frankly with sexual addictions and gives the procedure for overcoming sexual problems. Surveys and medical facts will convince you, "It's true! God's people really do make the best lovers!"

YOUR MARRIAGE WILL NEVER BE THE SAME!

Samuel G. Dawson

A physics and mathematics graduate from Texas Tech, Samuel G. Dawson did research in celestial mechanics and intercontinental missile guidance in the aerospace industry before preparing to preach the gospel of Christ. In twenty-two years of public teaching, he did extensive live call-in radio work daily for eight years and participated in a number of religious debates. Sam's scientific background has given him a logical and thorough approach to the scriptures and a reputation for making Bible students re-think teaching they've taken for granted.

Over one hundred thousand cassettes of his classes and sermons have been distributed across the nation. His most popular ones are now available in cassette albums: *Marriage, Divorce, & Remarriage* demonstrates how Moses, Jesus, and Paul all taught the same thing about this controversial subject. It deals frankly with issues confronting many Christians today and the people they are trying to teach. *The Teaching of Jesus* shows how many people take Jesus' teaching out of the context of the people he preached to and misapply it to our day. *How to Study the Bible* teaches dedicated Bible students how to study from choosing a dependable translation to rules for interpretation to solving difficulties in the Bible.

Sam drew on decades of experience working with local congregations to write *Fellowship: With God and His People (The Way of Christ Without Denominationalism)* and *Denominational Doctrines: Explained, Examined, Exposed.* He co-authored a *Handbook of Religious Quotations* and has written numerous tracts.

Sam worked mostly in the western part of the United States and presently lives in Texas with his wife Patsy, author of the *Marriage: A Taste of Heaven* series.